THE ACTIVIST HUMANIST

The Activist Humanist

FORM AND METHOD IN THE CLIMATE CRISIS

CAROLINE LEVINE

PRINCETON UNIVERSITY PRESS
PRINCETON & OXFORD

Published by Princeton University Press
41 William Street, Princeton, New Jersey 08540
99 Banbury Road, Oxford OX2 6JX

press.princeton.edu

ISBN: 978-0-691-25081-6
ISBN (pbk.): 978-0-691-25058-8
ISBN: (e-book): 978-0-691-25085-4

British Library Cataloging-in-Publication Data is available

Editorial: Anne Savarese and James Collier
Production Editorial: Jenny Wolkowicki
Cover design: Heather Hansen
Production: Lauren Reese
Publicity: William Pagdatoon

Cover images: *(From top to bottom)* Railroad tracks by Mike Eerie / Unsplash; row houses by iSky Films; Seeds by Steve Ausmus / USDA/ARS; farm by Azim Khan Ronnie; bikes by TonyV3112 / Shutterstock; boats by Azim Khan Ronnie

This book has been composed in Arno Pro

Printed and bound by CPI Group (UK) Ltd, Croydon, CR0 4YY

For Tyler Bradway and Jen Spitzer

CONTENTS

PREFACE

THE STUDENTS in my environmental humanities class feel bleak and terror-struck. The issue of climate change is so complex that it defeats them, they tell me. Most are science majors, but all of them know that the most powerful obstacles to meaningful change lie in culture, politics, and economics. And when they track the accelerating climate catastrophe to global corporations, long histories of racism and colonialism, and broken political systems, they feel panic: it will take years to unsettle these structures, they say, and the world is already on fire.

These students know that individual actions are not enough to halt the juggernaut of climate change, but every single one of them still tries valiantly to reduce their own carbon footprint. Most of them have already stopped eating meat. They recycle and compost. They wash their clothes in cold water and take short showers. They encourage family members and friends to buy sustainable goods and adopt eco-friendly habits. They strive for purity, and they are sharply critical of themselves when they fall short. One is ashamed for not being able to reduce his waste to zero. Another explains how guilty she feels when she shops for new clothes. They worry a lot about hypocrisy, unwilling to call themselves real environmentalists as long as they still use plastic cups or drive cars. The people they admire most are those who maintain the most austere standards of green living. Some look forward to a future without humans with a sense of relief.

These students embrace humility, open-endedness, undecidability, and complexity, some of the core values that I, as a literary studies scholar, have been working to teach for decades. I find myself feeling a growing unease about this work. Not wanting to risk an arrogant imposition of their own views on others, and overwhelmed by the prospect of dismantling the huge structures that enable climate change, my students fall back on policing their own actions. They cannot even imagine working at a scale larger than individual decision making, which is also, in this moment of climate catastrophe, the scale of isolation and hopelessness. They have no models of effective political action.

Turning to scholarship in the environmental humanities intensifies my unease. The most influential thinkers in the field urge us above all to open ourselves to wild possibilities, and to feel awe and wonder in the face of an overwhelming complexity. They argue that we must strive to undo dominant Euro-American ideas about the power of the human subject and recognize the intricate enmeshment of human bodies in ecologies composed of all kinds of non-human objects and forces, from rocks and birds to bacteria and fungi. We must resist the capitalist and colonialist imperatives to dominate and exploit otherness for the sake of profit. We must unlearn the illusion of progress and honor the vast suffering and loss that have resulted from naive techno-fixes and other illusions of a better future where humans remain in charge. The task, Donna Haraway says, is "to be truly present, not as a vanishing pivot between awful or edenic pasts and apocalyptic or salvific futures, but as moral critters entwined in myriad unfinished configurations of places, times, matters, meanings."[1]

This has been revelatory and exciting work for me, but I worry that it leads to the same hopelessness and powerlessness I see in my students. We find scholars across the environmental humanities moving back and forth between longings for a "wholesale dismantling," on the one hand, and an embrace of "the minor gesture" and "non-cumulative, self-erasing, processual experience" on the other.[2] Humanists speak of turns to beekeeping and gardening, arts of witnessing, and documenting local ecologies through memoir and photography.[3] "The anthropocene is no time for transcendent, definitive mappings, transparent knowledge systems, or confident epistemologies," writes Stacy Alaimo. "Surely all those things got us into this predicament to begin with."[4] Caught, like my students, between gloom about the prospects of a massive global transformation and small-scale actions too insubstantial to bring a halt to the runaway feedback loops of global warming, many humanists move directly to *mourning*, encouraging us to face the terrible, inevitable fact of overwhelming loss, both past and to come. Some argue that mourning is what the humanities are best equipped to offer.[5] A surprising number, horrified by histories of violence and exploitation, actively look forward to human extinction.[6]

At first it seems strange to find environmental humanists arriving at the same conclusions as undergraduates at Cornell majoring in plant science and environmental engineering. Maybe these similarities are an index of our success: could it be that the humanities are now powerfully influencing thinkers across fields? It seems more likely, instead, that this convergence is an index of our zeitgeist. From where I sit, the environmental humanities seem to be actively reinforcing one of the most dominant attitudes available to us in this neoliberal moment: a withdrawal from the public sphere.

After all, there is a whole register missing between dreams of a total global revolution and the small-scale act or gesture, and that is the *polis*—the scale of collective life. Politics in its most fundamental sense is the hard, messy work of living in common with lots and lots of others. It entails decisions about arrangements of space and time and the distribution of power and resources. This decision making is almost always disappointing, and often intolerably unjust. Even democratic decisions are often blunt instruments, covering over differences, reinforcing existing inequalities, and failing to envision genuinely radical or far-reaching changes. And it is true that most powerful institutions are corrupt and hierarchical, reproducing and reentrenching historical injuries over time. But can it be right that our only option, in this context, is to refuse political action, and in so doing effectively accede to massive extinction? Climate change is already magnifying the suffering of the world's most vulnerable bodies. To allow its predictable catastrophes to unfold is to acquiesce to unjust violence on an unprecedented scale, more immense than all past genocides.

But humanists, we often say, do not have the tools or the expertise to participate in the active, practical, strenuous work of politics on the ground. Scholars across my own home field of literary studies argue that the encounter with aesthetics is important because it teaches us to dwell in opacity and ambiguity, opening us up to radical imaginings that disrupt and resist the constraints of the status quo. Activism is not the proper work of the scholar of the arts. As Anahid Nersessian puts it: "For better or worse, works of art resist practical application or problem-solving," which means that the task of the aesthetic disciplines is to face the "traumatic knowledge that climate catastrophe is certain and unfathomable."[7]

As I struggle to come to terms with the insistence on political withdrawal and inaction all around me, I keep returning to a particular puzzle posed by scholarship on the arts: why do we start from the conviction that art is neither practical nor programmatic? It was in the eighteenth century that Europeans started to define art as a special realm, set apart from useful and simple objects. It is true that many scholars of art and literature have since clung to this definition, separating authentic art—complex, challenging, and open-ended—from its clumsier cousins: propaganda, didacticism, and design. But countless artists and writers around the world have also rejected this distinction, weaving creative art and political action together in a range of inventive ways—not just for protest and awareness but for structural and infrastructural building. We might think of Bertolt Brecht and Audre Lorde, Toni Cade Bambara and Augusto Boal, Project Row Houses and the Royal Chicano Air Force, to name just a few. Yet, the artists and writers most often taught in academic classrooms are those who question and unsettle existing norms and institutions rather than proposing plans and programs for political action. That is, the humanities tend to valorize the works of art that revolutionize consciousness—that wake us up to injustice and oppression—without advocating for any specific course of action to redress those wrongs. But why is that? Why do literary and cultural studies scholars so often remain committed to the separation of aesthetic study from the nitty-gritty of political change on the ground? This book seeks to answer this question and to sketch out an alternative—a justification for practical political action as an integral part of our work.

In my last book, *Forms*, I argued that formalist methods were especially well suited to understanding both art and politics, as well as the relations between them. I will build on those arguments, but I will also turn away from some of the conclusions I reached there. In *Forms*, I made the case that the formalist methods we have developed in literary and cultural studies are analytically useful far beyond the narrow sphere that is conventionally defined as art. These methods can help us make sense of all formed things in the world, all shapes and patterns and arrangements, from national borders to postal systems. My goal, in part, was to use formalist strategies drawn from the arts to redescribe political power. The multiple orderings and structurings at work on us in any given moment seemed to me to contradict conventional accounts of ideology. Did any single structure really dominate, organize, or cause all the others? I argued that gender, race, nation, and class, although they can work well together, do not always do so, in part because they take different, even incommensurable forms, and these have the capacity to destabilize each other. The more I looked, the more this instability started to appear true of other, smaller forms too. It began to seem like a strategic mistake to assume that we have to remake intractably deep structural causes first—like capitalism or racism—in order to create structural change. I hypothesized, instead, that all kinds of local rearrangements can result in the undoing of hegemonic structures. And so, I argued, there were radical opportunities at the sites where forms undermine one another, which I called "collisions."[8]

Like many other scholars of the arts, my attention was focused on instability, complexity, and open-endedness. All along, I simply assumed that collisions were waystations on the route to a more just society. But like other literary and cultural critics, I stopped short of sketching out shapes and arrangements that might take their place. This was not, I thought, the role of the literary scholar.

But stopping short also seemed like an evasion. It was so easy to take things apart; I was having a much harder time imagining how to create genuine alternatives. I started to push against the conclusions I reached in *Forms*. Was my insistence on aleatory openings just an accident of my disciplinary training, and was it getting in the way of the tougher work of figuring how to live in common? Anna Kornbluh's work persuaded me that collective life has always entailed structuration.[9] All human communities—and most non-human ones too—depend on orderings, shapes, and arrangements. For the ordinary project of day-to-day survival, all collectives rely on assigned spaces for shelter and gathering, appointed times for work and food and rest, and procedures for decision making. These orderings restrict but they also sustain us. And they are what make living in common possible. From this perspective, the *polis* cannot do without form.

But if we will always need forms, then it seems wrong to keep our scholarly eyes only on unsettling and dismantling them. It is especially urgent to rethink this impulse right now. We live in an age of acute precarity. As neoliberal economics undoes hopes of secure work, and as fossil fuels radically disrupt long-standing ecosystems, we are faced not with oppressive stasis but with rapid and destructive change—the warming of the upper atmosphere, the eruption of fast-moving wildfires and the melting of ice caps, the destruction of ecosystems, desertification, the extinction of species, the growing mass of plastics in the ocean, storms and droughts and floods both more frequent and more severe than ever before. This context has challenged my own long-standing embrace of disruption and prompted me to revalue terms I had long dismissed, like stability, security, and predictability. These have been bad words for artists and intellectuals, but they have also been much too easy for the privileged to take for granted. Right now, as all of us are threatened by rapid and multiplying forces of destruction, the unmaking of forms, so often the goal of artists and humanists, has become eerily consonant with domination and exploitation.

And so, as I was writing this book, I stopped trying to find gaps and openings and started looking, instead, for examples of social forms that could sustain collective life with some degree of fairness and mutual care. I asked: Are there some arrangements of space and time, some organizations of power and resources, some patterns of distribution and conservation, that are more supportive of the flourishing of bodies, equality, intimacy, pleasure, and creativity than others? Are there aesthetic forms that provide not the delights of surprise and complexity but practicable models we could put to use for climate justice? And are there more and less effective forms of organizing *ourselves* for political power? Can politics be something more than a despairing wail of pain?

The first chapter of this book focuses on theory. It argues that a single value—anti-instrumentality—subtends a surprising array of schools of thought in the humanities, from defenders of aesthetic autonomy to political revolutionaries. This value, I will argue, is now prompting us to work against sustainability, or what I will call, using a term coined by philosopher Kyle Powys Whyte, *collective continuance.*

Chapter 2 turns from theory to method. Here I show how formalist methods can help us both to analyze social forms and to design and build just and sustaining forms for collective life. This chapter offers an account of *formal survival,* which, I will argue, is crucial both to undoing unjust structures and to building lasting, reliable infrastructures for collective continuance.

Chapter 3 addresses the three major infrastructural forms that will be most essential to the work of keeping life going over time: routines, pathways, and enclosures. Routine provisions of food and rest are necessary to the project of keeping life going. All human collectives have also relied on pathways to carry food, water, and waste to and from the places where we live. Sheltering enclosures, too, are essential to a just *polis.* Too many people right now live precariously, wracked by heat and cold, unable to find safe spaces to sleep and gather. Reliable food, clean water, and places to rest and gather all are being radically disrupted in this time of anthropogenic climate change. None of these are subtle or exciting, but all are essential to collective continuance. Here I explore some existing examples of just and sustaining infrastructural forms. All of these are imperfect, but all of them are also better than the dominant structures that organize and disorganize so much of collective life right now. And all of the examples show that even in terrifying times, and even under regimes that are exploitative and cruel, it is possible to build just and sustaining forms.

Chapter 4 returns to the question of aesthetics to think about which works of art might help us to value infrastructures for collective life. I collect an unlikely assortment of cultural forms that value stability and predictability, and so have usually been dismissed by scholars as conservative, from realist narrative to pop songs, and from murals to happy endings.

I come back to the question of political action in chapter 5: how should we go about organizing ourselves to fight for collective continuance? Here I consider successful political movements for justice and make a case for the forms that helped them succeed. Where many activists in our own time have prized spontaneity and horizontality, I consider instead the importance of shared goals, the temporal turning point, and a form that can help us expand political movements to large scales: what I call here the *hinge*. I show how we might put all of these to use for climate justice.

In the final chapter, I bridge the usual gap between academic argument and practical politics by borrowing a deliberately mundane and practical form—the workbook. Meant for readers who do not know where to begin when it comes to overwhelming problems like the climate crisis, the workbook sets out a series of questions and exercises intended to help people get involved, and stay involved, in political action. This will seem like a strange ending for an academic book. Scholars have typically argued that it is our job to understand the past, to theorize and analyze rather than to try to change the world. But the binary opposition between scholarship and activism has boxed us into an unnecessary powerlessness.[10] And so, I end with a hands-on experiment in deconstructing the opposition between theory and practice.

The urgency of the climate crisis has shaped all of the arguments I sketch out here, but there is a broad claim about form and politics at work that goes well beyond an environmentalist frame. It is so easy to long for a freedom from structures, to dream of a world without constraints. What is much harder for humanists—and everyone else, for that matter—is designing, building, and maintaining the mundane forms that sustain collective life over time. That work is the focus of this book.

THE ACTIVIST HUMANIST

1

Toward an Affirmative Instrumentality

SCHOLARS ACROSS THE HUMANITIES RETURN, again and again, to three key moves: the pause, the rupture, and the dissolve. The pause: open-endedness, suspension, undecidability, illegibility, opacity, complexity. The rupture: revolution, resistance, fragmentation, shock, break, unsettling, dismantling, disorder. The dissolve: fluidity, process, liminality, hybridity, boundary-crossing, flow. These moves often overlap. Sometimes they are indistinguishable. Hybridity can rupture a system dependent on binaries. Dismantling the status quo can open a new space for reflection. Taken together, these three basic moves bespeak a single common purpose: to crack the world open to alternative ways of thinking and being—to get in the way of business as usual.

But what is it, exactly, that keeps humanists so focused on interrupting the settled routines of the administered world? This chapter will begin by making the case that there is one key value at work across schools of thought. It shapes and subtends all of the fields that I call the *aesthetic humanities*—literary studies, art history, musicology, and media and cultural studies. We find it guiding thinkers as different as Lionel Trilling and Fred Moten, Theodor Adorno and Gloria Anzaldúa, Stephen Greenblatt and Bill Brown, Rosi Braidotti and Kandice Chuh.[1] It is so pervasive across our fields that it does not even need to be justified: it seems to speak for itself. And so, like all norms, it carries its own limitations, repetitions, and exclusions. The name I will use for this value here is *anti-instrumentality*.

This chapter will investigate the appeal of anti-instrumentality across the aesthetic fields, and then it will argue for moving beyond it to the practical work of designing, building, and maintaining collective life. This will entail a new set of grounds for understanding art and politics and the connections between them. And it will mean recasting the pause, the rupture, and the dissolve as necessary preparatory work—but not as ends in themselves.

The Long Lure of Anti-instrumentality

Max Weber and, later, the thinkers of the Frankfurt School made a powerful case against what they called instrumental rationality—*Zweckrationalität.*[2] They argued that capitalism and totalitarianism rest on a kind of means-ends thinking that calculates value according to the efficient, rationalized achievement of economic and technical progress. Instrumental rationality emerged out of modern Europe, feeding the "hungry furnaces" of capitalist accumulation by turning the world into objects for its own use and profit.[3] For centuries, Europeans and their white inheritors have used instrumental rationality to justify themselves as the only real subjects of history and to treat non-European people and homelands as objects to be exploited for their ends.[4] *Zweckrationalität* has thus justified the destruction of Indigenous traditions, the abduction and enslavement of Black people, the expropriation of homelands, and the ravaging of ecologies.[5] And so, across politically minded scholarship in the humanities—including Marxist, deconstructive, critical race, postcolonial, queer, environmental, and feminist criticism—scholars for several decades have sought to unsettle and resist Western assumptions about the human subject: implicitly white, straight, adult, able-bodied, European "Man," who invokes his exclusive capacity for rationality to exploit all others.

This critique has been persuasive and significant. But the argument against instrumentality has gone a step further than Weber's *Zweckrationalität.* That is, the most influential theorists in the aesthetic humanities have warned against *all* instrumentality—not just Western-style instrumental rationality but all means-ends thinking. All plans and programs are dangerous. Even the most utopian visions of a revolutionary future, we are told, only reentrench existing dominations. As Michel Foucault puts it: "to imagine another system is to extend our participation in the present system."[6] Theodor Adorno, though deeply unlike Foucault in many ways, shares this position: "One may not cast a picture of utopia in a positive manner," he writes. What is productive instead is to draw attention to "what's missing": "the determined negation of that which merely is . . . which always points at the same time to what should be."[7] According to this logic, we do our best political work when we dwell in restless negativity, using imperfections to point beyond themselves to something other, the undefined to-come.

This argument has lasted robustly into our own time. For Fredric Jameson, it is crucial "to bring home, in local and determinate ways, and with a fullness of concrete detail, our constitutional inability to imagine Utopia itself; and this, not owing to any individual failure of imagination, but as the result of the systemic, cultural, and ideological closure of which we are all one way or another prisoners."[8] Jared Sexton argues against praxis, prescription, and prognosis in favor of reaching for "an indiscernible *something* beyond" Being: "imagining it in and as the ruins of Being, after the end of the world, in an entirely other relation to the nothing from whence it comes."[9] Or as Jack Halberstam puts it, "Revolution will come in a form we cannot yet imagine. . . . We cannot say what new structures will replace the ones we live with yet, because once we have torn shit down, we will inevitably see more and see differently and feel a new sense of wanting and being and becoming."[10]

For these thinkers, the resistance to instrumentality is political. But of course, anti-instrumentality also underpins major theories of aesthetics. Since Kant, up through Adorno and into our own time, theorists have defined the aesthetic precisely by its disturbance of means-ends thinking. Art cannot be reduced to exchange and profit or to the communication of moral values or information. It halts the reflexive rush to calculability, efficiency, and utility.[11] This is the definition of art that leads the aesthetic humanities—different from history and philosophy, in this respect—to return, again and again, to anti-instrumentality. Jonathan Kramnick, to give a recent example, argues that a disciplinary training in the arts means "spelling out the open-ended or the unresolved."[12]

From Marxist critique to Black and queer studies, and from deep ecology to aesthetic autonomy, the common logic of anti-instrumentality subtends otherwise conflicting schools of thought. And so, if you look at almost any essay or book in the aesthetic humanities, it will conclude with a kind of deliberate open-endedness—a soaring refusal to spell out the future. Catherine Gallagher and Stephen Greenblatt write: "we sincerely hope that you will not be able to say what it all adds up to; if you could, we would have failed." Sara Ahmed's *The Cultural Politics of Emotion* closes this way: "Justice involves feelings. . . . Where we go, with these feelings, remains an open question." For Derek Attridge, "the opening up of possibilities that had remained closed, is—however risky—a good in itself, particularly when the process is a continuous one, allowing no permanent settling of norms and habits." Robert McRuer concludes *Crip Theory* with the "promise that we will always comprehend disability otherwise and that we will, collectively, somehow access other worlds and other futures." The ending of Timothy Morton's *Hyperobjects* goes like this: "Heidegger said that only a god can save us now. . . . *We just don't know what sort of god.*" Dora Zhang reclaims the political potential of description on the grounds that it "challenges . . . teleology and instrumentality." Peter Boxall invites us to "think our way into the unpictured world to come" by way of literature's "unthought conjunctions." At the end of *Black Aliveness,* Kevin Quashie issues "a call that exists and vibrates beyond the scope of the rule of the world as we know it—an imaginary that inflects how we *can* behold ourselves and each other." And for Tim Bewes, the novel as a form is uniquely important because it gives us "access to a thought that, in its essence, refuses the ideological formulations of our world."[13] Critics of all stripes, that is, refuse the entrenched dominations of the status quo by beckoning to the indefinite, unmappable possibilities beyond.

Anti-instrumentality has proved an unusually tough and resilient underpinning for the aesthetic humanities, its basic presumptions managing to join critics who fiercely disagree with each other about everything else. Scholars who reject a traditional aesthetic canon in favor of popular culture, for example, like Ramzi Fawaz, will show how a superhero comic can unsettle dominant norms and systems,[14] while critics who are adamantly opposed to making political arguments for art, like Helen Vendler, will defend the most canonical artworks on the grounds that these rupture convention and expectation.[15]

But there is trouble lurking in these arguments. First and foremost, it should seem strange and surprising that anti-instrumentality can ground the most urgent political projects, from feminism to postcolonial theory, while it also provides the justification for anti-political arguments for aesthetic autonomy. But if anti-instrumentality seems to do the heroic work of uniting opposing camps—political revolutionaries and defenders of the aesthetic for its own sake—I will argue that in fact it falls short on both sides. First, because autonomous art serves political ends. And second, because anti-instrumental politics does not in fact yield the revolutionary justice critics have so often hoped and claimed for it.

The Implicit Politics of Aesthetic Autonomy

Champions of aesthetic anti-instrumentality return, again and again, to the freedom that art brings. In *The Poet's Freedom,* Susan Stewart argues that because art resists use, commodification, and mastery, the artist can embark on a "process of possibility without resolution."[16] For Attridge, it is the reader who is freed by the encounter with art: "To read a poem and feel one is entering a new world of thought and feeling, to find oneself laughing at a surprising passage in a novel, to have one's breath taken away by a speech performed on stage—these are experiences of alterity, of the impossible made suddenly possible, of the mind, and, sometimes, the body being changed by new configurations, new connections, new possibilities."[17] Nan Z. Da urges us to read closely for the many ways that "literature makes nothing happen," because an attention to the complexity of literary language is the only way to free ourselves from authoritarian and imperial propaganda.[18]

For all of these, art yields pleasures and thoughts and possibilities that push beyond dominant routines and assumptions. And as art breaks free from dogma and determination, it frees *us* from the torpid conventionality of the status quo. But what this means is that we are already fully in the domain of the political. After all, freedom is nothing if not a political value. And that is why political and aesthetic arguments can so easily be yoked together.

The politics of aesthetic anti-instrumentality is no mere academic affair. It was put to powerful use in the Cold War. In the 1940s and 1950s, the Soviets charged that the United States was a shallow and materialist nation, obsessed only with wealth and military might. The U.S. State Department responded by trying to showcase the many ways that the United States was a consummately free society and turned to art as a shining example. One effort was a traveling exhibition called *Advancing American Art*, which featured a range of innovative modern American painters, including Georgia O'Keefe and Jacob Lawrence. Reports suggested that these bold and unexpected paintings actually began to persuade audiences in Eastern Europe and Latin America that the United States was capable of original art. The State Department planned to take the show to Guatemala, Iran, and Cambodia. But when the U.S. Congress and the press found out about the exhibit, there was a huge public stink. Public pressure forced the State Department to cancel the show.[19]

Concerned that the global image of the United States as a beacon of freedom was suffering from episodes like these, the strategists of the newly formed CIA launched a covert arts program.[20] Its role in cultural life is now widely known, but at the time they largely kept their global operations secret through fake foundations and front organizations. The Congress for Cultural Freedom funneled resources to the literary magazine *Encounter* and to the Chekhov Publishing House, which printed the works of Nabokov and other Russian emigres. It supported the Nigerian magazine *Black Orpheus*, which published some of the most influential *négritude* writers, including Aimé Césaire and Léopold Senghor.[21] *El Mundo Nuevo,* the Paris quarterly of Latin American writing, was exposed as a CIA venture early on, though it also published the first chapters of Gabriel García Márquez's *Cien anos de soledad* in 1966 and new works by Octavio Paz and Mario Vargas Llosa.[22] The Cold War Program for Cultural Freedom was a major source of support not only for artists and writers but for the academic humanities. The CIA provided funding for programs in Asian and Latin American studies, foreign languages, and American literature.[23] MFA programs in creative writing drew support as weapons in the anti-Communist struggle.[24] Cold Warrior Richard Nixon poured vast sums into the National Endowment for the Arts (NEA) and the National Endowment for the Humanities (NEH).[25] Cuts to the NEA and NEH began in 1990—shortly after the Berlin Wall fell. If we look back nostalgically to a time when there was ample support for the arts and humanities, we should not forget how important it was for Western governments to make impressive worldwide displays of artistic freedom.

In other words, the CIA instrumentalized—we might even say, weaponized—the anti-instrumentality of the aesthetic. They saw that difficult, experimental art could stand for freedom from political ends and then they put that freedom to political ends. And this was not a misuse or misunderstanding of artistic anti-instrumentality. Freedom is the value that subtends arguments for aesthetic autonomy.

And yet, how could the same politics possibly unite thinkers as radically different as Jack Halberstam and Richard Nixon, Susan Stewart and Aimé Césaire? The answer is that aesthetic autonomy goes hand in hand with a specifically *indiscriminate* version of political negation. Peter Kalliney shows that African writers in the middle of the twentieth century embraced aesthetic autonomy for a wide variety of conflicting ends, including "emancipation from colonialism; independence from the postcolonial nation-state; avoidance of politics in order to foster collaboration among multiple constituencies; freedom from politics altogether as a professional disposition; and ideological neutrality in the Cold War."[26] Motivating anti-imperialists, nationalists, Cold War spies, and those keen to avoid politics altogether, anti-instrumentality can—and does—set itself against all constraints, all rules, all plans.

My central argument in this book is that this politics is too indiscriminate. Anti-instrumentality lends itself to dreams of freedom from any and all norms. It does not necessarily serve collective well-being. But it also remains the primary mode of political thinking we find across the aesthetic humanities today. It is what connects Afropessimism to the Frankfurt School's struggle against "the administered world" and what links deconstructive reading to Lionel Trilling's bleak humanism. While their political targets are crucially different, their moves bear a striking resemblance: point to repressive norms and call for their undoing; do not propose what should be built in their place. Susan Stanford Friedman refers to this political role as the "gadfly position."[27] As dominant institutions lumber along, imposing their oppressive norms, it is the job of the aesthetic humanities to act as constant irritants. But this means that the refusal of ends can go in any direction—resisting, unsettling, puncturing, any program at all.

It is especially clear in our own moment that the freedom from norms and constraints does not always align with the radical left or even with progressives. Authoritarian populist leaders have been celebrating resistance to rules in the interests—they say—of freeing people from state power. The Trump administration, for example, rolled back over one hundred environmental regulations, including fracking on Native lands, drilling in wildlife preserves, and dumping toxins in waterways. Brazil's Jair Bolsonaro has "gutted" the environmental agencies that limit and penalize deforestation. And Prime Minister Narendra Modi in India has deregulated the sale of crude oil.[28] From this perspective, the drive to resist norms has hastened the worst effects of climate catastrophe.

Climate denialism is itself oddly consonant with the humanistic values of opacity and open-endedness. Called "merchants of doubt" by historians Erik M. Conway and Naomi Oreskes, a small group of anti-communist strategists turned lobbyists set about undermining the policy prescriptions of scientists who had in fact come to a consensus about urgent dangers, their causes, and the need for government solutions: first tobacco, then acid rain and chlorofluorocarbons, and then, most destructively of all, climate change. They conducted a series of public campaigns that focused on scientific uncertainty and irresolution, and always called for more studies to delay large-scale public action.[29]

Tech companies, too, have vaunted open-endedness and disruption, claiming to free work from traditional office cubicles, regulations, bureaucracy, schedules, and hierarchies in favor of sharing, convenience, and "personal empowerment." This emancipation from traditional constraints has brought with it a terrible precarity for much of the labor force, as workers struggle to make ends meet by stringing together multiple unpredictable "gigs."[30] "Neoliberal subjects," as Wendy Brown puts it, "are controlled *through* their freedom."[31]

In all of these contexts, the pause, the rupture, and the dissolve have become perilously congruent with neoliberal precarity and onrushing climate catastrophe. This conclusion places particular pressure on the most influential thinking in the environmental humanities, which has put its most powerful emphasis on open-endedness. Jenny Odell's *How to Do Nothing*, for example, argues that we should withdraw ourselves from the push to productivity, pausing to focus on the places where we live, which in turn will open us to a new and more ecologically caring consciousness. Odell deliberately refrains from identifying any particular actions to follow from this new approach, ending instead with the celebration of "an aimless aim, or a project with no goal."[32] The practical work remains gestural, an appeal rather than a plan.[33]

Even when environmental humanists acknowledge the importance of practical politics, they often separate this from the open-endedness they see as proper to the humanities. Stephanie LeMenager, for example, entertains two different endings to *Living Oil*: the first, a single paragraph, invites us to "appreciate" political campaigns around renewable energy, including Germany's successful shift away from fossil fuels, and environmental justice and divestment struggles. The second ending draws far more of her attention: running over a dozen pages, it focuses on what academic humanists in particular can contribute to transforming the future of oil. The answer: "narrative itself."[34] Finishing with "an unresolved detective story" and a call for more stories, LeMenager says that the proliferation of narratives is "the humanistic complement to the work of engineers and geologists and hydrologists and city planners and county health agencies and environmental justice activists to create a more resilient energy regime."[35] Appreciating and supplementing the work of doers and makers and planners, the humanist dwells in narrative irresolution; no particular endings, but rather more and more stories to come.

Rob Nixon's *Slow Violence* ends in a similarly open-ended way. Nixon conjures up the image of a broad global coalition of constituencies coming together to demand action on climate change. He does not explore how this coalition will take shape and does not prescribe specific political aims or objectives for it. His focus remains on the writer-activist, who "will continue to play a critical role in drawing to the surface—and infusing with emotional force—submerged stories of injustice and resource rebellions." In the final line of the book, Nixon celebrates those writers who seek to transform society in ways that "their societies could never imagine, let alone demand"[36]—that is, the unknowable to-come.

Amitav Ghosh is more pessimistic than either LeMenager or Nixon. He ends *The Great Derangement* with a scathing critique of "a deadlocked public sphere, with the actual exercise of power being relegated to the interlocking complex of corporations and institutions of governance that has come to be known as the 'deep state.'" Ghosh is equally withering when it comes to climate marches and demonstrations, which amount to "little more than an orgy of democratic emotion, an activist-themed street fair, a real-world analogue to Twitter hashtag campaigns: something that gives you a nice feeling, says you belong in a certain group, and is completely divorced from actual legislation and governance." Ghosh holds out a glimmer of hope that global religious movements and climate activists might converge on the project of "drastically reducing emissions without sacrificing considerations of equity." But like Nixon, he tells us little about how this might take shape, and like Nixon and LeMenager, he ends with the open-ended possibilities of the aesthetic: the hope that a new generation will "rediscover their kinship with other beings, and that this vision, at once new and ancient, will find expression in a transformed and renewed art and literature."[37]

Scholars working at the interdisciplinary crossings of the sciences and the humanities, too, typically steer clear of specifying plans and programs on principle. Donna Haraway urges us to recognize our complex mutual entanglements with a range of beings—from pigeons to estrogen—in order to "cut the bonds of the Anthropocene and the Capitalocene."[38] New multispecies collaborations will then prompt us to refuse the usual "dictates of teleology, settled categories, and function"—that is, programmatic thinking—and shift us instead to "the realm of play."[39] In *A Billion Black Anthropocenes or None*, Kathryn Yusoff exposes the anti-Blackness that shapes geology as a discipline, and in that context urges a "destabilization of the mode of encounter" and "an insurgent geology for the end of the world."[40]

These are just a few examples. We might also think of Stacy Alaimo's invitation to "dwell in the dissolve," Chelsea Frazier's call to "construct alternative conceptions of ecological ethics within our present world and beyond it," and Kyle Devine's appeal to hear the environmental and political conditions of recorded music so that "we may be motivated to change them."[41] Across the environmental humanities, we find scholars calling for new modes of attentiveness and concluding with hopes—but not plans—for the transformations to follow.

All of this has been—and will continue to be—deeply important work. There is no question that as long as dominant structures of violence, dispossession, and oppression try to pass themselves off as nature or common sense, we will urgently need both critique and resistance. In this context, aesthetic objects that startle and surprise and baffle will help to stop us in the midst of other instrumentalizing pressures, to recognize the limits of dominant ideologies, and to imagine ways of being and thinking and feeling otherwise. For this reason, the particular strengths of the aesthetic humanities—pausing in the face of business as usual, envisioning alternative worlds, and telling many specific stories—remain indispensable.

What has come to concern me, however, is that these have become their own common sense across the aesthetic humanities—a set of unquestioned presumptions. I myself wrote three books that revolved around unsettling dominant structures before realizing how strange it was that I had never even *imagined* a different set of purposes. And as soon as I began to think directly about them, they seemed limiting and partial. And disturbing. What if open-endedness justifies an avoidance of planning and building, and reinforces the notion that it is not our job to find practical strategies to work against anthropogenic climate change and its calamitous and uneven consequences? That is, what if it disempowers all of us who are working across the aesthetic humanities?

In this book, I am, like other humanists, struggling to find alternatives to systems that reentrench injustice. I am also looking for effective ways to refuse the terrible rush to conquest and profit. In these respects I am building on the massive body of work that has been done in the past few decades in the aesthetic humanities, and in many ways, this book is not a break as much as a refocusing and a revaluing. But it is my hypothesis that the practice of concluding with calls to ever more complexity and possibility instead of sketching out plans of action is feeding the logic of climate denialism and neoliberal atomization. It is supporting collective inaction. As long as the aesthetic humanities stress humility, wild imaginings, the unmaking of prevailing values, and dense entanglements, we push off the work of organized collective action to another moment. Barbara Leckie argues that while this "preparatory work" can be rightly "slow and laborious," there comes a moment when "both individuals and collectives need to transition to . . . action."[42] But how? So far, the daily work of teaching and writing in the aesthetic humanities remains overwhelmingly caught in the pause before action, rarely focusing on how to gather forces, how to plan and strategize for a different set of conditions, how to face the tough, imperfect struggle of making collective decisions and reclaiming *res publica*—public goods.[43]

Environmentalist thinking, Ursula K. Heise argues, has long been caught up in contradictory temporal frames. On the one hand activists have encouraged a resistance to the technological speed of modern life, calling for slow food, slow reading, and long pauses for deep reflection. On the other hand, environmentalists have worried that current institutions are too slow to respond to the rapid pace of anthropogenic climate change. As Heise puts it: "The newbie environmentalist may be forgiven for wondering what the appropriate response is to the slowness of natural processes and the accelerated rhythms of global modernity—or is it the rapidity of ecological transformations and the foot-dragging responses of political actors?"[44] Both Leckie and Heise invite us to notice the temporal forms that organize and disorganize our relationship to climate catastrophe.

As delays and open-endedness are put to use by fossil fuel companies and climate denialists, it seems clear that there is no intrinsically resistant tempo, no way of approaching time that will itself get us out of climate trouble. But it also seems clear that the aesthetic humanities has become stuck on the preparatory moment. In response, this book adopts a specific temporal framework. In place of the unimaginable future, the evanescent gap or glimmer, the overwhelming complexity of densely entwined ecologies, and long histories of violence and dispossession, it gathers examples from all over the past, and it takes these as workable blueprints here and now—models that can guide building and making in the near future, and can shape conditions that are capable of lasting over time. That is, I keep my eye on the practical work that I and others can do, even in the painful conditions of the present, to create more just and sustainable conditions for intergenerational justice.

Collective Continuance

The first step is to reframe the problem of instrumentality. There is something attractively pure about refusing complicity with capitalism and colonialism, but the lure of an innocence that puts nothing other to use is also, quite literally, the logic of death. There can be no life that does not have effects on the world around it, and there can be no life that does not put otherness to use. That is, what if living bodies can never altogether avoid instrumentalizing? Anna Tsing distinguishes between two models of use—one that is necessary to ordinary survival, "eating and being eaten," and the other, a specifically capitalist instrumentality, that turns all kinds of lives into "resources for investment."[45]

In fact, any wholesale rejection of use—the notion that we could avoid instrumentalizing—may be itself a product of the Western mind-body split. The Indigenous peoples of the Columbia River Valley have articulated a philosophy that centers on water and the sustaining of a balanced ecosystem that can renew itself over generations. This philosophy both recognizes water as a value in itself *and* understands it as useful for the preservation of human life and health. For "the people of the river," writes Elizabeth Woody, "there is positively no concept of water as nonutilitarian."[46] The most serious dangers lie not in use in general, that is, but, as Haraway puts it, in "unidirectional relations of use, ruled by practices of calculation and self-sure of hierarchy."[47]

In this context, a resolute anti-instrumentality actually turns our attention away from the basic conditions that sustain collective life, such as water, food, and shelter. So: what is the alternative? What I propose is an *affirmative instrumentality* for the aesthetic humanities. I turn here to Potawatomi philosopher Kyle Powys Whyte's concept of "collective continuance," a framework for justice that does not dispense with use. Whyte defines collective continuance as "a society's overall adaptive capacity to maintain its members' cultural integrity, health, economic vitality, and political order into the future and avoid having its members experience preventable harms."[48] The continuity of food systems is one of Whyte's examples. Different societies will have different ways of finding, harvesting, and distributing food, but all will treat food in part as useful—necessary to the task of keeping bodies alive over time. Food systems will always be subject to external forces and sudden shocks, such as storms and floods. For this reason, some adaptation and some flexibility will always be necessary. Collectives will also have to plan for the future, not to overharvest a food supply, for example, or to store water for a dry spell. For Whyte, this means moving away from an opposition between conservation and innovation, and between traditional and modern societies, and toward the requirement to plan and build conditions for intergenerational flourishing in the face of inevitable change. A society is just if it prevents foreseeable harms to future generations.

This definition allows Whyte to specify the injustices of settler colonialism. Colonizing forces destroy "the capacities that the societies that were already there—Indigenous societies—rely on for the sake of exercising their own collective self-determination over their cultures, economies, health, and political order." For example, when European settlers built railroads or cleared land for timber and farms, they advanced their own interests while demolishing the conditions for the planting, hunting, and fishing practices developed by Indigenous communities to support collective health, strength, and political independence over the long term.[49] One especially violent settler strategy has involved forcibly moving Indigenous groups off traditional homelands where specific foods thrive and then dispensing and withholding food rations as a means of political control.[50] California settlers pushed Karuk people away from the river, a long-standing food source, and then criminalized practices that had sustained harvests over generations, including controlled forest burns. Around the world, working systems of collective continuance are violently disrupted by "dams, intensive agriculture, urban development, pollution from industry and other land-use practices, including recreational activities." The California Department of Fish and Game has in fact repeatedly favored fishing as a leisure activity over Karuk salmon harvesting.[51]

I rely on Whyte's definition of "collective continuance" throughout this book. I find it especially powerful because it points to a kind of means-ends thinking that does not immediately fall back into the trap of instrumental rationality. Collective continuance is a just end that is *also* an ongoing means. That is, collective continuance is the establishment of political, cultural, environmental, and economic conditions that allow collective life-worlds to flourish over time: it is a set of enabling conditions—an infrastructure. To reject all ends as constraining and oppressive is to miss the ways that some fundamental material conditions—clean water, fertile soil, breathable air—are the preconditions for all other activity. Or to put this another way: collective continuance is a *capacitating* end, a crucial means of affording a range of other ends.[52]

Another term for collective continuance might be "sustainability." This term has long drawn fire from humanists and activists.[53] As often embraced by businesses as by environmental activists, sustainability implies the continuation of life as we know it, which for many in business and politics includes expectations of ongoing economic growth, competition, and accumulation. If we work to sustain current systems—like global markets and extractive industries—we become complicit with the most rapacious forces on earth.[54] Yet in fact, these dominant systems are dramatically unsustainable: the pace of extraction and emission is making the planet uninhabitable for humans and vast numbers of other species. What I want to suggest here is that sustainability is in fact a kind of *neutral* term: it refers to the capacity to keep any state of affairs going over time. In this sense, sustainability can refer to just *or* unjust conditions. What climate change has made suddenly clear is that sustaining must be a goal on the left as well as the right. We are now faced with a struggle to keep collective life going at all. Collective continuance describes a *genuine* sustainability—the vast and urgent project of sustaining collective life over generations.

Amartya Sen's influential "capabilities approach" allows us to see why understanding ends as means is crucial to the work of global justice. Sen turns away from both abstract rights and the distribution of specific resources because these do not recognize or foster cultural heterogeneity: it does little good to have the right to a job if one cannot leave one's home, and it is not enabling to be offered food that it violates one's religion to eat. Justice lies in people's capacity to shape their lives according to a wide range of values. Most unjust are those constraints on specific groups that prevent them from pursuing the full array of possibilities that are available to others. It is unjust to force women to become dependent on male breadwinners for survival, for example, or to allow movement through the streets to remain unsafe for transgender people. For Sen, the ends must remain various: it is not for one group to decide and enforce a particular set of values for others.

Although Sen's model is deliberately pluralist, there is one set of conditions that he singles out as more fundamental than others. He assumes a broad global consensus around "basic capabilities": everyone needs minimal standards of health, food, shelter, and education as a precondition for achieving other ends.[55] These basic capabilities are what draw my attention in this book. They are not particularly complex or interesting to most philosophers, but climate change is threatening all of them right now, including air to breathe and water to drink. As homelands are made unlivable by droughts and floods, as arable land and safe shelter become scarce, and as violent conflicts over resources favor the armed, the powerful, and the rich, vast numbers of people will be forced to sacrifice other cherished ends—such as keeping families together or pursuing an education—for the sake of sheer survival. Whole populations will have to give up their homes in search of food and water. In Sen's terms, any acceptance of the onrushing consequences of global warming is therefore intolerably unjust. And so, I want to make the affirmative case here for capabilities, that is, a set of ends that are also a means: just and sustainable conditions that are themselves a means to allow a rich variety of lives to continue into the future.[56]

This definition of justice allows us to draw a precise distinction between right and left politics. The right often justifies some amount of starvation and homelessness as a necessary spur to economic productivity and argues that this is ultimately good for everyone,[57] while the entire span of the left, from progressives to radicals, argues that it is unjust to deny the most basic necessities of survival to anyone. In other words, *the most important difference between left and right in our time lies not in our relationship to norms and constraints but in the ways we understand enabling conditions—the infrastructures of collective life.*

Despite many and very substantive arguments among us, then, the whole span of the left could begin from a shared basic version of justice that is both an end and a means: the urgent work of guaranteeing basic capabilities for all. There is a universalism here, yes, but it is specifically a universalism of enabling conditions.[58] This is neither a top-down imposition of particular values nor an invitation to neglect racial and cultural difference. As Enzo Rossi and Olúfẹ́mi O. Táíwò argue, the temptation to privilege race at the expense of class or class at the expense of race misses the reason why it is crucial to address the two together, which is that anti-Blackness unjustly distributes the most basic capabilities that should be available to everyone—like adequate nutrition and health care—according to race. They make the case for "embedding antiracist policy within a universalist materialist politics."[59]

With collective continuance as our horizon, we do not have to choose between race and class. Nor do we have to choose between brutal exploitation and principled withdrawal, or between acquiescence to the status quo and change so radical that it is literally unimaginable. We can start doing the hard work of figuring out how to build durable material infrastructures for multiple life-worlds to flourish over time. It is true that we will need to break with dominant systems in order to get to new political and economic conditions, but it is my argument here that we should treat such ruptures not as goals in themselves but as waystations on the route to another, more just, set of ends. The struggle to build better conditions will be much harder and messier—much more imperfect and laborious—than resistance and negation, but to borrow Winnicottian terms, it will be a "good-enough" general guide for the political action that is urgent to undertake now, before so many of the globally devastating runaway effects of climate change have become irreversible.

Practical Action

Turning to the project of guaranteeing basic capabilities carries with it a new relation to political action. Instead of gesturing to unrepresentable futures, I ask: what materials, what agency, what strategies can build conditions for collective continuance here and now?

"Pragmatism" has often been a term of opprobrium in the aesthetic humanities, charged with confining us ever further within the brutal systems of the present. José Esteban Muñoz argues against "gay pragmatism" because it reentrenches the "corrupt and bankrupt social order," and Karen Pinkus warns environmentalists against the "tyranny of the practical."[60] Anything short of pulling this whole rotten society up by the roots is the same as quietism and complacency, wishy-washy liberalism, or worse, sinister neoliberalism. Radical thinkers call for "burning it all down,"[61] drawing on a long history of revolutionary thought that has opposed piecemeal reforms in favor of the shattering work of revolution.[62] At least as far back as Marx and Engels in 1850, leftists have worried that social welfare programs like health care and social security provide just enough in the way of comfort and security to prevent workers from rising up as an angry mass but without changing fundamental economic structures.[63] Accelerationists go so far as to argue that we should hasten the worsening of conditions because desperation is the necessary precondition for revolutionary change.[64] The more moderate—and more pervasive—version of this logic, which we can see in such different thinkers as Jack Halberstam and Giorgio Agamben, is that we should not work for small changes or half measures because these will prolong our acceptance of a fundamentally violent and exploitative system.

But what if this refusal of pragmatic action is wrong? What if institutional changes, techno-fixes, and legislative reforms do not necessarily get in the way of large-scale structural change and can in fact serve radical ends? A different tradition of revolutionary thinkers has understood organizing for achievable ends as important, even necessary, steps in a larger revolutionary struggle. For Rosa Luxemburg, famously, the opposition between revolution and reform was a false dilemma: "The struggle for reforms is its means; the social revolution, its aim." Women's suffrage was for Luxemburg a crucial example.[65] Raymond Williams, too, understood reformist tactics as more effective at mobilizing working-class people than the demand for an immediate smashing of capitalism.[66] In our own time, Chantal Mouffe advocates a "radical reformism" as a crucial tool for building a powerful populism of the left.[67] Against passionate arguments from fellow radicals, Angela Davis has defended the legal reforms of civil rights and the election of Barack Obama as important pieces of the Black radical struggle, not obstacles to it.[68] Similarly, Sherry Wolf, a socialist organizer for LGBTQ rights, has argued for the importance of gay marriage not as a concession to an assimilationist pressure but as part of a larger fight for civil rights for all.[69] And here, perhaps surprisingly, is Slavoj Žižek:

> In the developed Western societies, calls for a radical revolution have no mobilising power. Only a modest "wrong" choice can create the subjective conditions for an actual communist perspective: whether it fails or succeeds, it sets in motion a series of further demands ("in order to really have universal healthcare, we also need . . .") which will lead to the right choice. There is no shortcut here, the need for a radical universal chance has to

> emerge by way of mediation with particular demands. To begin straightaway with the right choice is therefore even worse than making a wrong choice, as it amounts to saying "I am right and the misery of the world which got it wrong just confirms how right I am."[70]

The insistence on revolution in wealthy countries actually turns into the opposite—a kind of perfectionism that gets stuck because it does not have sufficient mobilizing power. In this scenario, revolution *itself* gets in the way of revolution.

Despite many important differences, these thinkers agree that large numbers of people are most inclined to mobilize around immediate causes of suffering and concrete demands. And because revolutions take shape through the collective energy and organization of big groups, practical struggles to transform existing conditions and institutions, such as the fight for labor protections, voting rights, and same-sex marriage, are necessary to the building of the revolutionary left. Or to put this another way: it is a mistake not to recognize the revolutionary potential in any campaign that draws and mobilizes large numbers for expanding or transforming existing institutions, even if these ends are not thoroughgoing transformations of current conditions in their own right, like marriage equality or national health care.

The crucial question here is a strategic one—how social, economic, political, and cultural transformation actually comes about. In place of the fantasy of a spontaneous revolution where, as Bruce Robbins puts it, "Everything Is Suddenly and Utterly Changed,"[71] I turn to the revolutionary tradition that invites us all to struggle with imperfect and near-term political ends, to focus on mobilizing, organizing, and planning, and to engage in the unromantic, demanding work of social transformation through all existing channels for political struggle, including elections, battles for legal rights, and institutions like the university and the state. Practical politics is also crucial to building skills, organizations, and collective power on the left, all preconditions for radical structural change.

If no stark decision has to be made between revolution and reform, if movements across the left grow powerful by joining forces in messy, impure coalitions, and if short-term, practical struggles have the potential to serve long-term radical ends, then the wholesale refusal of pragmatism is troubling indeed.

But what kind of action will be most meaningful? When it comes to climate change, radicals have often been quick to critique political proposals. We should not hope for techno-fixes, for example—whether wind power, geoengineering, or wildlife reclamation projects—because an ongoing reliance on technical knowledge only reentrenches the assumption that human subjects can dominate and manipulate nature and deepens inequitable social relations.[72] Nor does it make sense to seek change through electoral politics, at least in the United States, because this "carbon democracy," dominated by a "politics of economic calculation," depends on fossil fuels.[73] We should not fight for carbon pricing, even if it will bring down emissions globally and quickly, because this reinforces the logic of capitalism.[74] The Green New Deal is troubling either because it does not go far enough or because it sustains the long history of Euro-American colonialism and the exploitation of the Global South.[75]

All of these critiques have merit. But too unflinching a focus on the problems obscures the ways that change actually happens. Kai Heron and Jodi Dean argue, for example, that three groups—scientists, social justice activists, and Indigenous leaders—have created a compelling coalition for environmental justice, despite serious differences in political and epistemic positions and methods: "Allied with science, environmentalists shed their eco-hippy personae to become representatives of a fact-based critique of mass consumption." Meanwhile, "the leadership of indigenous people [grew] to national and international prominence as they forged collective opposition to pipelines and fracking." And then "attention to sacrifice zones, slow death, and the persistent deprivations of environmental racism helped environmentalists move beyond the elitist image long associated with conservationism."[76] Increasing numbers of university scientists have found their knowledge transformed for the better by alliances with Indigenous communities, and racial justice organizations, from the NAACP to Black Lives Matter, have incorporated the fight against climate change and pollution into their daily work.[77] Heron and Dean argue that this coalition has successfully shifted the whole mainstream of public opinion away from climate denialism. In other words, different environmental movements, each marginal or troubling in isolation, have strengthened and transformed each other, and together have provided momentum for larger and larger scales of change.

"Left pessimism," according to Heron and Dean, is not only mistaken but outright dangerous. It has displaced climate denial from fossil fuel interests—where it began—onto the left's "own arguments, shielding themselves from the overwhelming burden of action."[78] The burden of action is overwhelming indeed if we assume that no work is worth doing apart from immediate and total revolution, demolishing every constraint and every institution, or if we must conduct pure and virtuous campaigns that avoid all imposition of human subjects on the world. But the burden lifts if we imagine ourselves as working with the conditions we have to build a larger and larger movement for collective continuance. That is where the hard, imperfect, meaningful, transformative work starts, and that work will be the focus of the pages that follow.

Cultivating New Aesthetic and Political Values

All of this will, of course, seem very far from the arts. But I have been making the case that there is always already a politics at work in aesthetic study, and that the art and politics favored by the aesthetic humanities sustain each other in kind of a circular logic. Ruptures and open-endedness are valuable in art; and art is valuable because it teaches us to break free from the known world into an unrepresentable otherness to come. The challenge, then, is to rethink the politics and the aesthetics together. Throughout this book I have turned to several traditions of thought that have helped to guide me away from a celebration of the pause, the rupture, and the dissolve and toward the work of sustaining collective life.

I have drawn particular inspiration from feminist thought, which has long argued that the art world's emphasis on revolutionary ruptures has meant too little respect for the mundane and repetitive tasks that are crucial to keeping bodies alive. Feminist thinkers like Mierle Laderman Ukeles, Silvia Federici, Luce Giard, bell hooks, Susan Fraiman, Talia Schaffer, and Marquis Bey have argued that artistic and political traditions have too often ignored or devalued the labor necessary to ordinary day-to-day survival, so often women's work—from literal reproduction to the ongoing care of bodies through the preparation of food, care for the sick, and the daily upkeep of environments. As Bey writes: "Is not the obliteration and ending of the world, the burning shit down, as it were—which, it seems, is one of nihilism's demands—a decidedly masculinist endeavor that forgoes black feminist movements of living in the turmoil (living here precisely because here is where we deserve to be) while refusing to concede that here must remain how it is, while bringing the kids, the laundry, the bills . . ."[79] The labor of material maintenance is not necessarily creative or heroic or radically emancipatory. It is practical and repetitive. It has to happen in many of the same ways every day. But no human sociality has ever taken shape without it. And to work for collective continuance will therefore mean revaluing the mundane work that keeps life going over time.

Against a long-standing insistence on rupture and innovation, repetitiveness itself emerges as an aesthetic and political value. It models endurance and persistence, rather than retreat or dissolution after an initial failure. This conclusion has prompted me to revalue the formulas of popular culture. The Frankfurt School's analysis of the "culture industry" as a top-down purveyor of oppressive ideology is particularly critical of repetition, and its arguments remain very much alive in the aesthetic humanities today.[80] For an alternative, I have looked to the Birmingham school of cultural studies, which has made the case for taking working-class people seriously, not as passive dupes of the culture industry but as thoughtful and self-conscious agents working through cultural materials, and translating these into a range of dynamic social practices.[81] This perspective has allowed me to see how repetitive mass pleasures might express authentic and politically productive desires and suggests that publics do not always need to be shaken into a new and unfamiliar consciousness.[82] Not all popular forms will encourage the making of just worlds, to be sure, but they can and some—already, sometimes—do.

It was something of a surprise to me that the questions I posed in this book kept returning me not only to the repetitive patterns of popular culture generally but specifically to realism. Realist fiction has been particularly out of favor with most thinkers in environmental studies until recently. Amitav Ghosh famously argues that the conventional scope and scale of realism are too limiting to capture the strangeness and vastness of climate change.[83] Both artists and critics have often turned to speculative fiction and fantasy for ways to imagine ourselves beyond the present. Afrofuturists have mostly been drawn to science fiction.[84] Elizabeth Chang makes the case that realism cannot push our imaginations to take up the perspectives of non-humans, including plants, which cannot be assimilated to human consciousness.[85]

And yet, several scholars, including Sourit Battacharya, Lynn Badia, Marija Cetinic, and Jeff Diamanti, have recently begun to reevaluate the importance of realist aesthetics for climate politics.[86] Realist art has often been condemned as conservative, making the world as it is seem inert and inevitable.[87] But as my own readings will show, far from naturalizing the tasks of everyday survival, realist texts often go to some trouble to *de*familiarize the ordinary struggle to keep life going over time—to draw our interest to this task. In this respect, realism is not so much conservative as *conservationist*.

Realism's confinement to the plausible is especially valuable, too, for thinking about practical political action. While fantasy, science fiction, and experimental art give shape to surprising and unfamiliar worlds, the conditions they imagine are often radically different from what we can make or build now. These works open our minds to new and exciting possibilities, but they also often reinforce the sense that we must wait for a radical rupture from the present before we can take meaningful action. In this context, I want to draw attention to *attainable* social worlds that we might in fact fight for and build here and now. Realist texts can be put to use as models—design blueprints—for real social formations.

And so, the aesthetic in this book will turn out to be, well, not very aesthetic in any traditional sense: it will be instrumental and popular and pragmatic, comforting and functional and quite deliberately mundane. My own canon of sustainable aesthetics includes Diego Rivera's murals and Mierle Laderman Ukeles's "Maintenance Art," protest chants and the BBC television series *Call the Midwife*, and a motley assortment of narratives, from Charles Dickens's *Oliver Twist* to the movie *Fame* to Chimimanda Ngozi Adichie's *Americanah.* It also includes shapes and patterns organizing experience that do not fall under the usual heading of the aesthetic at all, from the routines of toothbrushing to transportation infrastructures and from kneading bread to sewer systems.

But before we get to these social and aesthetic objects, I want to lay out a case for the importance of formalist methods to the project of collective continuance. Formalism does not belong to the arts, or in fact to any particular discipline, as we will see, but the aesthetic humanities have strong traditions of formalist thinking that will help us move back and forth between art and politics—and to design, build, and fight for sustainable forms for collective life.

2

Method

FORMALISM FOR SURVIVAL

OVER THE PAST HALF CENTURY, two methods have proved especially pervasive and resilient across the aesthetic humanities: close reading and historicizing. Even as scholars have turned their attention to new problems and new objects—from affect theory to animal studies—they have continued to put both close reading and historicizing to work, often together in the same project. What makes these two methods so durable? In keeping with the aesthetic and political values we explored in the last chapter, these methods are especially good at training us to resist prediction and expectation, surprising us out of conventional wisdom and beckoning us to an unknown beyond. That is, they sustain the long-standing commitment to anti-instrumentality.

Close reading involves concentrating slow and careful attention on a brief passage or detail and then connecting what we find there to the larger work.[1] Its defenders have long argued that as we dwell on the specific moment, the text reveals a radical alterity, which then resists and unsettles prevailing doctrines and systems of belief. This argument spans generations, going back as far as R. P. Blackmur, who argues that close analysis of texts produces a "bewilderment" devastating to dogma, up through Gayatri Chakravorty Spivak, who attends to the subtle details of texts as a way of countering the "monolingual, presentist, narcissistic" perspective of imperializing power, to Jane Gallop, who favors close reading as a way of "resisting and calling into question our inevitable tendency to bring things together in smug, overarching conclusions." Most recently, Nan Z. Da argues that reading for fine distinctions is the best way to resist the propaganda strategies of authoritarian regimes.[2]

Focusing on history, meanwhile, means analyzing cultural objects as responses to specific political and material contexts, from prevailing stereotypes and religious movements to state violence and media markets. Since the 1980s, most historicists in the aesthetic humanities have seen their work as seeking out "the singular, the specific, the individual"—the "myriad little connections, disjunctions, and conjunctions" that refuse monolithic or unifying accounts of social worlds.[3] Historical research thus reveals the contingency of practices and beliefs, disturbing imperializing and naturalizing assumptions in order to make way for a rich variety of alternatives. Like close reading, "History opens up the possibility of strangeness."[4]

The first chapter argued that opening up to strangeness is not the best framework for social and environmental justice now. In an age of precarity, the most basic needs, like clean water and safe shelter, are increasingly elusive and unpredictable. While close reading and historicism have been well-suited to interrupting entrenched habits and assumptions, other methods will be needed to follow these crucial moments of surprise and alterity—approaches to strategizing and building ongoing basic capabilities. For that, I will argue in this chapter, we will need an expansive version of formalism, one that is drawn in part from the study of the arts but also reaches beyond the aesthetic.

Formalist Premises

For critics in the arts, the word "form" typically refers to the patterns, shapes, and structures that organize aesthetic objects, from plot and meter to montage and vanishing-point perspective. In my own work, I have deliberately defined form more broadly than is usual in the arts—as any shape or configuration of materials, any arrangement of elements, any ordering or patterning. I have argued that it is useful to employ the same term for both aesthetic and social forms so that we can see how these work together, and how we are everywhere shaped by lots of different kinds of arrangements, from sonnets to public transportation systems.[5]

Politics, according to this definition, is very much a matter of form. Politics entails imposing order on space, for example, such as segregated neighborhoods or borders around nations. Power operates through organizations of time, too, from the age of consent and the forty-hour work week to the global pace of historical progress, with Europe famously imagining itself as the vanguard, consigning the rest of the world to the "waiting room of history."[6] Many of the worst injustices take shape as a third form—the hierarchy: a vertical order, one that ranks its elements according to their higher and lower relative status, giving shape to ongoing material inequalities, including the power of white over Black, masculine over feminine, rich over poor, and straight over queer. Politics involves distributions and arrangements. Or to put this another way: *politics is the work of giving form to collective life.*

Just as plots and rhyme schemes give shape to literature, zoning laws and racial hierarchies give shape to political communities. That does not mean that artistic and political orders are the same. It is clearly crucial to distinguish coercive political forms that are literally matters of life and death from imaginative and speculative works of art. But my point here is specifically *methodological.* Just as a historical scholar can give a rich contextualizing account of many kinds of events, from diplomacy to childbirth, and just as a statistician can track patterns across many different kinds of objects, from gene mutations to income disparities, a formalist scholar can analyze the shapes and patterns of a *Bildungsroman* or a school system. And that means that aesthetic critics have methodological tools that are portable beyond the aesthetic.

Some humanists have argued strenuously against an expansion of formalist reading to include politics,[7] but a movement back and forth between aesthetic and political forms is already one of the most ordinary practices in the aesthetic humanities. A scholar of poetry, for example, will attend to both the aesthetic and social orders at work in a given poem—connecting metrical patterns to the rhythms of industrial labor, for example—and will be particularly interested in how these intersect, sometimes reinforcing and sometimes undermining one another.

Let me offer a few deliberately various examples from recent scholarship to show how routine it is for scholars across media and periods to read for the relations between aesthetic and political arrangements. Barbara Fuchs understands the unreliable and meandering forms of the picaresque novel in early modern Spain as a challenge to the unified authority of imperial power. Juliana Hu Pegues reads Shoki Kayamori's early twentieth-century photographs as offering "multivalent expressions of space and time that extend beyond the limitations of settler colonial logic." Hongmei Sun shows how the first animated Chinese film, *Princess Iron Fan* (1941), made at the moment of the Japanese invasion and occupation of China, encouraged ordinary people to band together in a united collective to fend off foreign invaders. And Anthony Reed interprets Claudia Rankine's *Don't Let Me Be Lonely*—with its fragmented structure, its mix of visual and verbal media, and its multiple first-person perspectives—as indexing a shattered, partial, precarious, incoherent racialized subjectivity in the contemporary United States.[8]

In some of these readings, we are invited to see how the art form registers or reinforces a dominant political order, while in others the aesthetic form unsettles or cracks open the political form. But in all of these cases, the scholar is offering some account not only of the art object but of a specific political arrangement, whether that is the unified imperial state or the fragmented subject. Even in the aesthetic fields, in other words, form is not an exclusively aesthetic problem.

And yet, while critics insist on the importance of the shapes and patterns of sociopolitical life—the liberal subject, the rhythms of labor, the walled settlement—the aesthetic humanities do not give these as much careful analytic attention as the cultural forms that we take to be our primary objects of analysis. That is, while aesthetic scholars usually give a rich, complex account of the complexity of cultural forms, they leave an understanding of political forms thin—and, this chapter will argue, misleading.

For understandable political reasons, most critics focus attention on violent and oppressive structures and arrangements, celebrating texts that unsettle naturalized narratives of national progress, for example, or explore gender expressions beyond the dominant binary. But this practice also leads to the understanding, often left implicit, that *all* constraining forms are violent and coercive. It is for this reason that we find critics across schools of thought, from feminism to thing theory, arguing that we should refuse the fixity of forms in favor of ephemerality, fluidity, and dissolution.[9] We can see this logic at work in a powerful recent essay in my own home field, titled "Undisciplining Victorian Studies." Here, Ronjaunee Chatterjee, Alicia Mireles Christoff, and Amy R. Wong argue that Victorian studies has been built around two kinds of container: the aesthetics of "formal closures" and the "self-protective containments of race and geography." This form, they warn, entails "exclusion, especially of the non-canonical, the racialized, and the seemingly unrecognizable."[10] This is a deeply persuasive and, I would add, consummately formalist account: the authors single out a specific organizing form—the container—and point out that this succeeds in organizing politics, aesthetics, and scholarship in Victorian studies to troubling ongoing effect. But what is interesting is that the authors then use this formalist analysis to reject formalism as a method. Because form is *always* a matter of enclosing and excluding, they argue, Victorian studies should turn away from the study of forms. Implicit here is the logic that all forms are containers, and that all containers are politically repressive. The proper work of the critic, by this logic, is to resist form.

Many influential thinkers have taken the argument for the violence of formal constraints a step further, arguing that the various orders and arrangements that give shape to the social world—from architecture to law to romantic comedies—work together in dominant systems. For Foucault, this is the regime of the carceral. For Fredric Jameson it is late capitalism. For Lisa Lowe it is Western liberalism. For Jared Sexton it is anti-Blackness. For Lee Edelman it is reproductive futurism. Interestingly, all of these regimes both overlap and diverge. But whatever their relations, these models have helped to entrench a habit of thinking about political form: that different shapes and arrangements lock together in massive systems or structures of power.

Two assumptions about political forms, then, shape scholarship across the aesthetic humanities: first, that forms are oppressive instruments of control; and second, that very different forms, from police training to science fiction, work together to sustain regimes of domination. Are these assumptions justified? Attending to the *capacitating* potential of shapes and arrangements, this chapter argues otherwise. I ground my argument here in six formalist premises:

1. *No human collective can do without form.* Because humans are interdependent, we have always needed to figure out—and will probably always need to figure out—how to organize and distribute the materials of collective life. Even the most emancipatory *polis* of the future will require regular distributions of food and clean water, spaces for rest and sociability, and rules for decision making. This does not mean that there is a single, proper order for human life. As Anna Kornbluh argues, "Humans cannot exist without forms that scaffold sociability, even though the particular forms that human sociability takes are not fixed."[11]
2. No single form is necessary, but *there is a finite range of ways to organize materials for survival.* Living bodies need nutrients not once but over and over, which means that human communities have always revolved around repetitive rhythms—and especially the recurring labor of finding, growing, gathering, preparing, and serving food. Human collectives have also always depended on pathways to get food and water to the places where we live and to take waste away. And our bodies have always needed some form of enclosure to protect us from harsh weather and other dangers.
3. *Some ways of organizing the infrastructures of collective life are more just and capacitating than others.* Consider the difference between egalitarian

food-sharing to all members of a community and the allocation of the most nutritious food to men of property, or the difference between a thirty-five-hour work week and the continual forced labor of enslaved people. Egalitarian distributions and labor protections are not formless; they are tightly organized. If the *polis* always entails some structuring of sociability, then the goal is not to push beyond all constraints but figure out which specific shapes are better and worse for collective continuance.

4. *Forms carry with them a limited range of capacities, which I call affordances.* Affordances are the actions or uses latent in certain materials or designs.[12] Wax is good for pouring and molding, but it is not strong enough to use for building bridges. The shape of the dining table affords small-scale conversation, eating, and the paying of bills, but it does not lend itself to mass protests. Inventive people can certainly put things to work for unintended uses—like slicing a cake with dental floss. This is an expansion of the *intended* affordances of dental floss, but it is still an affordance—a use latent in the materiality and design of the object. What this means is that forms and materials have a limited range of capacities: they will always be able to do some things well and others badly or not at all.
5. *Form is a materialist concern.* Formalism has long been associated with disembodied abstraction, aesthetic transcendence, and a deliberate withdrawal from politics.[13] But a formalist analysis that focuses on the shapes of the material world, including the rhythms of labor and the contours of public spaces, attends to the body, the everyday, and the social.
6. *Social, political, and aesthetic patterns and arrangements do not typically lock together in coherent systems.* Different forms follow different logics of organization—boundaries do not impose the same order as routes or tempos. For this reason, forms often destabilize each other, getting in each other's way and creating openings for change. The emphasis of my own work in *Forms* was on these aleatory possibilities, which was very much in keeping with the field's long emphasis on rupture and open-endedness.[14] And yet, it was also always clear that some forms dominate, and have staying power. White supremacy and patriarchy are especially—obstinately—sticky, enduring despite changes in law, economics, and culture. But because of our strong emphasis on unmaking in the aesthetic humanities, our fields do not know enough about *why* some forms work together over long periods, while others

unsettle each other and come apart. Thus we need formalist methods to understand how different forms work together in both destabilizing *and* stabilizing ways.

Form and Ideology

So: where does a formalist account of politics begin? Most cultural critics start with ideology. That is, they understand social and aesthetic shapes and arrangements as effects of specific systems of value and belief. Lauren Berlant and Michael Warner argue, for example, that heteronormativity shapes "almost every aspect of the forms and arrangements of social life: nationality, the state, and the law; commerce; medicine; education; plus the conventions and affects of narrativity, romance, and other protected spaces of culture."[15]

The ideological explanation is persuasive. It is true, for instance, that a predominantly heteronormative culture produces and maintains some forms at the expense of others—like the sanitizing and policing of public spaces to make heterosexual couples and families feel safe and visible while concealing and criminalizing queerness.[16] But this account also assumes that forms follow from ideologies. Is it possible, instead, that beliefs and values grow out of material shapes and arrangements? For example, patriarchal values are clearly responsible for limiting women's wages, positions, and kinds of work. But does women's lower economic status then help to reinforce beliefs in male dominance? Could both be at work? If so, how would we know? Do forms and ideologies operate in a kind of feedback loop in which each reinforces the other? That is, could ideology sometimes be a cause and sometimes an effect?

It is my hypothesis here that material forms can in fact shape and engender some worldviews and practices of sociability while foreclosing others. That is, all kinds of arrangements—from occupied territories to environmental regulations to classroom seating—produce us as much as we produce them, not only organizing and constraining but also creating the very fabric of social relationships.

Imagine, for example, that you grow up in a city with inexpensive, safe, and accessible public transportation. As a teenager, you can explore the many corners of the city. You and your friends gawk at expensive homes, wander through queer neighborhoods, and sneak into music venues. You are crammed together with strangers on the bus every morning on your way to school, and on the way home you make up funny stories about the few scattered adults who are sleeping on the bus. When it comes time to find a job, you are able to look across the whole city.

Now, imagine instead that you live in a rural area without public transit, where houses are spaced so far from each other that you rarely see your neighbors. If as a teenager you want to see your friends, you might have to ask an adult for a ride, and most often you are stuck at home. Your local school may be full of people who look like you, racially and economically, and when you start looking for a job you will need to borrow or buy a car just to get to the interviews.

In other words, your worldview may flow at least in part from the shape of the transportation infrastructure that you have inherited, perhaps from several generations before you. From this perspective, power is not best described as the work of dominant groups intentionally exerting control. It is true, of course, that the public transportation system is the result of human intention and design in the first place: it had to be planned, fought for, and built. Like all infrastructures, it also needs to be maintained over time, and some groups will deliberately allow public transportation systems to crumble. In this sense, people can make, unmake, and remake forms. And yet, once the public transportation system is in place, it will also give shape to the lives of many who are not responsible for making it for years to come. Thus a form held over from the past maintains its power to direct experience and shape values now and into the future, molding neighborhoods, daily routines, education, work experience, the freedom to roam, and the understanding of lives unlike our own. That does not mean that agency is altogether foreclosed, but it does mean that building and installing durable forms can have formative effects on beliefs, values, and practices for long periods to come.

It will be clear from the argument so far that this book focuses most closely on the shapes of human communities and the possibilities of human action. Environmental and animal studies readers will probably object that this is too human-centered a project. Yet, the formalist methods at work here in fact emerge out of posthumanist and ecological theory. It is this thinking that has allowed me to see how arrangements of non-human materials—from sewer systems to classrooms to beehives—capacitate better and worse collectivities. But I also deliberately keep my sights on humans in this book for a few reasons. First, because a certain anthropocentrism seems unavoidable in scholarly debate. As Matthew Flisfeder puts it, posthumanists do not try "to convince a rock that it is noumenal." We write to convince each other about our ethical responsibilities.[17] Second, while the critique of the human subject that understands itself as separate from nature and seeks to master objects for its own use is persuasive and urgently important, it does not follow, as I argued in the first chapter, that all human action is conquest. And the desire to avoid all complicity is troubling in its own right, risking a principled inaction, a withdrawal from responsibility—and therefore an acquiescence to the violent forces of the status quo. "While it is obviously dangerous to overestimate human agency," Min Hyoung Song writes, "there is also grave danger in underestimating it."[18]

The definition of the human at work in this book is closest to Barbara Epstein's, who writes that "humans, like other animal species, have characteristics, including specific needs, abilities, and limits to those abilities." This account puts its emphasis not on mastery but on shared materiality, capacities, and constraints. "Socialist humanism," as Epstein defines it, "is based on the view that humans require social cooperation and support, are capable of collective effort and individual creativity, and are most likely to thrive in egalitarian communities dedicated to the common welfare rather than the pursuit of private profit."[19]

A formalist account can certainly work for multispecies collective continuance. Animals and plants, after all, also depend for their survival on forms, from seasonal cycles to sheltering spaces. Climate change is devastating for not only the forms that sustain human communities but those that support literally millions of other species as well. In this context, the goal is to figure out what I and whatever other willing humans can do, within the limits of our own capacities, to make the planet more livable for all species; and to see communities that include humans—and not only those narrowly counted as human by Euro-American settlers—survive, and do so with more justice than our current systems and practices allow.

Form across Disciplines

Aesthetic critics have analytic skills that we can take to the forms of social worlds, but we are not the only ones carrying a formalist toolbox. A vast range of objects, from sounds to neighborhoods to coral reefs, can be analyzed for their structures and patterns, which means that there are scholars attentive to shapes and structures working across fields, from religious studies to entomology to urban planning. In this respect, formalism belongs to all fields, or to none.

Formalism in fact has the potential to be a useful *metadisciplinary* method in two specific ways. First, a formalism that works across disciplines can help us recognize the limits and the possibilities of different forms of knowledge. My own disciplinary training has taught me to focus my attention on the novel, and in the past I, like many other critics, would have thought it was my job to ask how the novel seeks to understand and respond to a whole range of political problems, from gender inequality to racial capitalism. But a metadisciplinary formalism allows me to think as much about the limits as the capacities of the novel, and to see it as one form among others, with constraints that may be obstacles to both knowing and reshaping the *polis*.

The contemporary novel, according to Amitav Ghosh, "banishes the collective from the territory of the fictional imagination." He blames this limitation on the specific ideologies of our historical moment.[20] But it is also a long-standing problem of form. The realist novel has long been organized around plots and protagonists—exciting events and exceptional individuals—which makes it especially well suited to the scale of a few persons. Even when the classic nineteenth-century realist novel has aspirations to convey massive social structures and systems, as Alex Woloch has argued, it repeatedly narrows its attention to a small number of richly rounded characters at the expense of the mass.[21] A huge range of novels since then, from Virginia Woolf's *Mrs. Dalloway* and Mulk Raj Anand's *Untouchable* to Toni Morrison's *Beloved* and Yuri Herrera's *Señales que precederán al fin del mundo*, train our attention on a single protagonist or two in a specific historical situation. Many novels work in the Lukácsian mode, using one main character's experience to convey social structures or conflicts.[22] Sometimes the novel uses specific characters to stand for whole populations. The postbellum American novel, to give just one example, repeatedly joins a Confederate man with a Northern woman in its marriage plots, recruiting this narrative arc as an illusory resolution to the ongoing problem of national disunity.[23]

Janice Ho defines the novel *tout court* as "a genre preoccupied with the relationship between the protagonist and the social contexts in which he or she exists."[24] We could certainly cite experiments in the novel form that expand its usual cast of characters—from Honoré de Balzac's *Comédie Humaine* to Helena Maria Viramontes's *Their Dogs Came with Them*. But we could also begin from an altogether different starting point. Instead of analyzing a field of objects defined in advance as aesthetic—like the novel—and from that point trying to cross the gap between art and politics, we could ask which forms—both those that are conventionally aesthetic and those that are not—most readily invite an understanding of collective life.

Let's take the political problem of wealth inequality. The traditional plot-and-protagonist form of the novel is good at exploring some aspects of this problem—and bad at others. Capitalism and urbanization clearly shape experience in Charles Dickens's Britain and Chris Abani's Nigeria, for example, but *Oliver Twist* and *Graceland* tell us little about the forces, structures, and political decisions that produce these effects. What we do learn from the novels is what it is like to struggle to survive in these conditions, with desires repeatedly thwarted and serious dangers always threatening.

Contrast the novel's accounts to a very different form, a Center on Budget and Policy Priorities bar graph showing average gains and losses in U.S. incomes between 1979 and 2007. The graph divides the population into five groups and focuses on a single variable across those groups, showing simplified general trends that gather together huge numbers—reducing vast quantities of people, jobs, and dollars to one stark comparison. What is most striking, of course, is not the specifics of the numbers but the remarkable contrast—the *Gestalt*: that incomes lagged for the bottom four-fifths of the population, while skyrocketing for the top 1 percent. The graph uses color to set off the top 1 percent as a separable category: blue bars mark the five quintiles, but then an extra bar in red registers a single percent within the top quintile. This contrast in color foregrounds the startling difference—with red evoking stop signs and emergencies—between the 1 percent and the rest.

There is a powerful and striking—even, one might say, aesthetically compelling—account of inequality at work in this bar graph. At the same time, it has clear limitations when it comes to our knowledge of wealth and poverty. It does not tell us how structural inequality came to be, a task for historical narrative. And it cannot give us a rich sense of what it feels like to live within and against the many structural barriers of poverty, bumping up against obstacles to transportation and adequate nutrition and racial justice and homeownership and high-quality education. That is a task better left to the novel or the news story.

While some critics might insist that the novel does intrinsically better political work than the graph because it keeps us attentive to difference, refusing to agglomerate a vast range of situated experiences into knowable and governable categories, like "nation" or "population," a politics of social justice needs both. To understand poverty as a consequence of structural forces, rather than individual moral failure or bad decision making, we need to grasp the obstacles that constrain the lives of the pluckiest of characters. At the same time, any single case of hunger and hardship could be an anomaly; to

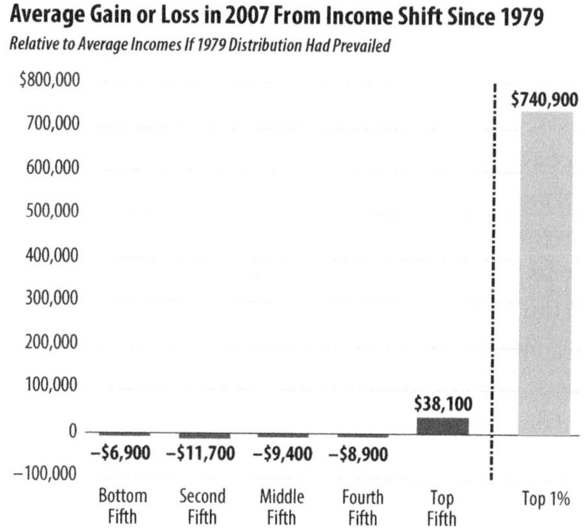

FIGURE 1. Center on Budget and Policy Priorities, https://www.cbpp.org/blog/enough-is-enough-on-tax-cuts-for-wealthy.

understand the reach of powerful structures like race and disability across social groups, we need to be able to recognize large-scale patterns. Both the novel and the graph thus afford a knowledge as well as an ignorance. And each reveals the limits of the other.

In the university today, our disciplines typically divide forms from one another—we put statistics in one department, history in a second, poetry in a third, visual images in a fourth, and the ethnographic interview in yet a fifth. Even within literary studies, we have experts in fiction who do not study drama, and vice versa. But what if we need all of these forms, precisely because each has powers and limits that the others do not? A map can show the distribution of world hunger, but it does not give us a sense of what it is like to wake up every day to an empty stomach; a photograph can show the devastating effects of war on a civilian scene, but it does not tell us how the violence started. In short, the first reason to use formalism to move across the disciplines is that we need many forms to know the world, and we need formalists to help us see what it is—and how it is—that we know.

If the first reason to turn to a metadisciplinary formalism concerns knowledge, the second has to do with action. Both the novel and the bar graph lead us to understand something about inequality, but neither form readily invites us to gather together or to pursue particular political strategies. Typically absorbed in silence and solitude, the material form of the paperback affords isolation and separation—even a temporary retreat from social pressures and responsibilities.[25] Novels can of course be read aloud in classrooms, clubs, pubs, and other collective spaces, and the serialized novel and unfolding news story afford the interruption of private absorption with pauses for collective reflection, as audiences gather over the water cooler or on the internet between episodes to reflect on the work so far and to speculate about what is coming. But other forms more readily afford the *production* of collectives. Live theater, for example, brings people together into a shared space, where audiences may be prompted to share laughter, applause, or song, and sometimes even erupt into riotous violence. The conflictual and dialogic forms of dramatic plots also afford radical questionings of authority and sovereignty, which together with its crowds have made drama seem like an especially threatening political form over the centuries.[26]

The public square, a less conventionally aesthetic form, has afforded many of the most famous political protests of recent years, including Tiananmen, Tahrir, and Trafalgar Squares, and New York's Zuccotti Park. Because these public spaces afford highly visible vast crowds, they are well suited to putting the sheer enormity of collective resistance on display. But the "movement of the squares," as we will see in a later chapter, has also been sporadic and ineffective at exerting and sustaining a lasting political force.

In short, all forms afford certain possibilities and foreclose others. And a formalism not limited by discipline can ask: what versions of collective life is it possible to know and build with different forms? This is not an aesthetic question, exactly, but it is not outside of aesthetics either. It allows us to ask how art forms interrelate with political arrangements and how they may give shape to worlds. But it does not prompt us to seek out works that are particularly innovative or beautiful or complex objects in themselves. It does not focus on the ways that cultural forms express specific contexts. It does not try to track the particular values and associations that different forms have accrued historically. Instead, this approach asks us to look for forms of all kinds that might help us fight for, design, build, and maintain a just and sustaining *polis*.

Formal Survival

Up to this point, I have argued that an expansive formalism can help us understand how some forms afford particular kinds of knowledge and action more effectively than others. Now let's turn to the particular challenge of collective continuance. Scholars in the aesthetic humanities have tended to privilege discomfiting processes, unruliness, and flux over fixed and stable structures. But collective continuance requires an understanding of that which lasts. What forms afford stability, reliability, and predictability over time? And are there ways to design and build just and capacitating forms—like public transportation or food security—so that they can take hold and endure?

For this we need an account of what I call *formal survival*. That is, we need to understand which social arrangements manage to stay in place over time. Many forms that take a robust material shape, like walls and roads, are built for the long term, but how do less literally inert forms, like racial hierarchies, manage to take hold and last over centuries, despite major changes in law, culture, and economics? My working hypothesis here is that *shapes and arrangements are most likely to endure when they operate in self-reinforcing configurations*—when material and ideological forms, for example, support each other, and so keep each other going over time.

A well-known example will help to make this clear. In 1934, the U.S. government established a system of defining certain neighborhoods as too risky for federal banks to invest in them. They drew red lines around these areas on city maps. The Federal Housing Administration was willing to guarantee loans only in neighborhoods occupied by "the race for which they are intended" and where local schools "should not be attended in large numbers by inharmonious racial groups."[27] This explicitly racist law subsidized mortgages for houses being built in neighborhoods in the suburbs, as long as only white people lived there, and blocked mortgages for prospective homeowners in urban Black and Latinx neighborhoods. Redlining then shaped other forms, like the construction of mass transit systems that linked downtowns to white suburbs while bypassing minority neighborhoods. Sewage treatment plants often ran to high-income subdivisions but offered no access to the urban poor.[28] Since public schooling in the United States is largely funded through local property and sales taxes, segregating neighborhoods deepened inequality between urban and suburban schools. Lack of access to public transportation and high-quality education in turn intensified poverty for Black and Latinx city dwellers.[29]

In this model, racial hierarchy organizes *other* forms. It starts by separating neighborhoods by race. It then directs the routes taken by roads, mass transit, and clean water. The lack of access to jobs and healthy food then entrenches and deepens poverty and inequality, which in turn feed a cultural myth of white superiority. Racism is an intentional ideological force in the first place, but then it persists by organizing *other* forms. And since rock and steel can outlast the intentions of their first construction, these material forms can prolong the work of racial hierarchy through later historical moments. A sewer is designed to be invisible, to function without the conscious attention of most of its users. It can therefore last well beyond the ideology that built it in the first place, continuing to shape and organize collective life without much in the way of ongoing justification, celebration, or consent to keep it going. With redlining, multiple durable forms of organization—housing law, school systems, sewer lines, trains, and roads—thus worked together to write racial hierarchy into the built environment for the long term. Simply to call this ideology is, I think, to miss the actual mechanisms of endurance, which depend on the arrangement of mutually reinforcing forms. The Fair Housing Act of 1968 could remedy some of the most unjust loan practices, but by that point racial hierarchy had written itself into the very shapes of the *polis*.

This story might well prompt us to want to fight forms and systems, but I am going to take the argument in the opposite direction, to make the case that the success and durability of this formal model also has a valuable lesson to offer to those working for justice. If we understand how portable, generalizable models work together to reinforce one another over time, those who want to work for collective continuance could use these lessons to develop our own sturdy alternatives—constellations of forms that could reliably produce and reproduce fairness over time.

To this end, let me offer the more hopeful model of Belo Horizonte, Brazil, nicknamed "the city that ended hunger." A leftist government in the early 1990s developed policies to guarantee food as a right for this city of more than 2.5 million. Nearly a fifth of all children in the city were suffering from malnutrition at the time, and there were high rates of child mortality.[30] Rather than proposing an emergency program or targeting a particular neighborhood or population, Belo Horizonte introduced a cluster of twenty integrated solutions across the city, which they call a "food security system." Elements include nutritious school meals, subsidies for fruits and vegetables, training programs for bakers and chefs, seed distribution to school and community gardens, and licenses for food trucks to move around the city with the stipulation they spend a certain amount of time in poor neighborhoods selling fresh foods at a fixed low price.[31]

Perhaps the best known of all the programs has been the "Popular Restaurants." Located in busy areas, these restaurants serve locally farmed, nutritious meals at very low prices. With high-quality food and a pub-like

FIGURE 2. Restaurante Popular in Belo Horizonte, Brazil (2011). Prefeitura de Belo Horizonte.

atmosphere—sometimes including live music—the Popular Restaurants attract people from across the socioeconomic spectrum, about a quarter from the middle and upper classes, with the consequence that eating there does not stigmatize the poor. Many people eat together at long tables, with students, elderly, professional, and unhoused people sitting side by side.[32]

Belo Horizonte's food security system has had some dramatic effects. Since the 1990s, infant mortality and child malnutrition have dropped by half, and poverty rates have declined significantly.[33] There is also evidence that Belo Horizonte's programs have contributed to local biodiversity by encouraging ecologically sound farming practices.[34]

But what is perhaps most notable about this food system is that it has long outlasted expectations. At the start, commentators predicted that it would fall apart as soon as the political pendulum swung right. They assumed that food security depended on a kind of political will that would simply disappear with the next election or economic crisis. Now that it has been in place for more than two decades, however, scholars are instead trying to find explanations for the food system's longevity. As food policy scholar Cecelia Rocha puts it, "Having more than 25 years of an approach to food and nutrition security is unique."[35]

A formalist analysis would have it that Belo Horizonte's food security system is sustainable because its different elements work so well together, as in the redlining example—in a kind of formal feedback loop. The Popular Restaurants offer all city dwellers affordable and healthy meals, for example, but they also bring people from different walks of life together to share food in a deliberately pleasant atmosphere, which—as opposed to so many deliberate forms of segregation—helps expand and deepen feelings of solidarity and connectedness across differences like race and class, which in turn encourages the political will for continuing collective solutions.

Or take Belo Horizonte's "Straight from the Countryside" program. Here, small family farmers in outlying areas receive government support for growing environmentally sustainable and nutritious fruits and vegetables, which they sell directly to urban consumers in designated public sites, cutting out corporate middlemen. A public process determines which farmers are eligible, based on the size of the farm and income level of the family; the government then requires certain sustainable farming methods from participants and sets low sale prices. The most important form here is the standardized quantity: small farms, low prices. But a different form—the network—also plays a crucial role. The program locates sales sites in busy urban thoroughfares where fresh food is otherwise scarce. These sites are places where two *different* networks cross: they are hubs for human movement, but they are gaps in the fresh food supply chain, or "food deserts." The various forms at work then reinforce one another. While city dwellers gain access to healthy food at low prices, rural farmers earn a decent living, which helps stem the migration of the rural poor to urban shantytowns, which in turn takes pressure off government programs, freeing up ongoing resources for the food system. The city can then train more chefs and urban gardeners, promote biodiversity, and put resources into keeping food quality high. Overall health, nutrition, and income rise; the need for city services to respond to poverty falls.[36]

Many of these elements exist separately in other cities, but part of what makes Belo Horizonte's program endure is the careful design of its administration across government departments. A single school gardening program could easily be cut by a new party in power, but to undo an integrated citywide system with multiple interconnecting forms that span neighborhoods and classes and municipal departments would involve a radical dismantling. So far it has lasted through multiple political parties, which suggests that it is indeed much more difficult to take apart a self-reinforcing system than a single ad hoc solution.

I have turned to these two examples, one deeply unjust, the other aimed at guaranteeing basic needs, to show how a formalist attention to social worlds can be useful to the project of sustaining collective life. I hope it is clear that I am reading cities in some of the same ways I would read a poem. Like the critic who connects Robert Browning's short end-stopped lines to the rhythms of train travel,[37] I am tracking different organizations of housing and the pathways of food and water through the *polis* as these interact and intersect. Sometimes social forms support one another, and at other times they get in each other's way, as when a food security system works against patterns of racialized poverty. But for the project of collective continuance, it is especially important to learn from mutually reinforcing forms. These are the formal feedback loops that afford sustainability over long stretches of time.

Designing for Collective Continuance

So far, we have seen how formalist methods are valuable in the effort to *analyze* sustainable social formations. Now I want to make the case that there is an aesthetic tradition that can help us to *participate* in the building of more just conditions. This is not the anti-instrumental canon of art that has been so central to the aesthetic humanities but rather the tradition of design, which is all about putting forms to practical use. In the work of design, forms move back and forth between aesthetic and social worlds. That is, designs are aesthetic in the sense that they are imagined and constructed, and they are material and social in that they give shape to matter, including the spaces, pathways, and objects that are everywhere organizing our lives.

Designers typically depend on *models*. A traditional architect, for example, might begin with a two-dimensional paper blueprint, which is then used to create an object in another medium, such as a skyscraper composed of steel and glass. As the design passes from sketch to building, what it is doing is abstracting forms—shapes and patterns—so that they can move from one material to another. The same rectangular shape organizes a small drawing of a window and a large glass pane framed by steel. Forms, in this sense, are portable.

In fact, the whole point of a designer's model is to be portable—from small to large, from possible to actual, from place to place. Models move across materials, media, scales. Think of a model of a city, shrinking and simplifying the vast and teeming reality. Or consider a model apartment, the same size as all the others but existing in more than one place. Some models remain imaginary and two-dimensional, like an architectural plan that never becomes a building. Models do not have to be static, either: in a Bayesian macroeconomic model or a board game like Pandemic, the task is to test out multiple scenarios. Models are used in aesthetic, scientific, and social domains: an artist might make clay models for a bronze sculpture; a scientist might use digital models to understand genetic interactions; and an urban planner might design a model for neighborhood revitalization. Models can also cross domains: engineers in Japan turned to the bills of kingfishers to help them design a high-speed train that runs quietly.[38]

The way that models work is that they sharpen or set in motion our knowledge of a reality that is not available to direct perception. They deliberately abstract relationships so that we can grasp those relationships apart from their details. That is, *models allow us to understand forms at work across contexts.* By detaching shapes, orders, arrangements from particular media and circumstances, they invite us to play out the work of forms, especially in their interactions with other forms. The kingfisher's wedge-shaped beak, which allows it to make sudden dives without splashing when it hits the water, inspired the shape of a train that can quietly manage the sudden change in air resistance when it enters a tunnel.

The portability of forms is what allows designers to move from imagination to built reality. It is also what allows us to make some predictions about what forms will do as they travel across time and space. In the aesthetic humanities, scholars have often read aesthetic forms as responses to specific historical contexts. But many of the most common sociopolitical forms never begin anywhere *in particular*: we can find hierarchies and enclosures, triads and binaries, rows and circles, in most social arrangements—ancient and modern, Western and non-Western. Bridges arise independently in many cultures, and so do wheels. We find narrative quests and repetitive song refrains in many places around the world too.

As forms crop up across contexts, they carry their affordances with them, organizing materials in the same limited range of ways, with the same finite array of affordances. Let me offer a brief example. The protest chant "Un pueblo, unido, será jamás vencido" began as part of a 1970s Chilean working-class political movement, but it has since traveled across borders and generations with surprising effortlessness, taken up by protesters for many causes and translated into Persian, English, German, Tagalog, and Portuguese.[39] I first chanted it myself in English as "A people, united, will never be defeated," marching against the anti-labor governor of Wisconsin in 2011. This short form affords easy memorization and recitation. Brief and catchy, rousing and rhythmic, it can pass quickly from protest to protest without instruction or explanation. It affords an experience of embodied solidarity, a joining of bodies and voices through shared spoken and marching rhythms. There is no question that the affordances of the chant will always be limited: it is too short and simple a form, for example, to do justice to the historical specificity of each protest, much less the particular perspective of each protester. It does not afford scientific evidence or plotted narration. But the affordances it does have are powerful: there are few forms better suited to quickly engendering a feeling of mass collective embodiment and purpose.

As each form moves from place to place, it will take its affordances with it, always able to do some things well and others badly or not at all. Borders will always enclose and contain, protect and exclude. A hierarchy of authority in one place and time will do some similar work to a similar hierarchy at another place and time. As Foucault says, "stones can make people docile and knowable," arguing that the arrangements of material in space produce and reproduce certain versions of subjectivity. But forms are not only troubling: they can also empower and enable a range of action. A network of durable tunnels underground, for example, affords the passage of clean water into my home and wastewater out, and in the process it also affords me certain freedoms: I do not need to walk hours each day to fetch water for washing and cooking, like many other women around the world, and I am not wracked by deadly waterborne diseases. The tunnels are an organizing form; they restrict and constrain matter, but, crucially, they also capacitate.

Drawing these claims together leads to a transhistorical and transcultural argument about politics and form. If collective life always depends on organizing forms, if similar forms can appear in multiple times and spaces, and if forms have general properties that they carry with them wherever they go, then it follows that *we can make some predictions about how political forms will work wherever they take shape*. We can then put that knowledge to use to design better forms for collective life.

Both redlining and the food system of Belo Horizonte are portable models. Redlining began as a federal program, replicated across the United States. Private banks then took their cue from government policy, denying loans to prospective homeowners in redlined neighborhoods. What followed was a similar pattern of white flight, suburban sprawl, school segregation, underfunded city services, and increasingly entrenched racial inequality across U.S. cities. The same interlocking of material forms yielded similar patterns of injustice from Los Angeles to Detroit to Memphis, affording both a ready replicability and a terrifying endurance over time, helping to sustain racial injustice across generations.

Belo Horizonte's food security system is portable too, at least in theory. It has inspired the cities of Cape Town in South Africa and Windhoek in Namibia to consider instituting a set of interconnected food security programs on the Belo Horizonte design.[40] It could also work in the United States, where redlined neighborhoods are typically food deserts and where cities are often ringed by struggling farmers trying to make ends meet.

Critics sometimes argue that design serves neoliberal agendas,[41] but it also has powerful revolutionary potential. As it crosses back and forth between aesthetic and social domains, between the imagination and the real, it draws attention to the artfulness and the artifices of our social worlds. Both sonnets and public transportation systems are designed and made, which means they can also be *re*designed and *re*made. Design offers a field of practices that build on an understanding of formal affordances to reimagine and remake the shapes and arrangements of collective life. The goal here is not to determine, once and for all, what will work in all cases but to make sense of organizing forms that have worked in the past and to think about how and why certain constellations might support collective continuance. That is, to experiment with forms and to use them as equipment for social transformation.

The Forms of Institutions

Formalism can give us the analytical tools we need to understand how forms of many different kinds work together, and design can help communities envision and craft better forms. But remaking the world for climate justice is obviously a tall order, and I have promised a determinedly pragmatic approach to this work. What does this mean in practice? It is my argument, here, that we should start by working to remake the forms of existing institutions.

An emphasis on institutions may sit uneasily with many thinkers in the aesthetic humanities. Influenced by Foucault, Althusser, and Bourdieu, our fields have worked hard to reveal the oppressive power of major modern institutions—the family, the school, the military, the hospital, the prison, and the state—as these produce, coerce, and manage subjects. Historical work across the aesthetic humanities has also shown how less obviously violent institutions, such as museums, archives, and novels, adopt techniques of imperial management and racial control.[42] Afropessimists have made particularly powerful arguments that dominant institutions have sedimented an inexorable anti-Blackness at their core. For Frank Wilderson III, the "White family and the White state" write anti-Blackness into "the genetic material of this organism called the United States of America."[43] And according to Stefano Harney and Fred Moten, all institutions, including universities, do the work of prisons: "In the clear, critical light of day, illusory administrators whisper of our need for institutions, and all institutions are political, and all politics is correctional, so it seems we need correctional institutions in the common, settling it, correcting us. But we won't stand corrected."[44] For Dylan Rodríguez, "the university (as a specific institutional site) and academy (as a shifting material network) themselves cannot be disentangled from the long historical apparatuses of genocidal and protogenocidal social organization."[45] And Nikki Sullivan has argued that queerness works against "the straitjacketing effects of institutionalization."[46] For thinkers like these, aesthetic anti-instrumentality is one of the few ways to emancipate ourselves from institutional coercions. And so, it has become commonplace to "measure artistic radicality by its degree of anti-institutionality."[47]

But what if institutions like the university and the state are not as unrelentingly oppressive as the aesthetic humanities have so often claimed? Understanding institutions as combinations of different kinds of forms allows us to see both how institutionalization will be essential to sustainable justice and how even current, oppressive institutions afford some of the crucial materials for major structural transformation. I build here on a range of recent affirmative reassessments of institutions by Jodi Dean, Shannon Jackson, Benjamin Kohlmann, Lisi Schoenbach, and Robyn Wiegman, all of whom point to the power of institutions as the best or perhaps even the only way to congeal radical change into lasting structures—to take the energies unleashed by crowds and protests and convert them into ongoing formations to support collective life.[48]

What is an institution? According to social scientists James March and Johan Olsen, it is "any relatively enduring collection of rules and organized practices, embedded in structures of meaning and resources that are relatively invariant in the face of turnover of individuals and relatively resilient to the idiosyncratic preferences and expectations of individuals and changing external circumstances."[49] Key concepts here are stability and organization—or, to translate these into my own terms, sustainability and form.

March and Olsen's definition certainly captures the oppressive institutions of a Euro-American modernity, like the mental asylum and the assembly line. But it also captures a range of less oppressive practices, like *satoyama*, the regular labor of preserving village forests in Japan described by Elaine Gan and Anna Tsing. These forests are rich in species, including ants and mushrooms that cannot thrive elsewhere. They depend on human labor—regular raking and pruning of tree branches and trunks—for their ongoing survival. When small farmers moved to cities in the twentieth century and stopped this work, new species took over these areas, creating dense forests where the older species could not survive. Satoyama revitalization groups are now deliberately working to reinstate these old agricultural practices and patterns. According to March and Olsen's definition, the mutually sustaining "multispecies collaborations" that make up satoyama forests are as much institutions as the modern factory or the prison.[50] They are a collection of practices organized and regulated over time, but they are neither exploitative nor punitive. Indeed, since all human collectives impose norms and patterns for the provision of food, including practices of finding, growing, distributing, and preparing food, it is impossible to imagine a total freedom from organizations that remain relatively stable over time—that is, a freedom from institutions.

Or to put this another way: both major qualities of institutions—stability and organization—are essential to sustaining life over time, and both will therefore be necessary to collective continuance. And even rigid regulations can be powerfully capacitating. While many contemporary businesses are proud of giving their workers freedom from old forms of temporal and spatial discipline, offering flexible work hours, creativity, and autonomy, these institutions are no less coercive for that. Employers can expect workers to internalize responsibility for productivity at all hours of the day and night. "Nimble" institutions can maximize profits by hiring workers only when they need them. Gig workers are increasingly forced to stitch together multiple unpredictable jobs to make ends meet. From this perspective, a rigid institutional form—such as the forty-hour work week—may be enclosing and limiting, but it also belongs in the tool kit of forms for sustainable justice.

March and Olsen's definition is deliberately loose and baggy: they call an institution "a collection of rules and organized practices." Hardly rock-solid and immovable, the word "collection" puts an emphasis on gatherings of separable parts, on the heterogeneous assembly. And this seems right. That is, even the most oppressive and hierarchical institutions cannot work as perfectly coordinated systems, as monoliths. They are composed of multiple and sometimes discordant forms that work against one another as often as they consolidate or reinforce each other. While scholars across the aesthetic humanities have imagined institutions as coherent engines of rigid ideologies, the daily work of institutions suggests the opposite—that coordinating every moving part for the sake of shared ends often feels arduous or downright impossible.

The state provides one example. Composed of police departments and food inspectorates, elected legislatures and credentialed civil servants, health care systems and tax incentives, the state is not a single homogenizing force, and its various bodies sometimes sustain and at other times undermine one another. The U.S. Environmental Protection Agency (EPA), for example, has been attacked by the presidency, sued in the courts, and sometimes even divided against itself. In one case, the air pollution department of the EPA pushed for "scrubbing," which turns coal particles in the air into solid form—thereby undermining those in the same agency fighting for reductions in solid waste.[51]

For an example closer to home for many readers, we might consider the university, an institution that has been the focus of much anti-institutional critique. Rodríguez wonders whether the university "ought to be completely abolished."[52] It is true that universities around the world are built on stolen Indigenous lands and have responded to financial pressures and a culture of economic efficiency and privatization by adopting an increasingly neoliberal logic, including a dependence on precarious adjunct faculty.[53] And yet, it is also true that universities have conserved a motley array of other institutional arrangements, many of them very old, including sabbatical leaves, which have their roots in the Old Testament Book of Leviticus; libraries, dining halls, and music ensembles, all of which have ancient and medieval roots; area studies programs, which date to the Cold War; and departments of gender studies and African American studies, which students and faculty fought to create in the late 1960s and early 1970s. Roderick Ferguson has argued, powerfully, that these fields have been incorporated into the institution in ways that co-opt them, converting them into servants of the state and capital seeking recognition and legitimation. New fields do not shift power, according to Ferguson, but allow power to "restyle" itself, "dreaming up ways to affirm difference and keep it in hand."[54] This claim rests on the assumption that different pieces of the institution work together, coherently, all serving the same fundamental order, whereas universities are in fact much messier and more plural constellations of forms, shot through with competing pressures and forms from different past moments that sometimes undermine and sometimes support each other. From general education requirements and core curricula, which require a broad exposure to a range of disciplines, to financial aid for students who cannot afford the full cost of a degree, which entails a limited redistribution of wealth, universities sustain a range of forms that do not exclusively serve genocidal or neoliberal agendas. And these "holdover forms" last in part because institutions preserve them.[55] That is, institutions are conservative in a stranger sense than we usually mean: they are engines of conservation, and so they conserve all kinds of forms that are not parts of the dominant order.

But they are not entirely inert either. Institutional forms from different moments tend to exert contradictory pressures that send them in different ideological directions. Raymond Williams famously points to "residual" formations, which are structures from the past that continue to shape institutions long after they have ceased to be dominant. One of his examples is organized religion, with its values of "absolute brotherhood" and "service to others without reward."[56] These are very old values—dominant under feudalism—but they also provide a critical rejoinder to dominant capitalist ideology, which would have it that private accumulation is the only real human drive. And so perhaps it is not surprising that the Black Lives Matter movement has conserved these residual values for its radical ends: "Our continued commitment to liberation for all Black people means we are continuing the work of our ancestors and fighting for our collective freedom because it is our duty."[57] For this new generation of activists, the fight for the future rests on a collective duty to the struggles of the past, which includes a service to others without reward and a sense of solidarity—values that date back many centuries. Conservation of the past can itself provide a vigorous alternative to prevailing values.

Or take the college-level teaching of literary studies today. Textual analysis can be traced back to the ancient practice of biblical hermeneutics, and much of our classroom reading focuses on—and preserves—texts from the past. The credits and degrees students earn from these studies then serve the dominant capitalist order by providing them with quantifiable workplace credentials. But at the same time, the humanities classroom invites students to explore aesthetic anti-instrumentality as a rich site for ways of living and feeling that challenge dominant assumptions and make room for what Williams calls "emergent" alternatives to the status quo. Teaching literature in an undergraduate class is therefore residual, dominant, and emergent all at once. And if these are all at work in the same moment, then it is not right to understand even one discipline within the university as serving a single coherent ideology.

The case for the importance of turning to institutions, then, is twofold: first, institutions preserve elements from the past in ways that can help us understand how sustainability happens; and second, the multiple forms of institutions tend to be jumbled together in ways that are incoherent, and often preserve capacitating and just forms as well as oppressive ones, sometimes over very long periods. From this perspective, a resistance to institutionalization as such feels like a falsifying distortion and a misleading direction for politics. And if we pay a formalist's attention to the ways that institutions are organized, we can see how specific institutional forms can be effectively mobilized for structural change.

Starting Here and Now, with Existing Institutions

We are surrounded by opportunities to reshape institutional forms. A household can organize its ordinary labors of maintenance around egalitarian routines, and a teacher can establish rules for inclusive participation. We might dismiss these as insignificant because they do not get at larger, what we often call "structural" forces, but even the smallest and most local reorderings are in fact precisely *structural*. That is, structure—understood as synonymous with form in this book[58]—refers to the imposition of one order rather than another. Both structure and form are terms for the shaping and organization of materials. The difference between them is not a difference in kind but a difference in scale and stability. The equal division of tasks in a household cannot easily scale up to organize a nation, and a single decision to distribute labor equally can easily fall away without an ongoing effort to sustain it.

But it is just as important to note that the largest-scale and most enduring structures operate by way of smaller forms. That is, capitalism, racism, and patriarchy all exert and consolidate their power precisely through a variety of local orderings, patterns, and arrangements, from segregated neighborhoods to the daily work of childcare. One effective route for politics, then, is to change the smaller structures that work together to sustain the larger ones.

For example, the massive and disproportionate incarceration of people of color in the United States helps swing elections toward white interests, since those with felony records in many states are not allowed to vote. But we could just as easily approach this from the opposite direction: the formal obstacles preventing African American voters from getting to the polls have meant that the people most affected by mass incarceration have a disproportionately small impact on political processes that might remake the justice system. Changes to either mass incarceration *or* voter suppression could have implications for the other. If racism is sustained by a cluster or constellation of mutually supportive forms, then reorganizing one form can also frustrate or hamper the others.

What this means is that effective political work involves keeping our eyes on mundane forms like congressional redistricting and school segregation—traditionally understood as "liberal" rather than "radical" approaches. But put another way, the work of revolutionary structural change can start with any number of organizing forms. Each structural shift may have implications for the strength and durability of other structures. To the most radical ends, then, I want to urge the formalist's sharp attention to the nuts and bolts of institutional arrangements—boundaries, regulations, tempos, norms, and pathways.

Specifically, let's consider the ways that existing institutional forms can be sites of meaningful and substantial change for climate justice. Individual actions like opting for hybrid cars and vegetarian diets are neither large enough nor structurally transformative. Meanwhile, many national governments have been swayed by energy interests, working to undo even the most relatively insignificant checks on fossil fuel emissions. Both scales often feel hopeless.

But it is possible to reshape the forms of many existing institutions, including universities, hospitals, churches, and even governments. I want to offer two promising models from my own experience with climate activism. The first is the movement for carbon pricing, an attempt to charge the real social cost of fossil fuels. The second is the divestment of institutions from fossil fuels. Neither of these will strike skeptical readers as sufficiently radical actions, but both have real and lasting impacts for climate justice and offer starting points for large-scale structural change.

Carbon pricing is divisive among leftists and environmentalists. Advocates argue that it will work to bring down emissions quickly and on a large scale: "Putting a price on carbon changes incentives. It encourages everyone—individuals, government agencies, and most importantly companies—to curtail their use of fossil fuels."[59] Detractors insist that calculating the cost of carbon in economic terms reinforces the dominant logic of capitalism and sustains the very modes of exploitation and extraction that caused the climate crisis in the first place.[60] Some carbon pricing models are rightly criticized as regressive—like the sudden rise in food and gas prices that prompted the "Yellow Vests" in France to organize mass protests in 2018 or the proposal to redistribute revenues to private interests that pushed Washington State environmental groups to reject carbon pricing when it was on the ballot in 2016.[61]

A formalist perspective can resolve both of these objections. If we understand capitalism not as a single massive juggernaut that must be shattered all at once but a complex system sustained over time through multiple forms as various as security forces, extractive technology, inheritance laws, and narrative protagonists, we can see how carbon pricing works both for and against other capitalist forms: on the one hand, it continues the pattern of calculating all costs in terms of market values, but on the other hand, it has the potential to protect many of the poorest communities of the world from the climate devastation that will follow from unchecked emissions, and it supports ongoing common goods like clean air and water. Stockholm, for example, has the highest carbon taxes in the world; the city not only taxes fossil fuels but puts high prices on traffic congestion and parking and has invested in a strong system of biogas-run public buses and subways, green spaces, and the building of high-density neighborhoods designed for walking and cycling. Together, these measures have brought dramatic reductions in air pollution and carbon emissions and new pleasures for those who walk or bike through city streets and parks.[62]

The second objection—that carbon pricing unjustly burdens the poor—can be solved by focusing on the specific design of the pricing model. The Citizens Climate Lobby's "carbon fee and dividend" model is particularly well designed for justice and sustainability: if imposed in the United States, it would have the capacity to bring down global emissions quickly while protecting the poorest people from rising prices. It works like this: first, the U.S. government puts a predictably rising fee on fossil fuels; second, it redistributes the income collected in equal amounts to all households; and third, it imposes a national border adjustment so that products imported from countries that do not impose a comparable price on carbon will be more expensive. The rising price on fossil fuels offers a broad incentive to shift to renewable energy, while the dividend itself benefits those with the least wealth: studies show that about two-thirds of U.S. households will receive more back in the form of a monthly dividend than they will pay in rising prices on fossil fuels.[63] The border adjustment then discourages businesses from moving overseas to less regulated economies and encourages other countries to introduce a carbon fee so that they can collect the tax rather than sending it to the United States.[64]

Since the United States is the world's largest economy, its adoption of border adjustments would have immediate ripple effects worldwide, bringing down emissions on a global scale. Because carbon pricing does not disrupt the market, it draws support from right-wing thinkers. And this bipartisan support in the United States is not negligible: it is what will allow the "carbon fee and dividend" to outlast shifts in governing parties—in short, to be sustainable over time.[65]

Predictable, pragmatic, progressive, and sustainable, the carbon fee and dividend model is not an exciting shattering of oppressive institutions or a remaking of consciousness for a new world. And yet, this particular model of interacting forms has the real potential to sustain human and non-human lives around the world for a substantial period—long enough, perhaps, to allow us to get a genuine revolution started.

My second example of institutional change is divestment. In 2019, I joined a group of Cornell faculty, students, and staff who were working to pressure the university to divest its $7.3 billion endowment from fossil fuels. Many of my colleagues in the aesthetic humanities met these efforts with immediate skepticism. Some insisted that the administration and the trustees would never agree to divest because Cornell had too much invested in fossil fuels to be able to afford the shift; others maintained the opposite—that there was so little invested that divestment would be purely symbolic and would have no substantial economic effect. Several had been discouraged by the failure of efforts to persuade the trustees to divest in 2016 and argued that the struggle against the neoliberal administration was hopeless. Many worried that it was hypocritical to ask the university to divest when we ourselves were still flying and driving cars, and quite a few worried about what divestment meant, exactly—was it even possible to figure out which companies were bound up in fossil fuels? A few claimed that divestment itself was counterproductive: it would just drive down the price of fossil fuel stocks, making them cheaper for other investors to snap up.

Most of my colleagues tried to convince me that there was no point in trying. But a small group of faculty and staff looked into each objection and concluded that even a symbolic move by a respected institution like Cornell could have meaningful ripple effects, sending the public message that fossil fuel companies were exceptionally dishonest and destructive actors and encouraging other institutions to join the growing movement. We knew that there had been a major shift in public opinion since 2016, with large universities like the University of California having divested, and 60 percent of

Americans claiming to have become either "concerned" or "alarmed" about climate change.[66] A majority of college-bound students in the United States now included environmental concerns in their decisions about where to apply.[67] Given the fast pace of climate change, it seemed to make sense to move sooner rather than later.

The trustees themselves had also created an opening for a new campaign. After they had voted against divesting from fossil fuels in 2016, the board laid out specific criteria they said would have to be met before they would consider divesting in the future.[68] They articulated a clear standard for us to meet. But how would we get to the trustees? The first form that mattered was an informal network of students, faculty, and staff who had met through other climate activist organizations. We met and pooled our knowledge of the various relevant institutional forms and developed a strategy to put them to work.

Cornell's by-laws stipulate that the trustees must consider any resolution that has gained the support of all five university governance assemblies—undergraduate, graduate and professional students, staff, faculty, and University Assembly, which joins representatives of all of these bodies. Robert Warren Howarth, a Cornell scientist and member of our informal network whose research had exposed links between methane emissions and global warming, had become chair of the University Assembly in order to hold Cornell to strict environmental standards. This position required him to meet regularly with the Cornell president, Martha Pollack, and they had developed a friendly and trusting relationship. Although the president had said that she was opposed to a divestment resolution, her conversations with Howarth began to shift her understanding of the science and of the importance of divesting. This form, the recurrent obligation to talk one-on-one, brought two kinds of power and knowledge together—a top university administrator in ongoing conversation with a leading climate scientist—and it proved surprisingly powerful. Howarth also had the power to appoint faculty representatives to the Campus Infrastructure Committee, where the last divestment resolution had gotten its start. He appointed me, and I drafted a document that was designed around the trustees' criteria for divestment, taking their explicitly articulated standards as its organizing form.[69]

Meanwhile, Climate Justice Cornell (CJC), a student group committed to divestment, had organized visible direct actions, deliberately disrupting trustee meetings and stopping campus traffic at busy crossroads to draw attention to the cause.[70] These events were intended to halt business-as-usual and grab attention, but they also depended on existing institutional forms to make their impact: they staged a mock wedding between the university and the fossil fuel industry at a busy network hub on campus, held a silent protest in one of the main libraries during its hours of heaviest use, and invited the daily student newspaper to report on these events.[71] This group is itself a durable institution, founded in 2001, after the United States rejected the Kyoto Protocol. With a long history of organizing sit-ins, demonstrations, educational campaigns, and petitions, CJC had been instrumental in pushing Cornell president Skorton to sign on to the American College and University Presidents Climate Commitment agreement and to become the first campus to commit to carbon neutrality.[72] Cornell has since garnered recognition as the most sustainable university in the Ivy League.[73]

Our team put all of these forms to work together. The Campus Infrastructure Committee brought a divestment resolution to the University Assembly for a vote in January 2020. Students, faculty, and staff asked questions and raised objections, but voted unanimously in favor of divestment. This was an entree to every other assembly. Representatives from different constituencies presented to all of the other bodies, urging them to adopt the same resolution for the sake of creating a united front and gaining formal access to the trustees. By March 2020, all five assemblies had passed the resolution.

At their May meeting, the trustees announced a moratorium on all new fossil fuel investments. Cornell University had divested its endowment. We will never know exactly which specific piece of this effort carried the most force—the shift in public opinion, the declining value of fossil fuel stocks, student protests, Cornell's eagerness to maintain its reputation as "the greenest Ivy," an open-minded president, the organizing of all five assemblies around a common resolution, or the trustees' recognition that their own criteria for divestment had been met. I propose to think of it as a kind of collaborative creative effort, a making of new social worlds out of the materials afforded by institutions. As in a symphony or theatrical production, we were working with existing scripts, materials, and instruments to craft new economic shapes and patterns at the level of the institution.

It is true that neither carbon pricing nor divestment from fossil fuels is enough in itself to stop climate change. But both are contributions to a large and growing movement, led most prominently by Bill McKibben, that is successfully diverting massive flows of money away from fossil fuels.[74] Both are much more politically significant than individual consumer actions. Both suggest that our most pessimistic colleagues may be wrong about the possibilities for institutional change. Both provide a training ground for participation in collective action going forward, which is crucial to building power on the left. And most importantly here, both campaigns give us formal models to work with to realize sustainable models for climate justice.

As we turn our attention to institutions, let's not forget the aesthetic humanities, with our own paradoxical institutionalization of anti-institutionalism, our sometimes anti-formalist forms of teaching, reading, publishing, debating, and convening. I have suggested that our long-standing insistence on anti-instrumentality has sustained a libertarian logic that draws us away from working together effectively for lasting political change. We teach and argue in favor of breaking the rules, and we rarely imagine crafting new rules; we celebrate disrupting organizations, and we do not often enough organize ourselves for change. "Left pessimism" can readily find theoretical support in the writing of the aesthetic humanities, from Adorno's "Resignation" to Lee Edelman's *No Future,* which offer explicit justifications for refusing to throw our energies into conventional political action. But also, more broadly and subtly, scholars have put our unrelenting emphasis on the virtues of the shimmering and the evanescent, glimpses of feeling or being in common that are valuable precisely because they are transitory, excessive, contingent, experimental, improvised—that is, free from the shackles of organization and institutionalization. It certainly makes sense to pause and take stock of the habits and pressures that might prompt a headlong rush into the wrong kind of action. It also makes sense to allow imagination to take flight, to break free from familiar worlds to envision them otherwise. As phases, as stepping-stones, as respites, this humanities thinking is indispensable. But not as an end in itself. The exciting anti-formalism at work in resisting organizations and institutions ultimately reinforces both solitude and powerlessness. What this book seeks to do, then, is to honor the importance of critique while countering the pessimistic, principled refusal to organize—and to get to work on designing and building lasting forms for climate justice.

3

Infrastructures for Collective Life

ROUTINE, PATHWAY, ENCLOSURE

THE MOST BASIC CONDITIONS of survival are an increasingly urgent site of political struggle. The people fighting hardest to sustain livelihoods and lifeworlds as climate catastrophes multiply are the world's poorest and most powerless—Black, Brown, Indigenous, female, queer, disabled. And as the right engages in a radical dismantling of institutions and regulations in the interests of intensifying mass precarity, sturdy conditions for collective survival become increasingly rare and precious. This chapter will make a case for the importance of three basic infrastructural forms for collective continuance.

Conventionally, the term "infrastructure" refers to the physical structures and pathways that allow a society to function. These forms afford the accommodation and movement of bodies, goods, energy, and information, such as buildings, roads, bridges, railways, and seaports; canals, electrical grids, fuel pipelines, and sewer systems; telephone cables, postal systems, and wireless connectivity. Many definitions of infrastructure include social services, such as schools, hospitals, and child- and eldercare.[1] While several recent humanities scholars have put an emphasis on the gaps where infrastructures fail and on the shifting meanings of infrastructures over time,[2] I keep my own eye here on the comparatively durable orders and arrangements of material infrastructures because these shape collective life over long periods, both directing and capacitating actions and relations.

This chapter will focus on three forms that have always been—and probably will always be—necessary to collective life. The first is the *routine*. Because human bodies have a periodic need for sleep, water, and food, we return, day in and day out, to face the same necessities. Human communities also rely on the repetitive labor that make those provisions possible.

The second major focus of this chapter is the *pathway*: human bodies depend on routes to carry nutrients, energy, and waste to and from the places where we live. Many communities have organized themselves around existing pathways, such as rivers; others have built complex aquifer systems. Either way, these routes matter, politically, because they are essential to the task of what political philosophers call "distributive justice"—the allocation of benefits and burdens across a collective.[3] Roads, waterways, and energy grids are quite literally the pathways of distribution.

The third form is the *enclosure*. Human groups have always needed protected spaces for rest and gathering, and so have imposed barriers of some kind—whether to keep out rain, noise, insects, or other intruders. As the planet warms, keeping a roof over one's head is becoming increasingly rare and difficult, and ever more destructive storms and uninhabitable temperatures—"thermal inequity" as well as dangerous cold—will push hundreds of millions of people out of their current living spaces to find adequate shelter elsewhere.[4] Any just society, I will argue, should provide stable shelter for all—not subject to sudden eviction or other threats of removal.

It is true that all of these forms have been readily put to use by despotic and oppressive regimes. Routines have been highly exploitative under industrial capitalism, with monotonous cycles of labor forcing human bodies to conform to the rapid and repetitive rhythms of machines. Railroads, highways, and gas pipelines are rightly understood as the "planned violence" of capitalist and colonialist states, displacing existing communities, ravaging ecologies, entrenching racial segregation, and feeding the catastrophic processes of climate change.[5] And I deliberately use the heavily freighted term "enclosure," here, to evoke a form which the humanities have long associated with the violence of private property, settler colonialism, militarized borders, and police surveillance. Since all of these infrastructures can last across long periods of time, Daniel Nemser writes—paraphrasing Marx—that "infrastructural pasts weigh like a nightmare on the circulation of the present."[6] And the longer they last, Rebecca Evans argues, the more "infrastructural access and infrastructural violence are rendered invisible, with racial violence naturalized and material causalities obscured."[7] In this context, humanists are right to remain critical, keeping our attention trained on the ongoing brutality of infrastructural forms.

And yet, if routines, pathways, and enclosures meet fundamental needs for human collectives—from keeping bodies nourished to social gathering—then we need analyses that recognize *both* the constraints and the capacities of these organizing forms. I follow a number of recent scholars and activists who understand infrastructure "as something that can be retooled for justice."[8] As Winona LaDuke and Deborah Cowen put it, "infrastructure is not inherently colonial—it is also essential for transformation; a pipe can carry fresh water as well as toxic sludge."[9]

There are several reasons why, although the current infrastructural landscape is inadequate and unjust, "burning it all down to begin again" is not the most just way forward.[10] First, since infrastructures keep collectives going in fundamental ways, their dismantling itself often causes acute suffering. Being without access to infrastructure, even for short periods, carries serious psychic, physical, and social costs. Hurricane Maria's devastating effects on Puerto Rican infrastructures prompted food riots, gas lines, waterborne illnesses, scarce drinking water, and hunger. People saw "winds peel back the roofs of their homes, tear off walls, smash windows, and blow in doors."[11] Rebuilding has been slow, with thousands still displaced from their homes, frequent power outages, and schools and hospitals still out of use years later.[12] Although many of the infrastructures in place before the hurricane, including water pump stations and electrical grids, were unequally distributed and kept in various states of neglect and disrepair, life has been, for most Puerto Ricans, much harder since the hurricane.[13] In this context, it seems crucial to recognize the ways that infrastructures may well be sustaining basic survival even when they are partial and inequitable.

Second, political movements that struggle against oppressive infrastructures use *other* infrastructures as resources for resistance. In apartheid South Africa, the government deliberately organized social space to keep Black people divided and powerless. Black townships did not have public squares, and roads were planned in ways that made travel between townships circuitous and time-consuming.[14] The state installed electric street lighting for the purpose of policing the township population, creating "tall light poles that enabled the surveillance of the townships at night."[15] Cheap and harsh, these created a "prison-camp effect," throwing a glaring light into homes and yards.[16] Seeking other ways to gather forces, the anti-apartheid struggle turned to institutions that connected sites around the country, including national churches, civic groups, and trade unions, which furnished the infrastructure to coordinate and mobilize people across South Africa.[17]

The third reason to focus on maintaining existing infrastructure is that the unglamorous work of keeping life going is often feminized—and devalued. Stories told about radical movements tend to celebrate the "people who give speeches, negotiate with bosses and politicians, get published, get elected, and otherwise become visible as actors in ways that align with dominant hierarchies."[18] This is certainly true of the men who led the "New Left" in the 1960s and 1970s, according to Lydia Sargent, who assumed that their women counterparts would quietly clean offices, prepare meals, care for children, drive men to demonstrations, and function as helpmates, "typing, filing, phoning, feeding, healing, supporting, loving, and occasionally even participating on the front lines."[19] Downplaying this mundane work behind the scenes is not only unjust; it is also a strategic mistake. As Dean Spade argues, when communities on the front lines provide stable infrastructure, including regular food, medical care, and safe shelter, they draw new participants to political action and help to sustain participation over time. The routines of mutual aid have been crucial to the expansion and endurance of social movements.[20] The Black Panthers are the most famous American example: FBI director J. Edgar Hoover called their free breakfasts for children, transportation, and health clinics "potentially the greatest threat to efforts by authorities to neutralize the BPP and destroy what it stands for."[21]

The final reason to focus on sustaining existing routines, pathways, and enclosures is that some of these enable collective pleasures. Routines organize patterns of sociability, including shared meals, breaks, and conversations. As bell hooks argues, routines of caregiving and cooking can themselves be a joyful corrective to the "stressful, dehumanizing, and degrading" work many African American women must perform outside of the home.[22] Public routes and squares gather people for parties, dancing, planning, and protest. Safe enclosures afford intimacy and debate. Everywhere sustaining, shaping, and conducting social experience, these are forms that afford practices of being together—the joys as well as the necessities of collective life.

Routine

There are few aspects of modern life which social critics have more roundly and frequently condemned than routine. The deadening, oppressive monotony of factory work, the unthinking acceptance of custom, the recycling of familiar images and ideas. Mechanization. Habit. Convention. Stereotype. Cliché. Social critics since the Romantics have insisted on the value of surprise and unpredictability. As Ralph Waldo Emerson put it in 1841, "People wish to be settled; only as far as they are unsettled is there any hope for them."[23] This strand of thought continues robustly into our own time, as contemporary critics follow "the urge to shake things up, to jolt people out of their everyday understandings of bodies and minds."[24] As we will see in the next chapter, this tradition has been particularly powerful for aesthetic thinkers. But I will argue here that too much insistence on disturbance and shock also blocks a recognition of the affirmative social and political affordances of routines.

Modern thinkers have most often associated routines with oppressive industrial labor. As Friedrich Engels puts it: "the worker's activity is reduced to some paltry, purely mechanical manipulation, repeated minute after minute, unchanged year after year. How much human feeling, what abilities can a man retain in his thirtieth year, who has made needle points or filed toothed wheels twelve hours every day from his early childhood?"[25] A century later, when Studs Terkel interviewed a spot welder in a Ford factory, the worker said: "Repetition is such that if you were to think about the job itself, you'd slowly go out of your mind."[26] The same objections remain strong into our own time, as enforced routines organize work globally, from sweatshops to electronics manufacture. Contemporary service work is highly monotonous, too, with servers in restaurants forced to clear waste off plates in five- to ten-second cycles.[27]

Dull, grueling, exploitative work has been rightly condemned. And yet, not all routines are equally oppressive. All cultures are in fact shaped by repetitive practices—from harvesting crops to religious observance to a weekly poker game—that keep social worlds going. Their repetitions establish predictable patterns over time. As we saw in the last chapter, Elaine Gan and Anna Tsing draw attention to the coordinated timing of human and non-human activity that contributes to the ongoing health of a Japanese forest. They argue that if we understand coordinated times only in terms of industrial modernity, we miss the ways that all kinds of coordination organize sustainable worlds.[28] And it is this aspect of routine that draws my attention here: predictable patterns of repeated action are necessary forms for the project of sustaining collective life—from eating and sleeping to providing vaccinations and keeping roads and pipes clear.

Let's begin by understanding routines in formal terms. Routines and habits are arrangements of action into predictable, repetitive sequences.[29] Since they maintain everyday life, both have been rightly cast as conservative. From gendered housekeeping to daily commutes by car, repetitive practices and expectations nourish whole regimes of injustice. "Everyday racism" is an especially troubling example: in the contemporary United States, anti-Blackness depends on the mutual reinforcement of multiple routinized practices, from discriminatory labor practices and police harassment to verbal assaults and microaggressions, all of which are so commonplace as to go unquestioned by many of those benefiting from racial hierarchy.[30] But while it is true that routines afford predictability, and so are conservative in that sense, a formalist analysis shows that they do not all sustain unjust social *hierarchies*. That is, we can distinguish routine from inequality on formal grounds. Both are forms, but they organize experience differently. Routines are arrangements of action and expectation into temporal sequences. Hierarchy is a stratification, a vertical ordering into levels or ranks, where highest is best—the position of most authority, power, value, prestige. Formally speaking, routines afford persistence over time, but there is no reason why routines must always and necessarily entail inequality.

Consider the mundane example of daily toothbrushing. This activity is not reserved for a superior or inferior class or race. It is conservative in the sense that it conserves the body's health, but it is also beneficial for all people with teeth, as well as cats and dogs. Far from imposing this practice on colonial subjects, Euro-Americans are latecomers to this daily routine, which has been practiced in China and the Islamic world for many centuries. In the *hadith*, the Prophet Muhammed advises the habitual use of *miswak*, a tooth-cleaning twig from the mustard tree with medicinal properties, before going to sleep and after waking up in the morning, before religious observance, and before any important gathering. The *miswak* is effective for dental hygiene, and is also organic and biodegradable—making it more sustainable than the plastic toothbrush. Some *miswak* users report brushing their teeth up to eight times a day.[31] In the United States, by contrast, it was not until soldiers brought the practice of toothbrushing home with them from World War II, where is was a military requirement, that it began to take hold as a widespread daily routine. A short film by the U.S. Public Health Service in 1941 urged Americans to take care of their teeth as essential to a healthy nation, regretting that regular routines of dental hygiene were far from widespread.[32] Political leaders were partly responsible for this lag in the first place. One member of Congress in 1912 said he would make it a "penal offence" for mothers to give their children toothbrushes because chewing tobacco and snuff were the only good dental health practices.[33] The point here is that toothbrushing might well be a repetitive, monotonous, even unthinking routine, but it also sustains healthy bodies, while it does not entrench global or local inequalities.

Now, let's take this argument a step further. Not only can we separate routines and hierarchies as forms; we can begin to imagine how routines could sustain more just and equitable social worlds. That is, if routines can train us into relatively stable patterns, could we use them precisely to *cultivate routines of equality*?

We already have some evidence that the answer is yes. Many political systems insist on regular rotations of leaders to prevent a consolidation of power. The ancient Mayans practiced a rotating schedule of sovereignty to ensure that no major kinship group would be able to dominate all the others, and all groups would have equal periods of power. The abstraction of temporal form into predictable sequences was crucial to this model of circulating authority: "Time itself was the sacred ruler; humans were merely its mortal and temporal custodians."[34] Today, the radical Zapatista movement in Mexico also insists on a routinized rotation of authority, requiring every adult to spend a fixed period of time serving on government councils, in part so that decision making will be shared equally and in part so that "people will no longer be mystified by the process of government."[35] Routine in this context affords the democratizing of political participation.

Cultures built around sharing resources have to work to maintain fair distributions, and for that they turn to routines of egalitarianism. Anthropologist Richard Lee focuses on the Kung San people of Southern Africa, a foraging society who put a high value on equality of distribution. This is neither natural nor effortless. In fact, they "browbeat each other constantly to be more generous and not to set themselves apart by hoarding a little nest-egg" and engage in "constant daily" habits of "puncturing the bubble of conceit," including "minimizing the size of others' kills, downplaying the value of others' gifts, and treating one's own efforts in a self-deprecating way."[36] It takes daily reinforcement to maintain equality as a value and a practice. But these routines also allow egalitarianism to become an ordinary element of culture, passed down through generations in part by means of its widespread repetition. As radicals have often charged, routines afford a troubling entrenchment. But if they serve just ends, then their capacity for endurance is all to the good.

Abstractions and enforcements—keeping track of time, ensuring everyone has had a turn—are not the usual desiderata of radical art and politics. They seem rigid, coercive, and artificial. And yet, this kind of routinization might also be one of the most effective formal strategies for building and maintaining social equality. As the example of Zapatista governance suggests, the most egalitarian model of power and authority is not a liberation from routine at all but an organization of repetitive periods that guarantees a fair distribution of collectively necessary work.

Yet, one might object, even if routines are good for constraining greed and power, they unfairly constrain us otherwise. William James makes the famous argument that "habit is . . . the enormous fly-wheel of society, its most precious conservative agent. It alone is what keeps us all within the bounds of ordinance, and saves the children of fortune from the envious uprisings of the poor."[37] In this respect, routines are crucial to keeping injustices in place.

But James also argues—less famously—that the total rejection of habit is not much better. Freed from all predictability, we get mired in an endlessly unpleasant kind of decision making over every dull detail:

> There is no more miserable human being than one in whom nothing is habitual but indecision, and for whom the lighting of every cigar, the drinking of every cup, the time of rising and going to bed every day, and the beginning of every bit of work, are subjects of express volitional deliberation. Full half the time of such a man goes to the deciding, or regretting, of matters which ought to be so ingrained in him as practically not to exist for his consciousness at all.[38]

Routine in small ordinary matters, he goes on, releases precious mental energy for more interesting activity.[39]

James points us back to the conflicting affordances of routines as forms. On the one hand, they have the capacity to force or lull us into reproducing the existing world. On the other hand, they allow us to perform uninteresting actions without thinking, producing time for thought and work of other kinds—daydreaming, ambitious planning, creativity, revolution itself. Since critics across the aesthetic humanities have so often emphasized the constraining and conservative power of routines, I want to turn our attention briefly here to some of the important freedoms that they also afford.

First, creativity. Artists have often stuck to rigid daily routines in order to protect the necessary time, space, and energy for making art. Franz Kafka set aside writing time late at night, after daily office work and dinner. [40] For Toni Morrison, "Writing before dawn began as a necessity," a period of quiet before her young children woke up, but as the years went on, she continued the routine, appreciating the morning hours as the best time for her work.[41] Maya Angelou also opted for a predictable daily schedule, which yielded not only writing but also pleasure: "I keep a hotel room in which I do my work—a tiny, mean room with just a bed, and sometimes, if I can find it, a face basin. I keep a dictionary, a Bible, a deck of cards and a bottle of sherry in the room. I try to get there around 7, and I work until 2 in the afternoon. . . . It's lonely, and it's marvelous."[42]

The U.S. Works Progress Administration in the 1930s and 1940s imposed fairly rigid routines on artists and writers. Some were required to clock in and out; some submitted time reports; and others had to show finished work at prescribed intervals.[43] Painters who worked for the Easel Division were expected to finish one canvas each month.[44] In return, they received a regular paycheck—a routine of its own that guaranteed day-to-day survival. The program was widely praised by those who took part, and it launched some of the most significant writers and artists of color in the twentieth century, including Jacob Lawrence, who called it a "turning point" when he began to earn $23.86 a week with the Federal Artists Project.[45] Both Richard Wright and Ralph Ellison first began to see themselves as professional writers when, employed by the Federal Writers Project, they could afford to spend every day writing.[46]

Second, the fair redistribution of wealth. As radicals insist on liberating people from the dominance of deadening routines, we might notice that political conservatives are attracted to a similar logic. Libertarian Robert Nozick writes famously that "taxation of earnings from labor is on a par with forced labor."[47] If people want to contribute money to social causes, the conservative argument goes, they should be free to choose among philanthropies. Taxation is the unfree alternative, repetitive and required, based in collective coercion rather than singular preferences. But if we recast taxation and philanthropy in Jamesian terms, a different set of freedoms and constraints emerges. On the largest and most significant scale, of course, the regular redistribution of wealth would be powerfully emancipatory for the poor, freeing them from painful, dangerous, and exploitative conditions, and from time and anxiety spent focusing on where to find the next meal or a safe place to sleep. But also: philanthropic decisions demand lots of thought and attention. Taxation takes away the excitement of these individual choices, but it also frees up the time and energy spent on choosing among multiple organizations, leaving the minute everyday decision making to government agencies, which assess spending programs and their impact on our collective behalf. It also frees more time for social work, since charities that are dependent on unpredictable gifts must invest substantial time in fundraising. As James suggests, then, routines of taxation will have liberating consequences even for the comfortable taxpayer—freeing them from spending substantial time and energy deciding where their money should go. I do not mean to make an argument for passive citizenship: it is surely good to know about how our tax money is spent and to participate in decisions concerning it. But I do want to point out that even the paying of taxes—the dullest, most coercive routine—brings freedoms with it.

The third reason to revalue routine has to do with radical politics and activism. Struggles for justice demand a lot of time and energy. Critical thought, historical knowledge, political protest, coalition-building, and experiments in living: we need all of these to shape alternatives to the terrors of the status quo. But it is no wonder that radical energies sometimes flag, as the demands of simply getting through each day—making a living, getting to and from work, child-rearing, cooking, coming down with the flu—take so many hours and so much focus that even the most privileged among us often experience the requirements of ordinary life as overwhelming.

From this perspective, systemic injustices already in place always have the advantage. They require not extra thought and action but unthinking acceptance. And that is why dismantling dominant regimes remains crucial. But it is equally counterproductive, politically, to put too singular an emphasis on undoing. Counterproductive because the undoing of routines is so laborious, so demanding of our every effort, that it is too tempting to give up in exhaustion and acquiesce—unless and until conditions come to feel truly intolerable. And intolerability is a high bar. Too high, in the sense that people may put up with an awful lot of suffering before they feel impelled to take action, and too high because the suffering itself is unevenly distributed, which means that an unjust system can accommodate a lot that is truly unendurable for some without actually toppling.

An affirmative alternative, in this context, is to fight *for* routines that make fairness and environmental justice easier, smoother, more unthinking, than unfairness. Routines are valuable precisely because they do not demand our constant and alert attention, running along so smoothly that they may even allow us to forget or ignore them. So: what if the privileged did not have to make the active decision to sacrifice comfort and convenience by choosing to take the train instead of flying, because the train was actually easier? What if nutritious and delectable food was more readily accessible to everyone than unhealthy and unsatisfying food? The goal is not only to undo systemic injustice, in other words, but *to make justice systemic.*

The fourth reason to reconsider routine has to do with labor. The body's repetitive, ongoing needs for food, water, and rest mean that human collectives cannot do without routine. The provision of food alone requires a range of recurring tasks, such as planting, pruning, picking, preserving, transporting, cooking, cleaning up, and disposing of waste. Add the many other ordinary labors of maintenance beyond food—including hauling water, supervising children, washing clothes, and caring for sick bodies. All of these can become both dreary and tyrannical. One nineteenth-century guide to farming warned that "a great many farmers' wives have been driven to insanity by the monotonous character of their work and the working seven days in a week."[48]

But there is another side to this story, too. While the tedium of repetitive labor certainly deserves critique, the twenty-first-century workplace suggests that the absence of routine is not in fact better for the worker. In this moment of "flexible capitalism," nearly 90 percent of workers in the United States will at some point work non-standard hours.[49] Employers now often require workers to be on call to meet spikes in demand. Hourly workers, from hotel housekeepers and teleworkers to restaurant servers and contingent faculty, get little advance notice about changes in scheduling. Not being able to count on regular wages, and having sleep and childcare constantly disrupted, workers "run from part-time job to part-time job and from unpredictable shift to unpredictable shift. They are economically insecure . . . but also frazzled from trying to coordinate a chaotic assemblage of irregular schedules."[50] Lacking security and predictability, "the precariat" spend substantial unpaid time seeking to fill paid hours, finding stopgap childcare, and commuting between jobs. Flexible capitalism thus demands that the worker spend many more hours away from family and leisure than their pay reflects.[51] Unpredictable shifts also disrupt bodily rhythms, including the need for regular sleep. And non-standard hours interfere with other patterns of sociability, like meals with friends and children's activities after school.[52] Studies show that women in hourly positions have especially little power to determine their work schedules.[53]

At the other end of the wage scale, high earners are also perpetually on call now, too, working long hours in electronic environments—"flexible workplaces"—that never allow them to be entirely free from the demands of work. Ironically, high- and low-wage workers alike feel perpetually harried, with both salaried and hourly women expressing the wish that they had more time to spend with their children.[54] Regularity and flexibility are both ways of organizing labor time—they are generalizable temporal forms. And while corporations often boast of flattening traditional bureaucratic hierarchies into quickly decomposable networks or "archipelagoes," few employees experience this new flexibility as a benefit.[55]

Of course, a wide variety of factors influence worker satisfaction—including culture, environment, economics, and temperament—but according to workers' own accounts, it is a mistake to single out routine as uniquely oppressive. A recent study of catering workers concluded with what the researcher called a "surprising result":

> When asked about the nature of their jobs and how they felt about them, all workers said that their jobs were repetitive but they were not bored. . . . One

> catering assistant said "I don't feel uncomfortable with the routine. You get yourself all set in a different way into a routine." . . . Routine seems to bring some measure of order to their work and helps them find security in predictability. One dishwasher said that he liked the routine because it was predictable. "It helps you to do things correctly . . . because you always know what to expect . . . you know what people expect of you, you know what to do."[56]

Similarly, while some of Studs Terkel's subjects loathed repetitive work, others expressed frustration at unpredictable interruptions. One worker compared the chaotic tempo of her work as a receptionist unfavorably to a more monotonous job she had done before:

> [For the receptionist] there isn't a ten-minute break in the whole day that's quiet. I once worked at a punch press. . . . You sat and watched it for four, five hours. You could make up stories about people and finish them. But you can't do that when you've only got a few minutes. You can't pick it up after the telephone call. You can't think, you can't even finish a letter.[57]

What accounts from workers suggest is that there are at least three different temporal forms at stake in oppressive labor: one is the *repetitive sequence* of actions; the second is the *rate* or speed of each task; and the third is the *duration* of work without rest. Workers often respond bitterly when management increases the speed of their tasks or the length of the working day, but express some enthusiasm for predictable routines, which suggests that fast pace and sustained duration are more painful than repetitive sequence.[58]

For some, the routines of work even afford active pleasures. A journalist recalls "learning to write to the typewriter's rhythms—the sounds of fingers striking the keys, metal typebars whacking the paper, the ring of the margin bell, the slam of the carriage return."[59] Feminist writer Alix Kates Shulman rejects the breadmaking machine for "usurping the pleasures of kneading and punching down."[60] Women in central Mexico set about the repetitive task of preparing daily meals collectively, "with devotion and with joy."[61] And a North American tuna factory worker reports that she actively enjoys the recurrent, sensuous rhythms of her work because these turn her mind to sex: "The most exciting thing is the dark meat. It comes in streaks. It's red-brown. And you have to pull it out with your knife. You pile it next to your loin and it's crumbly and dark red and moist like earth."[62]

Few of us, I think, are total strangers to the pleasures entailed by repetition, since these constitute so many of the joys of play and art, such as throwing and catching a ball, dance, song, and rhyme. In this context, we can imagine how even laborious activities such as kneading, knitting, sweeping, typing, chopping, stirring, smoothing, and hammering might afford pleasures as well as pains. And so, what I want to suggest here is that predictable, monotonous repetition can certainly be maddening and oppressive, but it also affords surprisingly pleasurable experiences of sensuous embodiment, time to daydream and plan, and even, sometimes, to make art and social change.

Pathway

When the term "infrastructure" was first coined in the twentieth century, it referred specifically to pathways—the new modern routes that connected and conducted people, objects, information, and energy across space, such as railroads, gas mains, sewers, mass transit, telephone systems, and electrical grids. Capitalist and colonialist states often unveiled these systems as gleaming symbols of progress. This has led some scholars to define infrastructure *tout court* as "co-constitutive" with modernity.[63]

Yet, defining these infrastructural pathways as quintessentially modern has given rise to two misunderstandings. First, premodern collectives certainly used and reshaped the material environment to direct the flow of bodies, resources, and actions. By 3000 BCE, the Minoan peoples had developed sophisticated systems to manage stormwater and sewage disposal,[64] while the Mayans built a suspension bridge over one hundred meters long across Usumacinta River in the seventh century.[65] Tricia Toso points to the complexity and sophistication of many forms of infrastructure designed by precontact Indigenous groups.[66]

Dominant narratives of progress occlude these earlier infrastructures, which were often better for collective continuance than their successors. Before railroads cut through the Rio Grande Valley in the nineteenth century, for example, water ran through a complex network of stone and earth structures designed and built by Pueblo people, including "contour terracing, cobblestone grids, gravel mulching, and small check dams and reservoirs."[67] These waterways were deliberately designed for distributive justice, with the goal of "equitable water sharing."[68] The modern system that replaced the Pueblo waterways was far less effective and also substantially less just than its Indigenous precursor. When British and U.S. investors built railroads through the Rio Grande Valley to spark growth in industry and agriculture, the area attracted massive new waves of workers in timber and livestock. These forces changed the very shape of the land, causing erosion and land deposits that resulted in frequent and damaging floods throughout the area, disrupting daily life in Albuquerque. Alarmed that these floods were prompting investors to flee and businesses to close, state officials built a new irrigation infrastructure to control water in the valley. They blamed the floods on the old ways of dealing with irrigation, which they cast as "primitive" and inadequate. This was a double error: first, because the existing irrigation system had been adequate to the needs of the region before capitalism and colonialism had transformed the landscape; and second, because the new, expensive infrastructure did not succeed in stopping the floods, which continued to wreak havoc on both urban and rural lives.[69] The first reason not to define infrastructure as co-constitutive with industrial modernity, then, is to invite attention to more just and less well-known pathways for distributive justice.

Second, in focusing exclusively on modern infrastructures, we overlook the endurance of pathway forms across long periods. Scholars have often paid attention to infrastructural installation—the building of London's Embankment, or the sudden appearance of electric light in Kano, Nigeria—as political events worthy of notice.[70] In these accounts, water and power networks are legible as intentional consequences of specific regimes of power. But if the water is still flowing through pipes under London, and the lights are still on in Kano, do these infrastructures belong to the past or to the present? Are they events then or facts now? How should we think about infrastructures that survive across political contexts, continuing to shape social life long after the end of the powerful groups that created them?[71]

We would do well to look backward in part because even the shiniest new infrastructures usually follow the pathways laid down in the past. Power lines and sewer pipes run along main roads, which themselves take older trade routes. Cell phone providers lease space on top of water towers. Optical fibers are built along railroad lines.[72] Some built infrastructures carry on for generations without notable interruption. An inscription on a Roman bridge built in Hispania in 106 AD reads, "pontem perpetui mansurum in saecula mundi fecit" (He has built a bridge that will remain into the ages of the everlasting world).[73] Although the bridge itself has been rebuilt several times, the current pathway continues the tracks of the old, still carrying bodies and goods across the Alcantará River. The route has continued to shape collective life for centuries. Or to put this another way: one of the crucial affordances of the pathway as a form is endurance, which is essential to the task of collective continuance.

The violence wrought by pathways can also last for long periods. The U.S. Federal Highway Act of 1956, for example, authorized the construction of more than forty thousand miles of interstate highways. This new network strengthened the automobile and fuel industries. Those who could afford to own cars shaped their lives around the daily routine of commuting from suburbs to dense downtown business districts. People of color, prevented from moving to suburban neighborhoods by redlining laws and discriminatory lending practices, became the dominant users of public transportation, which powerful elites deliberately left to disintegrate. The Highway Act therefore fostered "white flight" to the suburbs and powerfully reinforced the racial segregation of the Jim Crow era.

The new highways often cut through neighborhoods of color, destroying thriving communities. In New Orleans, the famous Treme neighborhood once revolved around a bustling boulevard lined with trees, businesses, homes, and churches—North Claiborne Avenue—which was demolished in 1966 to build an elevated interstate highway, now nicknamed "the Monster."[74] Like other noisy and polluting freeways—including those that sliced through Overtown in Miami and Jefferson Street in Nashville—Interstate 10 soars over African American residents in New Orleans, remaining largely inaccessible to those stuck beneath, thus dividing people from each other and from access to stores and services, and deepening the wealth gap between white and non-white Americans.[75] Writing both fossil fuels and racial segregation into the routines of commuting and shopping, the federal highway infrastructure has afforded the mutual sustaining of environmental and racial injustice over time.[76] And as Kaylla Cantilina points out, "these inequalities stack." She gives the example of "a woman in Detroit who spends three hours riding the bus with her kid to go to school every day. That's three hours she's not earning the money that might help her move closer to that school or buy a car to reduce the commute. It's three hours she can't spend preparing healthy food, from a grocery store that might be as inaccessible as the school, and could lead to long term health problems."[77]

Since infrastructural pathways are often built to last, they can be difficult to unsettle or reroute. Highways are made of such durable materials—concrete and steel—that shifting their routes must involve the literal demolition of existing homes and workplaces. This capacity for endurance thus drives vicious cycles, deepening inequalities and environmental destruction over time.

But does that mean we are doomed to conduct our lives along the pathways of the past? Not exactly. Even concrete and steel need ongoing maintenance and repair. A number of cities, when faced with deteriorating freeways, have launched effective campaigns to replace them with greener alternatives. San Francisco was one of the first. When an earthquake damaged State Route 480 in 1989, a double-decker freeway that carried over one hundred thousand cars and trucks a day while blocking views of the San Francisco Bay, the city decided to demolish it and in its place created walking and biking paths and a new streetcar route.[78] In 2003, Seoul tore out a highway to expose a creek beneath it. Now a greenway lined with pathways for pedestrians, Cheonggyecheon has encouraged public transit use and brought birds and other wildlife to downtown Seoul. It has also encouraged gentrification and has not fully restored ecological systems, but on balance it is still better for the city than its fossil fuel–intensive counterpart.[79]

Meanwhile, safe, affordable public transportation systems prove that well-designed pathways are widely capacitating, providing access to jobs, social gatherings, churches, health care, and education, while reducing fossil fuels and air pollution. The city of Bologna dramatically increased ridership on public transit by abolishing fares during rush hour, creating well-marked bicycle paths, and offering free bike-sharing to all residents. Pollution and traffic congestion both dropped significantly.[80] To reach rural and underserved households, some regions have been experimenting with flexible transit—like minibuses or taxis—that can carry people to major transit hubs on demand.[81] And the best models join temporal and spatial forms, connecting spaces not only equitably but also with speed and frequency.[82]

In other words, it is possible to design new pathways for social and environmental justice. My own hometown of Syracuse, New York, has recently been engaged in a battle over the future of Interstate Highway 81. In order to build an elevated stretch of this highway through downtown in the 1950s, the city bulldozed a thriving African American neighborhood, leaving vacant lots and grinding poverty in its place. Today, the elevated part of the highway is in a state of dangerous decay. It must be either repaired or razed. The New York State Department of Transportation has helped to fund a $1.3 billion plan for a redesigned infrastructural form, a "community grid," replacing the highway with streets filled with homes and stores. A consortium of business interests—including the huge suburban mall—are fighting against this plan, seeking to rebuild the elevated stretch of I-81 to the tune of $1.7 billion.[83] When it comes to the politics of climate justice, this is the kind of battle worth fighting—and winning.

Of course, transportation is not the only pathway that matters to collective continuance. Routes for clean and waste water are also essential to just social worlds. And pathways for energy are an urgent focus of politics in our time. On the one hand, there is ample evidence that "energy poverty" intensifies suffering and inequality. Communities without access to electricity infrastructure struggle to preserve food and medicine and to protect themselves from extreme heat and cold. People around the world rely on polluting fuels for cooking because they have no access to healthier alternatives.[84] On the other hand, gas pipelines are some of the most destructive pathways the world has ever known. Snaking through ancestral homelands, leaking toxins into waterways, laying waste to ecosystems, and shoving millions of tons of greenhouse gases into the upper atmosphere, these pathways spell destruction on an unthinkably massive scale. But natural gas is also comparatively affordable and meets some of the growing demand for energy in the Global South, leading some advocates to make arguments for it on behalf of the world's poor.[85] This tangle of competing pressures may seem overwhelming. But it is not hopeless. Rural communities in the Global South have already been successfully experimenting with a range of ways to build renewable energy to meet local needs, including solar-powered mini-grids in remote villages in the Indian states of Sunderban and Chattisgar.[86] Solar and wind power can be defined as commons in ways that would help to increase access.[87] Meanwhile, the real social cost of natural gas belies its current low price. It is not as cheap as subsidies and the disregard for externalities make it seem.[88] Much of the crucial work that needs to be done right now, then, is to design and build fossil-free pathways for distributive justice.

Enclosure

Like routines and pathways, enclosures are forms that social critics have long urged us to resist. There is no question that borders and walls are among the most oppressive historical forms—from the slave ship's hold to immigration camps and gated communities. For Stefano Harney and Fred Moten, the logic of enclosure everywhere sustains ongoing violence. Their response: "We are disruption and consent to disruption. We preserve upheaval."[89]

In this context, it might seem trivializing or downright wrong to focus on the affirmative affordances of enclosures. But human bodies need protective barriers of some kind—if only to keep out malarial mosquitoes and icy winds—and that means that even the best human collectives will never be able to make do with entirely free, unconstrained spaces. In this context, radical open-endedness reaches a literal limit. And the insistence on unsettling, drifting, resisting, and destabilizing across the aesthetic humanities ironically seems too soothing: it lulls us into a dream of pure openness freed from the hard work of securing shelter for all.

Building just shelter is not a simple matter. Private homeownership affords wealth inequality, domestic violence, racial segregation, and long, fuel-intensive daily commutes. Zoning laws that exclude all multifamily dwellings in some neighborhoods have limited the availability of affordable housing in the United States.[90] Setha Low describes the "fortress mentality" of white families in gated communities in the United States who increasingly opt to live behind walls and fences out of fear of non-white others.[91] Such walled communities have become increasingly common worldwide.[92] Victims of domestic abuse, including many queer and trans people, report feeling as unsafe inside homes and homeless shelters as they do outside on the streets.[93] And environmentalists themselves have been divided about the best forms of housing for a sustainable planet. Some have argued for dense housing near public transit, while others have fought strenuously against these designs on the grounds that this will hurt existing environments.[94]

At the same time, climate change has multiplied and intensified the difficulties of securing stable shelter. Storms, droughts, flooding, and wildfires have been driving new scales of dislocation around the world, with hundreds of millions of climate migrants expected by the year 2050.[95] Coastal flooding will make most of Vietnam, parts of China, and the Nile Delta uninhabitable by then. Droughts and crop failures have already been driving millions of people out of rural homelands in Africa and the Middle East. And by the year 2100, regions of India and China could become so hot that spending time outside for just a few hours "will result in death even for the fittest of humans."[96] Ensuing struggles over water and high food prices are likely to spur further political instability and violence—entailing even more displacements from homes.

Is it possible to design enclosures for environmental sustainability and collective justice? They certainly do not have to be organized around private property or the traditional family. Susan Fraiman focuses our attention on "extreme domesticity," cases where people on the margins—queer, economically insecure, homeless, and displaced—fight to make home-like shelters under inauspicious conditions. These are not attempts at conformity but struggles to create spaces that are safe and attractive for those most vulnerable to violence, extreme weather, and involuntary dislocation. "Desiring shelter," as Fraiman writes, "is not necessarily conservative."[97] She reads a passage near the end of Leslie Feinberg's *Stone Butch Blues* (1993), where the transgender character Jess creates a safe and comfortable home after a long period of homelessness. Jess paints, cleans, and buys linens and bath soaps at a department store. While critics have typically written off home decorating as weakly feminine and consumerist, Fraiman urges us to see Jess's homemaking as crucial to the struggle to survive: "an audacious effort to produce a basic sense of physical and psychic security by someone who has been repeatedly violated."[98]

Seeing from the perspective of hungry poverty and the constant threat of violence, I want to suggest that one of the most important infrastructural forms for sustainable justice will be well-designed social housing. In the United States, of course, public housing projects are notorious for their failures. Projects designed and built in the 1950s and 1960s, like the Cabrini-Green development in Chicago, quickly became infamous for poor building maintenance and violent crime. A long process of demolishing all of the Cabrini-Green buildings began in 1995. But it would be a mistake to conclude that public housing design is always doomed to failure. Recent scholarship suggests that even in the United States, public housing has succeeded better than public perception suggests.[99]

In fact, scholars around the world have shown that the most pressing problem with social housing is not that it is badly designed or maintained but that there is simply not enough of it. Architects, urban planners, and social justice activists are engaged in ongoing conversations about which housing plans work best for different sites and communities. Across the Global South, for example, massive numbers of poor people live in shantytowns on the outskirts of cities without access to reliable infrastructure. These residents are constantly building and repairing makeshift housing while they inhabit it, which means that access to materials and infrastructure are more urgent for them than new housing design.[100]

While political and economic conditions and solutions will differ, it is my argument here that adequate shelter for human bodies *itself* does not vary much in form.[101] It must afford sufficient space and quiet for rest and gathering; it must offer protective barriers from danger; and it must be reliable over time. The struggle for just forms of shelter will mean advocating for enclosures, then, but also resisting other organizing forms: for example, bodies have a right to be sheltered, but they should not be segregated by race; everyone should be protected from the elements, but barriers should not be especially confining to women or obstructive to people with disabilities; people should have the right to quiet and space away from others but also the freedom to share intimate spaces with those who are not conventional kin.

What draws my own formalist interest, then, are the ways that sheltering enclosures interact with other forms in self-reinforcing systems. In 2005, for example, the state of Utah launched a remarkably successful public housing initiative called "Housing First," which altered the conventional temporal and spatial forms for addressing homelessness. While most U.S. public housing requires that candidates pass tests for drugs or mental illness as a condition for inclusion—a pattern called "treatment first"—Utah reversed the usual sequence, providing shelter first and routines of treatment second. The theory was that people could address health and substance abuse problems better after they were securely housed. Apartments for participants were also deliberately scattered across buildings and neighborhoods, rather than clustered close in settings that resembled institutions. Over a ten-year span, rates of chronic homelessness dropped, the program proved less expensive than conventional ways of supporting chronically homeless people, and the new apartment-dwellers showed much higher rates of housing stability than those in "treatment first" programs or shelters.[102]

Another example from Boston offers an even more appealing constellation of forms. Politically effective, ethnically diverse, and durable over time, the Commonwealth Development is located in an unusually diverse neighborhood on a subway line. In the 1980s, its low-income renters were vocal and organized. They had been lobbying against leaks in the roofs, broken doors, high crime, and a lack of play space for children. When their buildings were targeted for demolition, they insisted that they did not want to be evicted and dispersed; they wanted to return to the new housing when it was ready. They set up a tenants' organization that elected fifteen members from among the residents. They published a monthly newsletter in both English and Spanish and held regular forums for information and debate. The Boston Housing Authority eventually conceded to the tenants, allowing them to negotiate the terms of the new complex. With the help of lawyers, the tenants succeeded in generating a 223-page contract. Its most important condition: the residents' association had the right to fire the management company. Today, Commonwealth is still entirely public housing and still run by the same private management company, continuing a "sense of shared governance." The space now includes a daycare, a senior center, and community gardens; and it remains of the best integrated neighborhoods in the city. The waiting list to join is long.[103]

The built forms at work here interconnect for collective continuance: stable shelter is linked to a public transportation network and to designated public spaces for gathering and play. It houses low-income people not segregated by race. But two social forms make this community especially just and durable. The first is routines of participatory governance, including elected representatives and regular meetings, and the second is a contract where decision making lodges with the residents: the private company that does the routine labor of maintaining the space has to provide satisfaction to those who live there.

An equally successful public housing experiment has taken shape in Vauban, a sustainable neighborhood housing about five thousand people in Freiburg, Germany. Once an empty French military barracks, the buildings used to house squatters and students. Local grassroots groups, including environmental organizations, lobbied for the design of the new community, which would come to include the squatters already living there. Housing, offices, stores, and parks are now located in dense proximity to each other, with easy access to walking trails and biking paths. Downtown Freiburg is connected by light rail and bus. The area does not allow parking on residential streets, and anyone who chooses to buy a car must pay for the construction of a parking space in one of its two garages. Seventy percent of households do not own cars.[104]

The work of designing housing is especially unusual in Vauban. Cooperatives of ten to fifty households, called *Baugruppen*, can apply to buy land for their residences, which they are allowed to design in a variety of ways, as long as they meet ecological standards. This has prevented large developers from buying up the area. One section, called the Solarsiedlung, or Solar Settlement, produces more energy than it consumes. Another development, called Sonnenhof, or Sun Court, is designed to serve humans and pets of all ages. It offers subsidized housing to families with children and ten residents with dementia, as well as market-rate units for other families. It is designed around a central courtyard, and it has an enclosed garden for the elderly tenants and one for small children. All of the apartments housing the residents with dementia have windows overlooking the courtyard or gardens.[105]

Multiple forms impose order on Vauban. Networks of pathways are overlaid: the train tracks follow a green swale—a long grassy channel—where ecological stormwater pipes also flow, and connect to the walking and cycling paths.[106] Driving and parking are tightly restricted to a small number of designated routes and spaces. Environmental standards for buildings are strict, and all applicants must follow the Baugruppe model of collective organizing. Otherwise, there is a lot of room for experimentation. The ongoing design of the whole neighborhood is a public, transparent process, involving multiple parties, including city government, representatives of citizen groups, and technical experts, including energy specialists and architects. As in Boston, the political forms are as important to the success of the project as the building design.

Portable Models

The Commonwealth and Vauban examples suggest room for a lot of creativity in the ways that constellations of infrastructural forms work together to sustain collective life over long periods. I end here by sketching out very briefly just a few models that show how these different infrastructural forms—routines, pathways, and enclosures—can work together in virtuous cycles to sustain justice over time. The goal is not to be exhaustive in my analysis but to suggest ways of combining forms that could give shape to political aspirations. All of these are real, and so demonstrate the genuine workability of these systems. All of them are also portable: designs that could shape the building of forms in other places.

Sustaining Networks

Curitiba, a city of nearly two million people in southern Brazil, has joined transportation and waste infrastructures in a mutually sustaining new order. Unlike many other "green" cities, Curitiba is not a wealthy place. In the 1960s, the population was expanding quickly, and the municipal government wanted to design public transportation to meet the city's needs. A new subway was too expensive, so planners designed a citywide bus system, which has proved successfully sustainable in four ways: it operates at a low cost, which means that residents pay a lower proportion of their wages for transportation than do residents of other cities; it is used by two-thirds of the population (1.2 million people every day); it is efficient, with the buses moving as quickly as trains along their own designated lanes; and the widespread use of the system allows Curitiba to boast the lowest air pollution of any city in Brazil.[107]

At the same time that the city was designing and building its bus system, Curitiba needed to address a different infrastructural problem. Poor people living in the *favelas* on the outskirts had no way to dispose of their waste and so were dumping their garbage on streets and in waterways, creating citywide health risks. Curitiba introduced a "Purchase for Garbage" program, which allowed residents to exchange bags of waste and recycling for bus tickets, as well as schoolbooks and food. Infant mortality and rates of disease dropped.

Less trash in streets and rivers helped to preserve the environmental health of the city. Curitiba started to treat its waste as a resource and now boasts the highest rate of recycling in the world, at 70 percent. The opera house was built from recycled materials, and the city reuses old buses as classrooms and health clinics.[108] Overall, the cost of this waste infrastructure program is no higher than it would have been if the city had paid a private company to collect the garbage.

What is most interesting for my purposes here is that the two infrastructures, one for transport and the other for waste, sustain one another over time. The "green trade" for public transportation means that many of the city's poor, though living on the outskirts, can afford to travel to jobs all around the city, which lowers poverty rates while deepening the city's commitment to public transport.[109] And these forms call for no painful sacrifice. Curitibans are rightly proud of their beautiful city, with its gorgeous opera house and many parks and gardens.

Routines and Pathways for Sustainable Agriculture

Contemporary agricultural business, dominated by a few huge global corporations, has thrown millions of small farmers into poverty, depleted soils, and increasingly introduced monocropping, which eradicates traditional plants and reduces biodiversity. One powerful alternative is a set of pathways that has helped to spread local practices of sustainable farming across distances—a transnational network called the Movimiento Campesino a Campesino, or the Farmer to Farmer Movement. Intentionally decentralized and horizontal, the movement revolves around "peasant pedagogy." Neighboring farmers share knowledge, experimenting with materials and techniques and then showing each other what works. Volunteers work as "promoters," holding workshops in their own and nearby communities. This grassroots pathway infrastructure, overcoming farmers' justifiable mistrust of government initiatives, has managed to spread sustainable farming to remote rural places. And yet, the movement has also run into obstacles afforded by its decentralized network form. In Cuba, for example, peasants in Pinar del Rio fighting a specific weed did not know that farmers in faraway Cienfuegos had found a solution. The crucial hinge between local networks was missing. And so, a centralized national infrastructure was formed to encourage and sustain the grassroots dissemination of knowledge. The Cuban government opted to provide coordinators to connect otherwise disparate local networks of farmers. Overall, this combined form—bringing together decentralized peasant pedagogy and centralized oversight of the gaps between networks—has been a success. National food production has increased; there has been a significant reduction in pesticide use; small farmers are showing signs of improved resilience to extreme storms; and more women have become active in decision making.[110]

La Via Campesina model has begun to reshape farming as far away as India, where small farmers have been falling more and more deeply into debt. In order to buy seeds and pesticides from private companies, they have had to borrow money at high rates of interest, and then, when hit by storms or a drop in global food prices, they cannot afford loan payments and plunge even further into debt. More than eleven thousand farmers died by suicide in India in 2016 alone.[111]

A grassroots movement has developed an alternative model, called Zero Budget Natural Farming, whereby farmers share indigenous seeds and learn from others how to farm without pesticides. Several forms are crucial to this model. One is the routine of the annual seed-sharing festival in Tamil Nadu, where a festival showcasing indigenous seeds is open to all. About six thousand farmers attend.[112] They are invited to collect a few pounds of seeds of different varieties and commit to return with double the amount they have taken the following year. More than half come back with the additional seeds to share.

Another form at work is the careful design of the farm. Subhash Palekar, the founder of the Zero Budget movement, favors what he calls a "five-layer model," which integrates combinations of trees and crops that need different amounts of sunlight and are harvested at different points in the year, helping each other to grow and freeing farmers from dependence on a single crop. The ongoing tasks of harvesting also mean that there are no dramatic rises and falls in the need for extra labor, and many families can handle the year-round work of the farm on their own. In order to work well, the combination of plants and the distances between them must follow a strict set of forms.

The Zero Budget model relies on numerous routinized farm practices that have been shown to have ecological benefits, including mulching, agroforestry, water conservation, and cover cropping. These help to prevent soil erosion and pests and do not depend on fossil fuels, leading to environmental sustainability and resilience through storms and droughts. Nearly all the farmers who were surveyed in Karnataka reported lower costs, higher incomes, reduced debt, and higher and better yields after adopting these methods.[113]

Crucial to the spread of the Zero Budget model so far has also been the grassroots pathway for information on the Via Campesina model. Here, knowledge spreads through a network of "lighthouses"—local farmers willing to try the method who then spread the word of its success to others. All of these volunteer their time, serving on a list of official mentors and offering their farms for demonstrations. Small farmers have also organized hundreds of training workshops and have set up social media sites. Local chapters do a lot of their own organizing, but they also link up through large-scale organizations, including La Via Campesina, which has helped to spread Indian designs and routines to farmers in Nepal and Sri Lanka. In 2016, the government of the state of Andhra Pradesh launched a formal state effort to spread Zero Budget farming to six million new farmers. They pay "master farmers" to train new farmers in the methods. Every day, these trainers follow a strict routine in each village: a morning leading a study session, an afternoon visiting farms to talk about problems and solutions, and evenings showing videos and leading group discussions. Andhra Pradesh, unlike Karnataka, has focused specific attention on women, "the poorest of the poor." It is too soon to tell how well this model will work across the state, but initial results have been positive.[114]

The struggle to spread sustainable routines of rice farming might benefit from pathways of information like those that connect Cuban and Indian farmers. Rice provides 20 percent of all the calories consumed globally, and it is especially important to the diet of the world's poor. Current rice farming practices also generate substantial carbon and methane emissions. In the 1980s, small farmers in Madagascar developed an efficient rice farming technique that involves planting rice seeds earlier than usual, draining the crops mid-season, and rotating them with a hand-operated hoe—low-tech methods that do not require significant investments to work, cut down on water and chemicals, and can quadruple yields while reducing greenhouse gas emissions. The techniques succeed even in poor soil conditions. The major obstacle to the spread of this "System of Rice Intensification" (SRI) is what Norman Uphoff calls "mental inputs": millions of small farmers will need to learn new techniques and be willing to change their usual practices.[115] It is here that drawing formal inspiration from the networks of La Via Campesina might offer an important solution.

To be sure, some readers might object to the very idea of improved rice cultivation as imperialist—a classic example of a Eurocentric modernity insisting on a single, rational solution around the world to replace generations of established practices. Generalizable and portable, it surely cannot be sensitive to local cultural needs and values. But while improved rice cultivation is a generalizing model, it was developed by Malagasy farmers. It does not find its roots in Europe. In fact, SRI's defenders allege that it has been unfairly questioned and criticized precisely because it is *not* the brainchild of academics or corporations but a genuine grassroots innovation.[116] It helps small local farmers rather than massive agribusinesses and replaces rice cultivation techniques that are already standardized around the globe. Currently dominant techniques of rice farming were transmitted in part by enslaved Africans who brought indigenous practices of rice growing to the Americas,[117] and in part by trade expeditions that spread rice cultivation from its origins in China to India and then eventually to Europe. That is, most rice farming as it is practiced today is itself a legacy of imperialism. Water- and space-intensive, it is best suited to environments where there is ample land and lots of rain. Both land and water are under increasing pressure now, and with exploding global populations dependent on rice as a basic dietary staple, the need for more efficient rice farming is in fact not only a good but an urgent requirement for food security and food justice worldwide. From this perspective, it seems worth experimenting with forms—like routines of crop rotation and pathways of information—in order to sustain the lives of millions of people over time.

Pathways to Equality: Women and Mobility

Electric light has often been hailed as a symbol of European modernity, producing new and unnatural rhythms—including nightlife, third shifts, and *flanerie* through pulsing city streets. Scholars have linked electric lighting specifically to imperial power. Queen Wilhelmina of the Netherlands, for example, put on elaborate illuminated displays in Java to celebrate the enlightenment brought by the Dutch to their colonies.[118] Light pollution, disrupted sleep, round-the-clock industrial production, and heightened police and military security are among the serious burdens of this infrastructural development. It has become commonplace across the Global North to flick a switch and immediately illuminate a space, combining a kind of instantaneity with control at a distance that reaffirms an ideology of individual power.[119]

But electric light has affirmative affordances too. Today, around the world, girls and women are especially energy poor, which means that they often lack access to an adequate education for self-sufficiency. In South Asia, Latin America, and Africa, there are many communities where household work is gendered feminine, and girls have so many routines to perform during the day that they do not have time to study. Their families also worry about the dangers of the streets and so keep them inside the home at night. Unable to engage in educational routines of different kinds—from doing their homework to walking to classes or meetings at night—they drop out of school early, lack literacy and numeracy skills, and become dependent on male breadwinners for survival.[120]

After an NGO called Little Sun distributed solar lamps to girls between the ages of fifteen and eighteen in Yemen, the girls reported having time to study and increased motivation to learn.[121] Similarly, a program offering handheld solar lamps to girls in a refugee camp in Haiti reduced the rate of violence against them, which afforded them a new mobility and autonomy.[122] Development economists Lupin Rahman and Vijayendra Rao compared various factors limiting gender equality in North and South India and discovered that villages with better road and energy infrastructures afforded more autonomy and mobility for women: "If the village approach road is of better quality, women are significantly less likely to need permission to visit health clinics. If a bus station is nearby or the village is located close to town, the probability that a woman will require permission to leave the house is reduced. Interestingly, the presence of electric street lighting, which reduces the fear of venturing out in the dark, is positively correlated with higher female mobility across the board."[123]

Networks of energy and mobility matter for gender equality, and the shape of women's lives, in turn, has surprisingly important consequences for environmental sustainability. Educating girls leads to lower rates of child marriage, fewer children, and better strategies for resilience in the face of storms and droughts, all crucial aspects of a globally sustainable collective life. Paul Hawken's "drawdown" project estimates that educating girls would reduce carbon-equivalent emissions by 68.9 gigatons globally over the next three decades.[124] This is a case where a hierarchy of oppression reinforced by energy poverty and household routines can be answered by a constellation of other forms, including energy pathways to light the way to women's education.

Conclusion

The infrastructural forms brought together in this chapter emerge from very different ideological sources. Some are centralized state projects, like dams and railroads; others are highly critical of the work of formal government, like the Black Panthers, or operate outside of the purview of the state, like daily habits of tooth-cleaning across the Islamic world. Some models are the consequences of clear and consistent ideologies, like sanitation infrastructures designed to showcase the progress of a nation, while others have adapted to competing value systems and ends, like roads originally built for military purposes that eventually become major trade routes and still later conduits for resistance. Some infrastructural constraints have had surprisingly radical results, like the strict work schedules that have encouraged the making of innovative works of art. Some are the results of grassroots organizing, including the Zero Budget farming movement and the Commonwealth housing development in Boston. Others are very much top-down affairs. Jaime Lerner, the radical mayor-architect of Curitiba, was first appointed by Brazil's military regime. He believes in imposing change fast, rather than engaging in long and inclusive processes of deliberation. In 1972, when Lerner wanted to transform a busy commercial street into a pedestrian mall, he was met with strong opposition from store owners who thought that blocking car traffic would hurt business. He decided to work fast: "the initial block would have to be built from Friday night through Monday morning to avoid an injunction, so that it would be ready for the people to use once the shops reopened early on Monday," Lerner explains. From the start, the pedestrian zone proved enormously popular, and later the same businesses petitioned to extend it.[125] Although Lerner believes in citizen feedback and participation, he argues for imposing innovative designs first to see how well they work, correcting them later if necessary. "Changes need to be quick," he says.[126]

The models offered here also operate at different scales. Some, like Boston's Commonwealth Development, are ways of organizing neighborhoods. Others are citywide projects, like Curitiba's interlinked waste and transportation infrastructures. Still others scale up to the level of the nation, like electrical grids and highway systems. And some forms travel successfully across borders, like the Via Campesina peasant farming network.

My point in gathering these disparate examples is to think clearly about which forms can work together to support just distributions, sustaining routines, and sheltering enclosures over time. This is very different from the work of most aesthetic humanists, who tend to focus on the ideological origins of infrastructures. And since so many existing forms can be traced back to hierarchical regimes, this focus on origins has helped contribute to a pervasive pessimism among humanists. Looking back to intentions will necessarily miss the affirmative, and sometimes unintentional, potential of the orders and arrangements that might happen to have been set in place along the way. Perhaps an authoritarian state builds a smooth and environmentally friendly transportation system that might sustain a more democratic collective too. Maybe tracks laid down by an oppressive empire end up affording the successful mass gathering of anticolonial radicals. Bounded spaces may exclude some people but still afford safety for vulnerable bodies, including those of women, trans, and queer people. For this reason, I proceed, like the most famous literary formalists—the New Critics—by focusing not on origins and intentions but on what the forms actually *do*, and on figuring out how to use and rearrange the formal landscape going forward. Instead of tracing genealogies, that is, I have been posing a more future-oriented kind of question: not a focus on who created each system and why but an attention to what systems of collective life it is possible to do or make with the basic forms of the routine, the pathway, and the enclosure.

4

Aesthetic Challenges

IT IS DIFFICULT for writers and artists to capture the "slow violence" of climate change, Rob Nixon argues, because it takes such unsensational forms:

> Violence is customarily conceived as an event or action that is immediate in time, explosive and spectacular in space, and erupting into instant sensational visibility. We need, I believe, to engage a different kind of violence, a violence that is neither spectacular nor instantaneous, but rather incremental and accretive, its calamitous repercussions playing out across a range of temporal scales. In so doing, we also need to engage the representational, narrative, and strategic challenges posed by the relative invisibility of slow violence. Climate change, the thawing cryosphere, toxic drift, biomagnification, deforestation, the radioactive aftermaths of wars, acidifying oceans, and a host of other slowly unfolding environmental catastrophes present formidable representational obstacles that can hinder our efforts to mobilize and act decisively.[1]

So gradual that they are often imperceptible, processes of climate change do not lend themselves to the shock and excitement of the news story, the spectacle, or plotted narrative.

The same can be said for collective continuance. It is not particularly subtle or exciting to keep things running smoothly, and for a long time. Continuity does not lend itself to thrilling or sensational forms. Social worlds that ensure that everyone has enough food, clean air, shelter, and water can be, as many a utopian text has shown us, boring. And yet, monotonous and stable fairness is profoundly desirable, especially in a time of climate calamity. And a canon of aesthetic objects that puts its highest value on ruptures with convention and expectation is not ideally suited to this work. Are there cultural forms, then, that could prompt us to feel aesthetic desire and appreciation even for the boring predictability of having a safe place to sleep or flushing a working toilet?

This chapter proposes an unfamiliar canon for an age of precarity, a set of aesthetic objects that might help us revalue stability and predictability, and especially the ongoing, repetitive work of collectively sustaining infrastructures that mostly operate uneventfully and out of sight, like well-functioning sewer systems and electrical grids. The better they work, the more difficult it is to recognize and appreciate them. Even visible infrastructures, like bridges, tend to invite attention only once they have started to break under the strain of too much use. As comedian John Oliver puts it: "Infrastructure: If Anything Exciting Happens, We've Done It Wrong."[2]

Several scholars have challenged the idea that drives this chapter—that stable infrastructures are too easy to overlook. They point out that they are impossible to forget or ignore for those who lack access to them—like inhabitants of a *favela* without access to clean water or wheelchair users faced with a staircase.[3] Some infrastructures are also very much intended to be seen.[4] Consider "Lenin's Light," the Soviet electrification of Mongolia, which was supposed to inspire awe and bring the peasants out of darkness, both literally and figuratively.[5] Spectacles like these purposefully invite a visual attention to infrastructures for ideological ends.

Scholars have also been arguing recently that infrastructures are not stable; they are dynamic fields of meaning, "sites of representation and aspiration," which can be reworked, improvised, and put to unexpected uses.[6] For Lauren Berlant, they are characterized by variation and adaptation, unlike institutions, which "congeal power and interest."[7] And AbdouMaliq Simone has famously argued that people themselves have had to *become* infrastructure in Johannesburg, filling the gaps where official infrastructures have failed.[8] For these scholars, infrastructures are pliable and adaptive conditions rather than brute material facts.

But it would be a mistake, this book has argued, to underestimate the lasting and shaping force of material infrastructures on human communities. "They consist of metal and machines as much as by meanings and discourse," writes Casper Bruun Jensen.[9] I keep my own attention here on their capacity for stability. Many infrastructures are not particularly flexible or malleable, and the sturdy shapes these take afford some versions of collective life while precluding others, directing access to clean water, adequate food, laboring patterns, flows of energy, safe rest, and social gathering over long periods. A new subway line in a city, for example, "changes the time that it takes for people to commute from their homes to workplaces, or from one part of the city to another. It also changes the urban form, as new housing, offices, and shops spring up along the metro line."[10] Although it is certainly possible to make multiple meanings out of the subway, to let it deteriorate, to use it for something other than travel, or to avoid it altogether, its physical shape will still impose order on collective life, including the distributions of homes, labor, goods, and services. In many cases, these will keep roughly the same shapes for generations to come.

While it is certainly true that the meanings and values of particular infrastructures vary, then, my own argument here is that their physical structures organize collectives in ways that matter, often regardless of their perceptibility. And while some are highly noticeable, the best-functioning infrastructures—the ones most crucial to collective continuance—are also those most likely to be taken for granted. After all, infrastructures are capacitating forms: they smooth the way for other activity—which means that they allow people to focus on other, more exciting, ends.[11] We might think of the bus that carries us to our beloved, the electric lighting that allows us to throw a nighttime dance party, the network of public streets and squares that bring queer and trans bodies into visibility and contact. When infrastructures are oppressive and constraining, it is difficult to ignore them, but precisely when they are at their most enabling, they function as means to other activity and so lend themselves to being undervalued or disregarded. And since attention to infrastructural forms is most likely to flag when they are working well, the people most likely to be breezily unappreciative of them are precisely those who benefit most from them. If you have to walk miles to a river for water, you might wish for an indoor faucet; if your drain is backed up, you might well long for it to be in working order; but if you can expect clean water to flow in your home because it does so many times a day every day, you will have to go to some trouble to appreciate the ease that affords you. The more smoothly infrastructural forms function, the more we are free to let our attention wander to other matters, including the many varied ends which these forms make possible. It is work to focus on the very freedom you have not to focus. This is why rich communities routinely allow their own infrastructures to crumble.[12] And it is why, I suspect, we have seen an uptick in scholarship on infrastructure in North America and Europe at the very moment when subway systems, water pipes, and electrical grids are breaking down from the strain of long years of public underfunding and inadequate maintenance. We notice them most readily when they begin to fail.

Quite a few infrastructures are literally hidden from view, like the sewer pipes that run beneath the streets or the global network of undersea cables that even communications experts do not know are there.[13] And as Brian Larkin notes, even when we notice some aspects of infrastructure, we are probably missing others: "we often see computers not cables, light not electricity, taps and water but not pipes and sewers."[14] But that is precisely why it is politically important to keep our eye on infrastructural forms. So crucial to collective survival and yet so desperately inequitable, so fundamental and yet so unexciting, well-functioning infrastructures do not readily draw the cultural and political attention they deserve.

Cultivating an appreciation for infrastructural forms will be especially tough for scholars in the aesthetic humanities. For more than two centuries, theorists of aesthetics have reviled routines for their deadening reinstantiation of the status quo. Clear pathways, we know, smooth the operations of military and police violence, capitalist accumulation, and petroleum and fracked gas. And enclosures have been recurring targets of aesthetic critique, from national boundaries to settler colonies to domestic walls. So: why bring the arts into the argument at all? This chapter will make the case that art can work with smoothly functioning infrastructures in mutually sustaining systems that support collective life over the long term. Aesthetic forms that lend themselves especially well to an appreciation for infrastructure, as we will see, include the regular patterns of rhythm, rhyme, and ritual, the descriptive plainness of realist narrative, colorful public murals, and the endings of domestic fiction, all of which critics have cast as politically conservative. I will argue that these forms not only serve dominant elites; they also register the genuine pleasures of finding stability in the midst of precarious conditions, pleasures that can be put to work for the political struggle for collective continuance.

Aesthetic Routines

For more than two centuries, artists and writers have argued that the aesthetic is the best antidote to the oppressive power of routine. Poetry is valuable, according to Percy Shelley, because it "strips the veil of familiarity from the world."[15] For Russian formalist Viktor Shklovsky, what defines art is its disruption of the automatism of habit.[16] John Dewey agrees: "Art throws off the covers that hide the expressiveness of experienced things; it quickens us from the slackness of routine."[17] The painter Jean Dubuffet wrote that it is the property of art "to smash all the crust of routine, to crack open the shell of policed and socialized man, to unblock the channels through which the voices of his internal wild man can express themselves."[18] Adorno and Horkheimer single out the repetitiveness of the culture industry—"infecting everything with sameness"—as lulling us into a deathly acquiescence to capitalist modernity.[19] Even Michel de Certeau, the great theorist of everyday life, understands it as a "battleground" for disrupting routines.[20]

This tradition of setting art against routinization continues, very much alive, into our own time. We find Derek Attridge, for example, arguing that literature jolts us out of ordinary expectations and conventions.[21] Choreographer Alka Nauman says that she "is faithful to the idea that art needs to disrupt people's daily routines."[22] And Fred Moten celebrates the unruly "auto-explosions" of lyric.[23]

If Euro-American criticism for two centuries has repeatedly valorized—and canonized—the artist who invents new forms, experiments with generic conventions, subverts norms, or surprises us with fresh images and ideas, it is not so easy to train our aesthetic attention on routine. But there are some cultural forms that do exactly that. In a move that risks sounding hypocritical, I am going to argue for a break from humanistic business as usual—but with a slight twist: I aim to disrupt the disruption so routine in the aesthetic humanities in order to revalue routine.

Rhyme and Rhythm

Which art forms might help us to appreciate and celebrate the routines of daily labor? The nineteenth-century realist novel, the field of my own training, is surprisingly disinclined to represent the day-to-day experience of factory work. Even the so-called "industrial novel" displays "a marked *absence* of representations of work or workers working."[24] Most scholars have assumed that these fictions avoid representing labor for ideological reasons.[25] But the challenge for the novel is as much formal as ideological: it is difficult to represent routine in narrative without miring a plot in intolerable monotony. In Emile Zola's *Germinal*, to take a famous example, the narrator follows a stranger into the mines for his first day of work, and describes at length his shock at the overwhelming heat, the backbreaking labor, and the enormity of his hunger and fatigue. The novel gives us the horror of this, but precisely as *new*, and then never returns to the description of mine work for a second or third time, though Etienne goes back every single day. That is, the novel never repeats the experience *as* routine. Zola certainly criticizes the painful repetitiveness of the miners' lives, but we readers encounter the routines of labor in their least routinized form—as novelty.[26] As Gerard Genette explains, narrative is not "condemned to reproduce [repeating phenomena] in its discourse" because it can opt for synthetic formulations like "every day" or "for years."[27] Similarly, Elaine Scarry has argued that plotted narratives typically avoid "perpetual, repetitive, habitual" action in favor of exciting and exceptional events.[28] Or to put this another way, narratives usually condense the experience of repetition into a single description which they then subordinate to the arc of the singular events we call "the plot."

One reason to find the formal account more persuasive than the ideological one is that many nineteenth-century British poets—of similar classes and educational backgrounds to their novelist contemporaries—did often represent repetitive industrial labor. Thomas Hood's 1843 poem, "Song of the Shirt," for example, is spoken by an exhausted seamstress who must work around the clock:

> Work—work—work!
> From weary chime to chime,
> Work—work—work,
> As prisoners work for crime!
> Band, and gusset, and seam,
> Seam, and gusset, and band,
> Till the heart is sick, and the brain benumbed,
> As well as the weary hand.[29]

Hood clearly is not trying to avoid the monotony of routine here; his verse positively wallows in it. The speaker repeats the word "work" three times in the first line to establish the rhythm of the lines to follow, and then rhymes the word "work" with itself in lines 1 and 3. Using the repetitiveness of rhythm to reinforce the repetitiveness of rhyme, and vice versa, he maximizes the repetitive affordances of poetic form.

Since Hood is deliberately focusing our attention on the deadly routinization of labor, it is not surprising that he overwhelms us with repetitiveness. The point of representing monotony here is to critique and reject it. But it is interesting that "Song of the Shirt" was hugely popular. It tripled the circulation of the journal where it first appeared. It was translated into German, French, Italian, and Russian, turned into a street ballad, memorized by schoolchildren, parodied, and even printed on handkerchiefs.[30] Regular rhythms and rhymes here have two affordances that seem curiously at odds: on the one hand, they reveal the oppressiveness of monotonous labor practices; on the other, they create appealing entertainment, with their pleasurable, catchy repetitions.

Hood is by no means the only poet to have used rhyme and rhythm to call attention to the oppressive routines of industrialized labor. British poets across the political spectrum did so, including Elizabeth Barrett Browning, a liberal, Caroline Norton, a Tory, and William Morris, a Socialist.[31] The connections between the repetitive patternings of poetic and laboring forms also extend well beyond nineteenth-century Britain. We might think of Heinrich Heine's "Die armen Weber" ("Silesian Weavers"), Langston Hughes's "Brass Spittoons," Maya Angelou's "Woman Work," and Rhina Espaillat's "Find Work."

If repetitive poetic forms are well suited to conveying the painful monotony of industrial labor, they also afford an attention to the more sustaining, affirmative affordance of work routines. This passage from "Goblin Market" (1862) by Hood's contemporary, Christina Rossetti, suggests a pleasurable model of routine labor:

> Early in the morning
> When the first cock crow'd his warning,
> Neat like bees, as sweet and busy,
> Laura rose with Lizzie:
> Fetch'd in honey, milk'd the cows,
> Air'd and set to rights the house,
> Kneaded cakes of whitest wheat,
> Cakes for dainty mouths to eat,
> Next churn'd butter, whipp'd up cream,
> Fed their poultry, sat and sew'd;
> Talk'd as modest maidens should . . . [32]

Some of the daily tasks involve imposing order. At other times the characters create pleasures for the body—cakes and butter and cream. Rossetti's main form here is the rhyming couplet, which gets us into habits of expecting recurrence, as it describes tasks, like milking and cooking, that are part of daily routines. There is also repetition on the level of syntax, as one past tense verb follows another in a rapid sequence of tasks: fetch'd, milk'd, air'd, set, kneaded, and so on. But unlike Hood's unending present, Rossetti's verbs are mostly past participles, making it clear that each task can come to an end, that patterns of recurrence can afford rest as well as movement. The characters have opportunities for sociability in the daily round; they sit and talk, not simply forced into deadening sameness but afforded chances for rest and companionship.

Rossetti's rhythm and rhyme scheme are famously irregular throughout the poem. Even in the short passage I have quoted that describes Laura and Lizzie at work, the last three lines break the couplet pattern with a line that does not rhyme and then an off-rhyme. "Sew'd" and "should" still preserves some echoing repetitiveness, but it is about as far as possible from Hood's null rhyme of "work" chiming with "work." And yet, this moment in the poem is not an example of radical disruption either. It is repetition without deadening monotony.

"Goblin Market" is not only organized by rhythm and rhyme. It has a plot too. And in keeping with the usual affordances of plotted narrative, Rossetti organizes the story around a major interruption, when Laura eats the goblin fruits and can no longer be satisfied with her daily labor. Here we can see how rhyme and rhythm model repetitions, while plot affords a heightened focus on singular events.

Most importantly for a formalist interested in infrastructure, Rossetti turns to rhyme and rhythm to suggest that repetition does not only afford mindless monotony. Recurrence can be braided with variety and rest. This attention to the affirmative affordances of routine is not limited to nineteenth-century poetry either. Recent Anglophone examples include Naomi Shihab Nye's "Daily" and "Loving Working," Al Maginnes's "The Dignity of Ushers," and Laura Da's "Bead Workers."

Of course, it is quite possible that the idyllic model of agrarian work Rossetti imagines never actually existed. Or that it was not so idyllic.[33] Neither of these critiques matters for my purposes here. I am suggesting that "Song of the Shirt" and "Goblin Market" raise for us a different kind of question, a question not about the truth of the past but about the generalizable affordances of aesthetic forms for the future. If we accept the necessity of some repetitive labor to the maintenance of collective life, then poetic forms will be better suited to modeling the various rhythmic forms that daily life and labor might take than plotted ones. If we wanted to sketch out an optimal rhythm for workers that would avoid the radical unpredictability of poverty as well as mind-numbing monotony of industrialization, we might well lay out a pattern that looked something like Rossetti's, one that would involve some variety as well as some repetition, some completed tasks and some ongoing maintenance, some ordering the environment and some making things for ours and others' sensuous pleasure, a pattern characterized by variation and rest within necessary repetitions. Or to put this another way, rather than pointing a way beyond routine, rhyme and rhythm allow us to recognize *as forms* the difference between a working regimen so rigidly routinized that workers are not allowed to chat or take bathroom breaks and a laboring rhythm that incorporates time to rest, think, and socialize.

Song

Music, like poetry, readily affords the repetitive rhythms of labor, and for many of the same formal reasons. Hood's "Song of the Shirt" was put to music and reportedly sung by seamstresses themselves.[34] Surprisingly often, in fact, popular music, like poetry, entwines the double affordances of laboring routines: it can be coercive; it can be pleasurable. And it can be both.

Numerous scholars have pointed to music's troubling power to discipline and control workers. The most painful examples come from the antebellum U.S. South, where slave drivers demanded that enslaved people sing in time with their work to maintain a steady pace. Later, the BBC launched a daily radio show in 1940 called *Music While You Work*, in an effort to boost factory productivity for the war effort.[35] In *Swinging the Machine*, Joel Dinerstein argues that the "propulsive, fast, fluid, and precise" rhythms of big band swing music schooled human bodies to conform to the new pace of assembly line labor.[36]

It is tempting to stop here, with a recognition of the exploitative affordances of music for workers. But if some routines of maintenance will be required simply to keep our bodies alive, then music might offer us a way not only to move beyond repetition but also to bring out its collective and embodied pleasures. That is, music points us to the potential joys that might characterize routinized experience, such as moving to a beat, joining with a collective, and singing a familiar refrain.

In the western islands of Scotland, women traditionally sang to coordinate the collective work of shrinking and thickening cloth, called "waulking":

> They would pass their portion of cloth on to their right-hand neighbour on every third beat, so that the cloth always moved around in a clockwise circle as they sang the songs of waulking. The woman of the house measured the progress of their work by how many songs it needed, though the pace

> of the songs varied according to the tune and the stage reached in the proceedings. The women's bodies swung in unison as the infectious call-and-response lines provided the coordinated physical movement characteristic of work song.[37]

This highly routinized song shows not only the subordination of workers to repetitive routines but also the coordination of movements into a smooth and pleasurable harmony.

Of course, there is danger in covering over dangerous or exploitative labor with the pleasures of song. In a study of a window-blind factory in Britain, ethnographer Marek Korczynski found that popular music played on the shop floor invited the workers to tolerate an alienating kind of labor they might have rejected otherwise. Specifically, it fostered a communal and participatory culture, where workers invited one another into patterns of call-and-response, teased one another about their musical tastes and talents, and joined together in bursts of song and dance, helping to create a "richly supportive, caring, laughing, singing, dancing, and talking culture." Music played "an important role in creating, expressing, and sustaining a sense of community."[38]

These two affordances of musical rhythm—conveying painful labor and producing embodied pleasures—come together in an extreme form in Sam Cooke's 1960 hit, "Chain Gang." On the one hand, the song was enormously popular, reaching number two on the U.S. Billboard Hot 100 and number nine on the UK singles chart. With its bouncy beat and catchy chorus, the song might almost seem to invite audiences to overlook its content, an explicit account of prisoners forced into hard labor, "moanin' their lives away."[39] And yet, while prison gang labor might seem like an odd topic for a light dance tune, Cooke's lyrics draw attention to their shared forms. Vocalists sing "ooh" and "ah" in the voices of workers on the chain gang, followed by hammering clangs that imitate the sound of a pick hitting rock. Cooke sings, "That's the sound of the men working on the chain gang." According to the song itself, then, the sound of the music *is* the sound of the chain gang. Listeners are drawn to move their bodies in pleasure to the hypnotic patterns of oppressive work, which are also the patterns of popular song.[40]

Pop songs and prison labor are not, in fact, the same at all. What the song has in common with backbreaking work is form: a predictable pattern of sound. And while we might use this analysis to condemn popular music and to resist predictable patterns everywhere,[41] I want to do the opposite, and argue that the pleasures of music prove that regular repetitions are not always and necessarily themselves oppressive. It is misleading, as we saw in the last chapter, to understand regularized patterns as themselves what make labor intolerable. And since it seems likely that some regular work will always be necessary to maintaining collective life, we might turn our attention to its potential for shared pleasures and ask how those can be separated from hierarchy and exploitation. In other words, it is too easy to conflate repetition with domination, and from there to miss the affirmative affordances of predictable rhythms, including the crucial role song has played in building solidarity, joining bodies and voices in infectiously, joyfully shared tempos.

Songs have often helped to rouse and sustain political movements. Because their forms afford easy transmission and memorization, catchy songs are especially well suited to the work of energizing crowds and bringing bodies and voices together to march for a common purpose. Political songs have shown a surprising capacity for resilience across time and space, too, providing resources from old struggles for new and emerging movements. British workers drew on the rousing and familiar anthem of the French Revolution, with the Chartists and others singing "La Marseillaise" at local meetings through the nineteenth century.[42] Suffragists then rewrote the lyrics in the early twentieth century for "The Women's Marseillaise."[43] And "L'Internationale," the communist international, was first sung to the tune of "La Marseillaise"—until it got its own, which has itself crossed over into popular culture, from the erotic montage sequence in the 1981 film *Reds* to the swing version sung by Tony Babino.[44]

Another portable example is Friedrich Schiller's poem "An Die Freude" ("Ode to Joy"), made most famous by Beethoven's Ninth Symphony, which speaks to the joys of a "brotherhood" united against tyranny. This call to solidarity proved inspiring to Chilean protestors, who sang the "Ode to Joy" during demonstrations against Augusto Pinochet.[45] Later, Chinese students would rig up loudspeakers to broadcast the song loudly as the military descended on Tiananmen Square. "We used the Ninth to create an ambience of solidarity and hope, for ourselves and for the people of China," explained Tiananmen leader Feng Congde.[46]

Stirring songs afford not only the temporary joining of voices but also the sustaining of political movements across time. James Weldon Johnson's "Lift Every Voice and Sing" was originally written in 1900 for schoolchildren to honor Abraham Lincoln's birthday. In the early twentieth century it became popular across the South, where many African American children sang it every morning at school. Black churches and civic clubs soon took it up. In the 1920s, the NAACP adopted it as their official song, and by the 1950s, it was known as the "Negro National Anthem" and regularly stirred crowds at civil rights marches and demonstrations.[47] Here are the words to the first stanza:

> Lift every voice and sing
> Till earth and heaven ring,
> Ring with the harmonies of Liberty;
> Let our rejoicing rise
> High as the listening skies,
> Let it resound loud as the rolling sea.
> Sing a song full of the faith that the dark past has taught us,
> Sing a song full of the hope that the present has brought us.
> Facing the rising sun of our new day begun,
> Let us march on till victory is won.[48]

Most of the lines are couplets, but there is a quatrain in the middle: AA BCCB DD EE. The ninth line also contains an internal rhyme (sun and begun), which suggests it too could be split into two. In fact, if we listen for the sounds, we can hear a second rhyme scheme haunting the first: AA BCCB DE FE GGG. Echoing sounds also shape the beginnings of lines: "Let our . . ." "Let it . . ." "Let us . . ." Weldon gives us lyrics that are saturated in repetition, explicitly inviting us to "let it resound"—that is, literally, to *sound again.*

In other words, this is a song that everywhere insists on the political power of reverberation. Rhyme affords memorization, which allows the song to travel readily from protest to protest down through generations. The words also tie past to future, calling voices to sing the song over and over across time—from dark past to future freedom. And the song calls for every voice to be lifted, summoning a collective through the experience of a song that resounds across bodies. Nothing is singular here; everything must be repeated; and with repetition comes collective power.

Recently, Black Lives Matter protesters have turned to Kendrick Lamar's 2015 song "Alright" for "an updated theme song for Black folks."[49] Unlike "Lift Every Voice" in many respects, it does share with the earlier song a thematic stress on the endurance of Black people through long struggle and hope for a better future. "God's got us," Lamar sings: "We gon' be alright." Formally, too, the song is similarly saturated in repetition, with rhymes throughout and then repetitions of the same phrase—"We gon' be alright"—eight times in the eight-line refrain. This line reportedly electrified the first

Black Lives Matter conference at Cleveland State University. "The whole damn place went nuts," said one of the attendees. "You were moved. There was no way you could just sit back and not feel the effect of that song. Everybody was singing in unison. It was like being at church."[50] Now called the "unifying soundtrack to Black Lives Matter protests nationwide," "Alright" has become the unofficial anthem of the movement, sung repeatedly at protests against police brutality from Ferguson to Sacramento.[51] Unifying, inspiring, and deliberately, insistently repetitive, "Alright" has become a portable rallying cry for racial justice.

If critics since the Frankfurt School have argued that repetitive mass culture keeps workers from resisting domination through unsatisfying distraction and empty amusement, and so have paid the bulk of our scholarly attention to challenging, unfamiliar experiments, we have missed one of the other affordances of the catchy refrain, which is to train us for endurance, to sustain bodies and minds for the long haul, and to draw people together in shared rhythmic joy.

Visualizing Routines

While rhyme lends itself to the repetitive forms of labor and music affords the joining together of bodies and voices in ways that are powerful for collective action, traditional paintings and photographs are still forms, better suited to affording "the pregnant moment" than the ongoing routine.[52] But visual forms are especially good at capturing crowds and masses, inviting us literally to see collective life on the large scale. My focus here will be large mural paintings that seek to convey the immensity of the labor necessary to collective continuance.

In the 1920s and 1930s, three radical Mexican artists, David Alfaro Siqueiros, José Clemente Orozco, and Diego Rivera, all experimented with ways of conveying masses of ordinary people—not special individuals but the vast collectivity of workers. In 1924, Siqueiros created a woodcut for the militant newspaper *La Machete,* which shows a solider, a laborer, and a peasant hand in hand in the foreground. Their faces are indistinguishable from each other, and behind them an uncountable series of figures packs together into the distance. Evoking throngs of workers in a crowd without a clear end, Siqueiros suggests solidarity on a mass scale through an insistent pattern of similarity that extends beyond the frame.

FIGURE 3. Woodcut by David Alfaro Siqueiros. Photograph by John Lear. © 2022 Artists Rights Society (ARS), New York/SOMAAP, Mexico City.

While Siqueiros's woodcut offers a direct frontal perspective, which pushes the figures up close against the picture plane in a kind of iconic flatness, Diego Rivera, in murals for the Education Ministry in Mexico City (1923–28), opts for a fuller illusion of depth with an upward-thrusting vanishing-point perspective. Human eyes typically see parallel lines, like railroad tracks, approaching one another into the distance until they seem to disappear at a single point. Perspectival images simulate human depth perception, organized around lines that move closer to each other as they recede, and so appear to converge in the distance. Invented by Italian Renaissance architects, one-point perspective is famous for implying an imperialist European subjectivity; it "makes the single eye the centre of the visible world," and so assumes a transcendent, coherent viewer gazing at an objectified world under its control.[53] And yet, the form has another affordance also: organized around lines so long that they move out of sight, vanishing-point perspective is good at conveying huge scales.

Rivera's *Market*, for example, affords the vastness of a crowd by repeating the same shape and color—a round yellow sombrero—in an echoing pattern that disappears into a distance beyond the frame.

The more complex *Good Friday on the Santa Anita Canal* layers repetitions on top of repetitions—the single vanishing point of the canal, with countless people in lines along the banks, reverberates with details that also echo backward into the distance, such as the white lilies miming the shapes of men rowing a faraway barge. In both images, Rivera uses the receding view to capture a huge populace that extends beyond what we can count or know.

The U.S. artists of the New Deal would draw inspiration from these Mexican artists. And like Rivera, they would paint the walls of bureaucratic buildings, like post offices, where people go about their most ordinary routines. One of the few women artists supported by the New Deal arts program was Maxine Albro, born in Iowa and educated in San Francisco, New York, and Paris. In the late 1920s, she went to Mexico to learn from Rivera.[54] Although she never studied with him directly, she learned techniques of fresco painting from his circle of associates. Albro was employed by the short-lived Public Works Art Project, the first of the New Deal arts relief programs, to work on San Francisco's Coit Tower.

Assigned an inside wall, Albro decided that she wanted to paint the bounty of local agriculture. Her mural is called *California* (1934). Here, Albro plays with vanishing-point perspective by using it multiple times across a single wall. This form refuses the coherent single gaze while allowing multiple vistas of ceaseless repetition to extend into the distance. As in Siqueiros and Rivera, rows of workers recede. But here they recede into different distances—women harvest off to the left horizon, men to the right and in the middle in multiple rows. And what repeats most clearly is the production of food: not only workers but fruit, tilled fields, livestock, hay. Rows of orchard trees and sheep repeat endlessly down to the vanishing point at the center of the painting, just as we viewers ourselves might disappear through the door in the wall.

What this mural offers is not the exciting event but the monotony of massive social reproduction, the labor of providing enough food to keep collective life going. Albro's repetitive figures in multiple vanishing-point perspective are thus well suited to conveying both the interminability of the labor of growing food and its reiteration across groups and sectors. Everywhere we look, surrounding us on the walls and receding well beyond the horizon, all we can see is the endless, repetitive work of sustaining life.

FIGURE 4. Diego Rivera, *The Market*. © 2022 Banco de México Diego Rivera Frida Kahlo Museums Trust, Mexico, D.F./Artists Rights Society (ARS), New York.

FIGURE 5. Diego Rivera, *Good Friday on the Santa Anita Canal.*

FIGURE 6. Maxine Albro, *California* (1934). Collection of the City and County of San Francisco; commissioned by the Public Works of Art Project for Coit Tower.

My last example of an artist who visualizes routine, here, is Mierle Laderman Ukeles. In her 1969 "Manifesto for Maintenance Art," Ukeles argues that our obsession with newness and rupture is complicit in current systems of domination and oppression: "make something new, always move forward. Capitalism is like that."[55] The art world, in keeping with these values, prizes "pure individual creation; the new; change; progress; advance; excitement." And yet it is women who do the routine tasks of maintenance that free the heroic (white, male) artist to create art in the first place.[56] Ukeles's early art involved having herself photographed dusting the art and cleaning the floors of the Wadsworth Atheneum, to show that even the most radical and anti-instrumental aesthetic objects cannot survive without the feminized labor of maintaining infrastructure. "MY WORKING WILL BE THE WORK," she wrote.[57]

Ukeles has since created "work ballets," performance art and photography with the New York Sanitation Department, where she has been an unpaid

artist in residence for decades. In "Touch Sanitation," for example, she had herself photographed shaking hands with 8,500 sanitation employees, saying to each one: "Thank you for keeping New York City alive."[58] Here she develops a routinized performance, repeated 8,500 times, to show respect and recognition for the most denigrated daily work routines, which are also, she points out, necessary to the collective continuance of the city. For Ukeles, the regular labor of upkeep is worthy of our appreciation, and it will always have to be done, even in the most radical future. "After the revolution," she asks, "who's going to pick up the garbage on Monday morning?"[59]

Ritual

Rituals, like routines, are repetitive actions performed at prescribed intervals. But while routines are semi-conscious or altogether unthinking, rituals are forms that alert us to the repetitive patterning of collective life. That is, rituals deliberately solicit attention to the routines that sustain us over time, slowing us down to pay attention to their meaning and value. If for Shklovsky art defamiliarizes objects and experiences that have become too routinized, ritual defamiliarizes routine itself.

The study of ritual is a vast and complex field, and I will touch on it only briefly here, focusing particular attention on practices designed to keep groups alert to the importance of repetition to collective continuance. A whole range of communities that have struggled to prevent over-fishing, from Micronesia to Maine, have rituals celebrating timed and organized labor practices to sustain shared resources over time.[60] Indigenous groups who live in the Klamath River Basin in Northern California, for example, have coordinated restrictions on harvesting salmon: no one is allowed to fish until an annual ten-day ceremony is complete. This annual rite, which includes prayers, fasting, and dancing, demonstrates "respect, up and down the river, for that system of management that allows for . . . adequate spawning or escapement . . . meeting the needs of the resource first, prior to thinking about the needs of your own folks."[61] Sustained over time, this practice is also crucially sustaining: it has successfully nourished the human communities who live in the basin; it has supported the fish population; and it has nurtured a worldview that repeatedly solicits an active respect for collective resources and coordinated survival over generations.

To protect a mountain from being turned into a profit-making quarry, to give another example, Indigenous Mi'kmaq people who live in Nova Scotia deliberately combine rituals of science—including the publication of statistics about mining—with the performance of sacred rites, such as drumming and dancing, both of which they understand as ritual practices.[62] Mayan groups in Guatemala have successfully fought off the Monsanto corporation by gathering together around rituals of seed conservation, selection, sowing, and harvesting, all of which support long-term community resilience against neoliberal globalization.[63]

The predictability and repetitiveness of ritual matter to collective continuance in three ways. First, belonging to groups rather than individuals, they survive across long periods precisely by repeating shared knowledge and value over generations. Second, since individuals can be tempted to take too much for themselves and deplete resources for collective life in the future, rituals bring people together at regular intervals to remind them of their enmeshment in ongoing collectives. Third, rituals lend meaningfulness to ordinary practices of maintaining life that might otherwise become rote and unthinking—and so taken for granted.

Some readers might be inclined to dismiss rituals as over-romanticized traditional forms, but they have been part of effective secular political movements for climate justice in recent years. In 2018, Swedish teenager Greta Thunberg launched the "Friday for Futures" movement, inviting students around the world to walk out of school every Friday to protest against government inaction on climate change. Leah Namugerwa, a fourteen-year-old student striker inspired to join Thunberg's movement, carries her placard with a group of fellow nonviolent strikers every Friday in Kampala, Uganda. "Friday used to be ordinary, but now it is the busiest day of the week," she says.[64] This secular environmentalist ritual, like its spiritual counterparts, is repetitive, coordinated, and sustained over time, and like religious rituals, it affords a respectful, alert attention to the project of sustaining collective life.

Pathways: Realist Defamiliarization

Pathway forms, like routines, are prone to fade into the background. One aesthetic option for bringing them to public attention is to make them highly visible—grand and magnificent. Nineteenth-century train stations were designed to feel as glorious as cathedrals—London's Gothic Saint Pancras or the Chhatrapati Shivaji Terminus in Mumbai—not only hubs for departures and arrivals but resplendent destinations in their own right. They invite a visual attention to infrastructure as a triumph of modern civilization.

But that might not be such a ready solution for all infrastructural pathways, including waste removal, which is probably best left out of sight. And I want to suggest that even when we build a splendid railway terminus or water tower, we are not attending to the most important work that the pathways do, which is to enable *flow*. When we encounter the Chicago Water Tower, we are stuck admiring the end rather than the middle. A beautiful railway terminus can easily hide deteriorating tracks. And so, the decision to build spectacular infrastructural displays also allows us to overlook the great bulk of the labor involved in keeping infrastructures going, which is operation and maintenance.[65] The steady, reliable passage and distribution of bodies, fluids, and energy might never be awe-inspiringly and visually arresting because its crucial affordance is an ongoing capillary movement across sites.

This section will make the case that realism, with its long tradition of valorizing ordinary life, has techniques for drawing attention to pathways that function smoothly and without incident. Science fiction has often focused on the design of radically new infrastructures, and apocalyptic and dystopian fictions have invited an anxiety and excitement in imagining their destruction, but realism is especially well suited to representing the humdrum middle.

I will focus on a particular strategy that I will call here *realist defamiliarization,* a reworking of Viktor Shklovsky's concept. "The technique of art," Shklovsky writes, "is to make objects 'unfamiliar,' to make forms difficult, to increase the difficulty and length of perception."[66] Critics have often turned to experimental art for their examples of defamiliarization. Rita Felski writes: "Modernism especially, with its roughened verbal textures and often startling juxtapositions, can inject a sense of strangeness and surprise into its portrayal of the most commonplace phenomena."[67] Realist fiction, by contrast, has been taken to task for naturalizing and thereby reaffirming and conserving social structures. Franco Moretti claims that realism tries "to inscribe the present so deeply in the past that alternatives became simply unimaginable."[68] But since realist writers are often interested in describing ordinariness, they also repeatedly struggle to make that ordinariness feel meaningful—*worthy of attention.* Thus one of realism's goals is to interrupt a reader's tendency to be too interested in exciting and exceptional experience. If Shklovsky worries that we have dulled our perceptions in the face of an interesting world, realist writers work to generate an alert, attentive perception to the world's very dullness.[69]

Nineteenth-century realism in particular is explicit about its goal of moving away from a reflexive enthusiasm for exciting events and extraordinary persons and toward the ordinary. Consider, for example, one of the most famous passages in *Middlemarch,* where we find Dorothea surprised to be sobbing on her honeymoon:

> Not that this inward amazement of Dorothea's was anything very exceptional: many souls in their young nudity are tumbled out among incongruities and left to "find their feet" among them, while their elders go about their business. Nor can I suppose that when Mrs. Casaubon is discovered in a fit of weeping six weeks after her wedding, the situation will be regarded as tragic. Some discouragement, some faintness of heart at the new real future which replaces the imaginary, is not unusual, and we do not expect people to be deeply moved by what is not unusual. That element of tragedy which lies in the very fact of frequency, has not yet wrought itself into the coarse emotion of mankind; and perhaps our frames could hardly bear much of it. If we had a keen vision and feeling of all ordinary human life, it would be like hearing the grass grow and the squirrel's heart beat, and we should die of that roar which lies on the other side of silence. As it is, the quickest of us walk about well wadded with stupidity.[70]

Dorothea is astonished to find herself miserable, but hers is actually a very routine kind of unhappiness, so frequent that older people, immersed in their own routines, will ignore it and just "go about their business." Meanwhile, we readers too are "well wadded with stupidity." We cannot focus on ordinary unhappiness because it is just too common. Eventually, perhaps, we might develop new habits of perception, as the tragedy of ordinary suffering gets "wrought" into our emotions. In the meanwhile, however, the realist novelist has to develop aesthetic strategies that register the frequency of ordinary experience while also making it interesting, worthy of our notice.

A similar logic drives the famous passage in Charles Dickens's *Bleak House* where Jo the crossing-sweeper is dying from poverty and neglect:

> He is not one of Mrs. Pardiggle's Tockahoopo Indians; he is not one of Mrs. Jellyby's lambs, being wholly unconnected with Borrioboola-Gha; he is not softened by distance and unfamiliarity; he is not a genuine foreign-grown savage; he is the ordinary home-made article. Dirty, ugly, disagreeable to all the senses, in body a common creature of the common streets, only in soul a heathen. Homely filth begrimes him, homely parasites devour him, homely sores are in him, homely rags are on him: native ignorance, the growth of English soil and climate, sinks his immortal nature lower than the beasts that perish. Stand forth, Jo, in uncompromising colours! From the sole of thy foot to the crown of thy head, there is nothing interesting about thee.[71]

Distance and unfamiliarity, according to Dickens, "soften" our image of the remote and exotic person. By contrast, Jo's closeness and familiarity make him both repellent *and* uninteresting. There is a kind of circular logic at work here: first we ignore the poor because they are all around us and so feel too familiar for us to take any interest; then we become so used to ignoring poverty that we fail to notice how shockingly everyday it is. Boys like Jo are "dying thus around us every day."[72] It is the common things we are inclined to ignore, but their commonness is, in fact, precisely what is shocking about them. What Dickens tries to do, then, is to jolt us into a recognition of the familiar as both everyday *and* shocking.

Neither Eliot nor Dickens seeks to naturalize the commonplace; nor do they struggle to reject the everyday in favor of radical newness and unfamiliarity. Rather, both novelists seek to freshen perception of what is precisely not fresh—to jolt us into alertness to the "very fact of frequency," the "nothing interesting" that is human suffering. Since the ordinary is worse and more horrifying than the exceptional, the point is to shock us into recognizing the vast scale of its sheer unremarkableness.

In some ways, this is the opposite of revaluing infrastructure. Eliot and Dickens are trying to draw attention to the horrors, not the benefits, of the humdrum. But as these realist texts defamiliarize the ordinary, they help us to see how realist fictions might bring mundane infrastructural pathways from the background into the spotlight so that we can appreciate the work that they do.

I turn here to two recent examples that take up this challenge: Chimimanda Ngozi Adichie's 2013 novel *Americanah*, about middle-class Nigerian migrants, and the BBC series *Call the Midwife* (2012–present), based on the memoir of Jennifer Worth, a midwife working for the new British National Health Service in the 1950s. Both use techniques of realist defamiliarization to register the smooth functioning of infrastructural pathways.

Whenever characters in *Americanah* find themselves living in comfort, they lose their capacity to perceive the conduits that once drew their notice. After Ifemulu's Aunty Uju becomes the mistress of a powerful and wealthy general, for example, she says: "Do you know I've forgotten what it feels like to be in a bus? It's so easy to get used to all this."[73] Similarly, Ifemulu's friend Ranyinudo grows accustomed to gifts from her wealthy lovers, and starts to live "a life in which she waved a hand and things fell from the sky, things that she quite simply expected should fall from the sky" (481).

As the two protagonists, Ifemulu and Obinze, move across borders and rise and fall in personal wealth, they find themselves shaped by new habits of attention and inattention. And unlike the people around them, both work hard to refuse the habituation of too much comfort. Ifemulu leaves her wealthy boyfriend Curt in part because "the gift of contentment and ease" has dulled her perceptions: "How quickly she had become used to their life" (246).

One of the easy aspects of life in Britain and the United States that both protagonists struggle to keep in mind is the smooth flow of electricity. Ifemulu realizes that she has started to take it for granted only when she is reminded of what it was like not to have it back home: "When her mother said there had been no light for two weeks, it seemed suddenly foreign to her, and home itself a distant place" (196). Later, when Ifemulu first returns to Lagos, she is struck by "the loud, discordant drone of generators, too many generators." Electricity here is impossible to ignore because the absence of a smoothly running public infrastructure literally makes a lot of noise. When Ifemulu visits a wealthy home with a "completely noiseless" generator, Ranyinudo teases her about the fact that she has not noticed it, and this shocks Ifemulu into the uncomfortable recognition that she has become Americanized: "a true Lagosian should have noticed: the generator house, the generator size" (485).

The difference between electricity flow in the two nations—the United States and Nigeria—is not strictly a matter of wealth: rich Nigerians can pay to provide their own electricity. What the noisy Lagosian generators indicate is the absence of public investment in an electricity infrastructure. Or to put this another way: a smoothly working electrical grid leads, perhaps even *necessarily*, to a deadening of perception on the part of those who benefit from it. Habituated to the quiet flow of electricity, well-off Americans can afford to treat it as uninteresting. Thus Adichie's turn to a plot organized around mobility across national borders could well sharpen U.S. readers' attention to their own habits of taking public investment for granted.

For Adichie, the antidote to inattentiveness is the classic realist technique of plain description. From earliest childhood, Ifemulu shocks people who are used to deception and self-deception with her plain speaking. She is frustrated with those adults, like her mother, "who denied that things were as they were" (63). The problem grows only more acute when she moves to the United States, where Ifemulu objects both to misperceptions of racism on the part of white friends and acquaintances and to misleading "mythologies of home" nursed by Nigerian migrants (143–44). Two of the major turning points in the novel are moments when Ifemulu rejects her own facades and concealments: first, when she decides not to fake an American accent any longer; and second, when she chooses to let her hair grow naturally, without relaxers or weaves. Obinze, meanwhile, is fascinated and troubled by the lies told by Nigerians in Britain, like his old friend Emenike, who has married a white British woman and "completely absorbed his own disguise" (333), hiding his rage to keep his white friends comfortable and adapting the very tone of his voice to please them.

Ifemulu eventually becomes a blogger whose goal is simply to observe ordinary patterns of race and racism in the United States and Nigeria. Her American blog posts in the novel appear in a sans serif font—plainer than the rest of the text. When the protagonist starts a second blog in Nigeria, she explicitly opts for "a stark, readable font" (514).

But why is aesthetic plainness so important? Adichie suggests at one point that too much nuance and complexity prevent us from grasping patterns and arrangements—*forms*. When Shan, a young Black writer, tries to describe a racist encounter in a memoir, her editor objects that it is not subtle enough. "He thinks we should complicate it, so it's not race alone. And I say, but it *was* race":

> "Nuance" means keep people comfortable and everyone is free to think of themselves as *individuals* and everyone got where they are because of their *achievement*. . . . So if you're going to write about race, you have to make sure it's so lyrical and subtle that the reader who doesn't read between the lines won't even know it's about race. You know, a Proustian meditation, all watery and fuzzy, that at the end just leaves you feeling watery and fuzzy. (416–17)

Proustian style here is what conserves structures, and it does so by permitting a misapprehension of race as fluid or indistinct. Far from watery or fuzzy, race in the United States should be understood, Ifemulu explains, as imposing a simple and painful order, "a ladder of racial hierarchy" where "White is always on top . . . and American Black is always on the bottom" (227). If it is a struggle to recognize and reject the falsehoods that come with habituation, then aesthetic indistinctness, complexity, and ambiguity may actually cloud our apprehension, making principles of social organization seem more "watery and fuzzy" than they are. This is a case not only for realism but for realism's affordances for formalist analysis. Adichie suggests that it is not the richness or the complexity of structural racism that should draw our attention but the often straightforward shapes that it takes, which are too readily obscured or dismissed.

Plainness, in this novel, turns out to be both rare and precious. It encounters resistance from Ifemulu's academic lover, Blaine, who looks down his nose at her taste in novels that "don't push the boundaries," feels contempt for her friend "who says ordinary things," and urges her to add details of "government policy and redistricting" to her blog posts about urban Black poverty. Ifemulu remains adamant: "I don't want to explain, I want to observe" (386–87). Similarly, Obinze is the only person he knows to keep a careful distance from his own wealth through an emphatic plainness of style: "all this exaggerated politeness, exaggerated praise, even exaggerated respect that you haven't earned at all, and it's so fake and so garish, it's like a bad overcolored painting" (532).

Aesthetic plainness and an appreciation for infrastructure come together in a moment when Obinze starts to worry that his own riches are corrupting him. He grows nostalgic for a past when he could not take the smooth running of electricity for granted: when the "neighbor downstairs used to shout, 'Praise the Lord!' whenever the light came back and how even for me there was something so beautiful about the light coming back, when it's out of your control because you don't have a generator" (533). Obinze's invocation of beauty here is in keeping with the larger aesthetic aims of this novel, a valuing not of splendor or subtlety but of the most ordinary electric light, which allows one literally to perceive the ordinariness of one's surroundings but which, in becoming too routine, loses its capacity to move us. By recalling a different ordinariness, Obinze distances himself from the one he has. Or to put this another way: there are really two overlapping strategies at work here. Adichie defamiliarizes infrastructure by imagining its absence, and she defamiliarizes *habituation* to infrastructure by pointing to a loss of desire for it when it is working smoothly and well.

Like *Americanah, Call the Midwife* is a realist narrative that strives to defamiliarize smoothly functioning pathways. In this case, the focus is the infrastructure of the British welfare state—no easy task, as Benjamin Kohlmann points out: "It is hard to see . . . how a state that is imagined as an ensemble of administrative functions and redistributive mechanisms can become the object of affective investments."[74] But this is exactly what *Call the Midwife* does well.

I want to point to three particular realist strategies at work in the series. The first is its unusual protagonist, which is the National Health Service itself, founded in 1948, to provide public health care across Britain. When one new mother thanks God for saving her, the doctor corrects her: "credit should go" not to God or to any god-like doctor but "to the National Health—ten years ago we'd have had none of this; no obstetric flying squad, no ambulance—no chance."[75] Although the series focalizes many of its scenes through Jenny Lee, a new midwife, it carefully rejects the idea that any single exceptional character could lead or save a community. What saves lives is a complex form of social organization that includes fleets of ambulances and bicycles, standardized equipment and supplies, teams of trained nurses and physicians, prenatal clinics and emergency services. The midwives themselves are explicitly interchangeable. When they answer the phone, they say, "Midwife speaking," and their patients call them all "Nurse."

In short, the show displaces the problem of heroism from persons to infrastructure. It does so in part by repeatedly drawing our attention to the pathways essential to the National Health Service—the connective work of streets and telephones, for example, which link laboring mothers to state services. Even the title of the show foregrounds the act of networked contact with the state, and its opening credits focus on a nurse riding her bicycle through the streets as she makes her way to the scene of need. If childbirth itself could be said to be a kind of infrastructure—the embodied pathway by which collectives are literally reproduced—in *Call the Midwife* this event takes place within a network of other infrastructural networks, coordinated by a single large safety net of social services.

The second formal technique the show employs is what I call *historical defamiliarization*—the repeated invitation to think back and forth between historical moments. The BBC series is clear about how the welfare state of the 1950s was built on existing networks of charitable health care institutions, and especially the Anglican Sisters of St. John the Divine, who had been offering home visits and emergency care to the poor since the 1860s.[76] As in many other cases, the modern, secular infrastructure of the welfare state was laid along the pathways of older systems. *Call the Midwife* explicitly makes this part of its plots, revealing the many ways that the National Health Service took advantage of the earlier infrastructure—the experienced Anglican midwives themselves, and also their district-level organization, their training, and their distribution of nursing tasks. Repeatedly, we see the new midwives of the welfare state benefiting from the trust already established between the neighborhood and the Anglican sisters.

But the series is also perfectly clear—perhaps too clear for readers who like subtlety and complexity—that the welfare state infrastructure is far better for the well-being of the most vulnerable people than the Victorian workhouse system that preceded it. As one character in *Call the Midwife* says, "It was a roof over people's heads. They didn't starve." But this was a far cry from supporting their well-being. "I imagine none of you girls have ever been inside a workhouse," Sister Evangelina scolds the young nurses. "They were designed to break the spirit, worse than dying."[77]

In one early episode, we hear the story of two orphans, a brother and sister, who have spent their lives trying to repair the damage done to them by the workhouse system. "It got a hold on you. Got inside your head," says Peg, who still finds herself muttering compulsive apologies to the workhouse administrators decades after she is free of them. The most painful aspect of the workhouse for Peg and her brother is that it deliberately separated family members. They are so traumatized by their childhood separation that they refuse to leave each other's sides even in death.[78] By contrast, the new public health infrastructure is organized around home visits, which bring the state to the family. The goal of the midwife in particular is to support the integrity and well-being of life within the home, as the laboring mothers give birth in their own beds, surrounded by friends and relatives, and are encouraged to form loving bonds with their newborns. The crucial difference between the two state infrastructures ends up having everything to do with their capacity to sustain relationships: while the Victorian workhouse enforced separation, the modern welfare state works to support intimate connections.

This social form could certainly be criticized for being too focused on the traditional heterosexual family—with mostly married mothers laboring inside domestic walls. But *Call the Midwife* deliberately offers a more inclusive politics than that. It shows us over and over that it is not only the conventional married couple who are entitled to connectedness. Even after we learn that Peg's relation to her brother is incestuous, for example, we are invited to understand it as a worthy form of love relation, better in many ways than a conventional marriage. And we are asked to sympathize with Mary, a fifteen-year-old Irish sex worker, who is thrown into unbearable misery by her enforced separation from her child by a welfare state that notably fails in this case, refusing to nurture the bond between the unwed adolescent mother and her newborn. The show makes it clear that in this case the state system should have done better.

The third form that nurtures an appreciation for infrastructural pathways in *Call the Midwife* is seriality. As Eliot or Dickens might remind us, critical illness and childbirth are ordinary across a population, but for any given person, these will feel like dramatic events. It is the genius of *Call the Midwife* to combine these. It organizes most of its episodes around one major suspenseful event—like the birth of a child. This plot is then resolved, usually, by the crucial infrastructural forms that stand by, ready for each crisis, including the team of midwives, the sisters who supervise them, and the networks of doctors, ambulances, telephones, and bicycles. The standing infrastructure of a reliable health care system brings characters together, saves lives in danger, and carries maternal and infant bodies successfully through the traumas of childbirth. That is, each episode shows us how important it is, in cases of emergency, to be able to rely on what is continuous across them all: a functioning welfare system humming along in the background. The national health system itself takes two major temporal forms: ongoing care, including vaccinations and check-ups, and bursts of sudden action in situations of crisis. The series thus manages to combine the long temporal span of reliable, continuous infrastructure—going into an eleventh season as I write—with punctual moments of crisis that keep each episode's narrative thrilling and eventful.[79] And in a world of vulnerable bodies, the ongoing provision of care itself is the protagonist of the story.

Like Adichie, the show invites us to appreciate public infrastructures by asking us to keep in mind what it is like not to have them, and implicitly, *Call the Midwife* invites us to contrast the welfare state not only to an earlier time but also to contemporary Britain, where home health visits and public housing have become a distant memory. Like Adichie, then, *Call the Midwife* teaches audiences to feel desire for the ordinary workings of a smoothly functioning public infrastructure. And it reminds us that what we are tempted to understand as the dreary conduits can, if they are well designed, carry not only basic services but also—a little shockingly—love.

Closure and Enclosure

It is one of the "axiomatic assumptions in contemporary left cultural criticism," Susan Fraiman writes, "that the home is invariably a site of indolent consumption, bourgeois individualism, private property, and conservative values."[80] But if shelter is a fundamental social good that is desirable and just, then home might be not only politically distracting or illusory but crucial for the affirmative work of social justice. I am going to make an unfashionable argument, then, for revaluing the happy endings of domestic fiction.

This argument works against more than a century of criticism that has rejected happy endings as naive and dangerously illusory. Any promise of "happily ever after" is said to cover over the ongoing conflict and instability produced by psychic, economic, and political forces. Wrapping up with marriage and financial stability for the individual protagonist, happy endings are also famous for cruelly disposing of other characters along the way—the madwoman in the attic, the queer lover—without proposing structural alternatives to the status quo. Comforting resolutions cloak real social contradictions, critics say, and lull us into accepting the world as it is.[81]

Perhaps it is not surprising, then, that we continue to find celebrations of open-endedness at the heart of the most recent scholarship on narrative. Comics are politically and aesthetically valuable, according to Hillary Chute, because they disrupt linear structures, with frames arranged in such a way that "reading can happen in all directions."[82] Ramzi Fawaz agrees: the fact that the graphic text "is fundamentally nonteleological and opposed to narrative foreclosure, and it requires no relation between unfolding panels," makes comics a "queer medium," a form well suited to deviations from prescribed social and moral codes.[83] Even Tyler Bradway, who critiques the anti-narrative traditions of queer theory, remains critical of teleology.[84] Clare Pettitt and Derrick R. Spires have also recently praised the open-endedness of serialized forms on political grounds. Nineteenth-century British serials invited a whole new class of readers to see themselves as actors in the unfolding arc of history, Pettitt shows us, while African American writers saw serials as forms that marked the unfinished project of democracy, Spires argues, allowing them to look forward to "new installments in an ongoing literary cultural agenda tied directly to imagining a robust and insurgent Black citizenship."[85]

But this celebration of open-endedness has drawn our attention away from the affirmative affordances of happy endings, which are sites where narratives can and often do outline the shape of a sustainable life.[86] D. A. Miller famously defines the "narratable" as dependent on "a logic of disequilibrium, deficiency, and deferral."[87] In order to launch the propulsion forward we call plot, narratives require insufficiency and instability; they revolve around the desire to fill a lack. To put this another way, *the form of the narratable is also the form of precarity*: a deficiency that yearns for a resolution. Plotted forms readily afford the uncertainty of hunger and homelessness, and use these instabilities to propel the plot forward toward a resolution that sketches out the conditions necessary to supporting life into the future.

Domestic fiction, in particular, establishes a longing for two different infrastructural forms that are essential to collective continuance: stable shelter and sustaining routines. Both, like smoothly working electrical grids and clean water pipes, are too readily taken for granted by those who have them. It is easy to crave disruptions of routines when your next meal is not in question, and easy to think shelter is boring when you are not facing the daily struggle to find a safe place to sleep. Plotted narrative is particularly good at registering the distressing insecurity of hunger and homelessness and reminding comfortable readers to value reliable food and shelter. Michael Parrish Lee argues that the most canonical nineteenth-century fictions revolve much more around literal appetite—what he calls "the food plot"—than scholars have recognized. Criticism has too often missed the basic importance of eating in the realist novel.[88]

What inaugurates plotted action in *Oliver Twist*, after all, is ravenous hunger. The boys in the workhouse "suffered the tortures of slow starvation for three months: at last they got so voracious and wild with hunger, that one boy, who was tall for his age, and hadn't been used to that sort of thing (for his father had kept a small cook-shop), hinted darkly to his companions, that unless he had another basin of gruel per diem, he was afraid he might some night happen to eat the boy who slept next him, who happened to be a weakly youth of tender age." The threat of violence here prompts Oliver, "desperate with hunger, and reckless with misery," to make his famous request. "'Please, sir, I want some more.'"[89] This is not a demand for radical change but for repetition—more of the same. And yet, the shock of even such a minimal request gets the plotted adventure going in earnest. After being imprisoned, Oliver escapes into the streets and is forced into exploitative and criminal labor in order to survive, eventually to be saved by the beneficent Mr. Brownlow who, by adopting him, guarantees him shelter and food. Drawing public attention to the cruelty of the Poor Laws and the workhouse system, Dickens uses Oliver's story to make poverty appear both innocent—the angelic Oliver is certainly not at fault for his hunger—and intolerable: a boy so hungry that he threatens to eat another instigates a whole novel's worth of excitement. And it will only come to an end once Oliver is settled into a stable home and the promise of ongoing plenty.

The term "closure" suggests that plotted narrative endings bring all action to a close. But that is not, in fact, accurate. Coming to an end often means precisely showing us stable routines that extend predictably forward. The conclusion to *Oliver Twist* brings our previously precarious protagonist to a stable home in the serenity of a small country village, where he can settle into a life of safety, comfort, peace, learning, and music, all of it organized around a stable set of routines:

> The days were peaceful and serene; the nights brought with them neither fear nor care; no languishing in a wretched prison, or associating with wretched men; nothing but pleasant and happy thoughts. Every morning he went to a white-headed old gentleman, who lived near the little church: who taught him to read better, and to write: and who spoke so kindly, and took such pains, that Oliver could never try enough to please him. . . . Then, he had his own lesson for the next day to prepare; and at this, he would work hard, in a little room which looked into the garden, till evening came slowly on.[90]

George Moore's 1894 novel about an illiterate servant, *Esther Waters*, provides a more critical example. For most of the novel, we follow this economically precarious character through numerous dramatic crises, including a pregnancy out of wedlock, an abusive stepfather, a spell in the workhouse, starvation wages, gambling wins and losses, and trouble with the police. The novel ends, however, with a widowed Esther falling into a life of regularity with her employer. "In the evening they sat in the library sewing, or Mrs. Barfield read aloud, or they talked of their sons. On Sundays they had their meetings." In this smooth final stage of the novel, Esther's employer asks her if she would like to marry, and she responds: "Marry and begin life over again! All the worry and bother over again! Why should I marry?"[91] In place of the "worry and bother" of the marriage plot, the two women agree to "Work on, work on to the end," the exact duplication of the phrase conveying the sameness of the sequence to follow.[92] This is not the stuff of narratable adventure, but it is for Esther the first genuine prospect of a sustainable life—reliable food and the regular rituals of labor and religious observance. It is hard-won relief from the trials of poverty, the pleasurable prospect of predictable work rather than plotted worry. And Moore's ending explicitly refuses the illusion that women will find stability in marriage, drawing attention instead to the material routines that actually sustain bodies and communities.

Of course, the traditional realist novel, organized around plots and protagonists, struggles to convey large-scale collectives. Many happy endings, including those of *Oliver Twist* and *Esther Waters,* bring comforts only to the "deserving" protagonist, leaving in place the economic structures that keep masses of others precarious. Oliver's own situation is resolved by a series of unlikely coincidences, Mr. Brownlow's personal kindness, and his own angelic goodness. At one intriguing moment, Dickens does go out of his way to point out that his own ending is insufficient, taking care of only one child while leaving equally deserving others to a sadder fate. Oliver tries to save Dick, a childhood friend from the workhouse, but Oliver arrives too late, and Dick cannot be saved. Doing his best in the novel form to gesture to the fact of other children living with hunger and homelessness who are not as lucky in their endings as our hero, Dickens gives us Dick as a kind of a shadow Oliver, an ungraspable echo of the child we have come to know well, reproducing needs and conditions just beyond our perceptual frame.

Since the traditional ending to the domestic novel usually falls short when it comes to offering structural solutions to hunger and homelessness, my final example in this section offers a twist on domestic fiction. It is a particularly inventive nonfiction narrative that incorporates many strategies drawn from realist fiction, including domestic endings, but also moves beyond these to sketch out collective solutions. Matthew Desmond's Pulitzer Prize–winning *Evicted: Poverty and Profit in the American City* is a 2016 ethnography of rental housing in poor areas of Milwaukee. Critics have repeatedly called the work "novelistic," and Desmond puts several characteristically novelistic forms—protagonists, free indirect speech, focalization, a villain, and especially the quest for a happy domestic ending—to compelling political use. Thus *Evicted* not only helps me to make my case for narratives that teach us to appreciate the security of safe and reliable shelter but also allows me to foreground the value of a transdisciplinary formalist analysis, which tracks particular forms and their affordances as they move across domains of knowledge and experience.

Desmond's *Evicted* tracks eight struggling renters, some Black and some white, most in rundown city neighborhoods and a few in a trailer park on the outskirts. Specific episodes reveal the painful hurdles that they face in their quest for a sustainable life. Arleen, a single mother of two boys, is evicted because a stranger has broken down her front door, and the landlord holds her responsible for the damage. As she struggles to keep her children under a stable roof, she will have to choose first between rent and food, then between rent and her sister's funeral costs, and later between rent and school clothes for the kids. Vanetta, also threatened with eviction, worries that her three children will be taken away from her if she loses her home, and so participates in a robbery to cover her rent. She is arrested, fired from her job, and evicted. She loses her children. Scott, a nurse who has become addicted to drugs, decides to get clean, only to discover that too many people are ahead of him on line at the rehab clinic to bother trying to secure a place.

In all of these examples, Desmond moves between scenes where his protagonists trudge through long, wearisome days spent looking for jobs or apartments and intense, devastating moments of drama. After being sentenced to fifteen months in jail, for example, Vanetta turns, "tears streaming down her cheeks," to look at her oldest child. "Kendal stared back stone-faced, strong, just like his momma had taught him."[93] Here, the quintessentially novelistic technique of free indirect speech translates Kendal's expressionless face for us: this is a boy who might look as if he has been hardened against his mother, but in fact he has internalized her voice only too well, a voice that has taught him, in response to unspeakable pain, to hold himself together. In another haunting scene we see a young renter named Kamala who has lost her infant in a deadly fire. She is described as "writhing on the floor, screaming, '*My baby! My baby!*' Her hair had burnt off on one side. She arched her back and pressed her face into the ground. An older woman nobody recognized tried to hold her. 'Whoa!' she would say as Kamala lurched. 'Whoa.' When the old woman grew tired, she let go, and Kamala collapsed on the floor, wailing" (201). Starting out as an ethnographer's description, this passage switches to focalize the experience of Kamala's anguish through the eyes of a sympathetic stranger whose desire to soothe is exhausted by the inflexible power of the mother's overwhelming grief.

These novelistic passages focus our attention on the emotions of specific people desperate to solve problems in painful conditions, inviting us to understand what it feels like to experience impossible choices and the suffering that follows. That is, they offer not only a heart-rending account of distress but also the kind of *knowledge* we need to unsettle a certain moralizing middle-class complacency: against the common assumption that the poor are responsible for their own suffering, we see hardworking, well-meaning Arleen trudging through the streets looking for housing, and a sober, self-disciplined Scott working for years to regain his nursing license. Quantitative researchers argue that we need large data sets because it is always risky to generalize from a single case—each might be an anomaly. But even one instance of a struggling, suffering, irreproachable figure who faces no alternatives disproves the argument that the poor are *always and necessarily* answerable for their own poverty. This is a kind of knowledge that narrative protagonists readily afford. And cannily, Desmond gives us eight protagonists rather than one. This formal decision allows him to counter a skepticism about the single case while keeping our attention trained on the painful texture of poverty as it is experienced by sympathetic people forced into tight corners by conditions beyond their control.

Perhaps surprisingly for a social scientist, Desmond gives us not only a set of sympathetic victims but also a villain. One of *Evicted*'s most compelling characters is the landlord Sherrena, who is determined to make as much money as possible off the poorest neighborhoods in Milwaukee. She evicts anyone who reports her for failures to keep up the property, including broken plumbing. After the fire that kills Kamala's baby in one of her rental units, she celebrates the fact that she is not liable for any damages and decides to refuse to return rent money to the tenants made homeless by the fire. "The only positive thing I can say is happening out of all of this is that I may get a huge chunk of money," she says, only moments after we have seen Kamala writhing in uncontrollable misery (203). Sherrena understands herself as a smart entrepreneur, always looking for opportunities to make money from the poor. Occasionally she has moral qualms, but she quickly quells them with self-serving justifications.

Sherrena is a truly repellent character. And yet, Desmond makes it clear that her greed and selfishness are not in fact the primary cause of her tenants' woes. He shows how legal and economic conditions are what allow landlords like Sherrena to profit from the poor. Organizing forms—from segregated housing laws to police violence in Black neighborhoods, from housing vouchers to Supplemental Social Security Income, from fair market rents to the collapse of the industrial sector—constrain the lives of both victims and villains. For example, landlords are allowed to reject potential tenants who have been evicted before, which means that a population desperate for housing will have to pay high rates for poor conditions because they have no alternatives. Arleen, who is in no way responsible for her eviction, is later rejected eighty-nine times in her search for an apartment she can afford. We learn, too, that after the 2008 foreclosure crisis, when properties were going cheap, landlords like Sherrena could buy rundown properties in the poorest neighborhoods for cash and then take advantage of an endless supply of tenants, like Arleen, desperate for a place to live. Landlords are not the only ones to discover that eviction is profitable, either: companies that manage foreclosures, store household goods for evicted tenants, and help voucher recipients find housing readily take advantage of a deep pool of people living always on the brink of homelessness.

What most clearly differentiates *Evicted* from *Oliver Twist*, then, is that Desmond shows in detail how government programs, laws, and economic patterns together afford the shape of the lives of both the mean-spirited rich and the deserving poor. *Evicted*'s combination of novelistic forms—like scenes of wrenching disappointment for Scott or Arleen—and descriptions of social forms—like eviction laws and kin support systems—offers a powerful analysis of the relations between feelings like grief and desperation and social forms like housing vouchers and trailer parks.

We might seem to have wandered far from the question of narrative closure, but Desmond's ethnography matters particularly to this chapter because its narratives are organized around the same lack and longing that structure so many realist novels—the desire for a stable home. It is not surprising that sociologists and realist novelists should find common formal ground here. On one hand, both are both interested in grasping some of the same *social forms*, like class hierarchy and the racializing of public spaces, and on the other hand, they present that knowledge in some of the same *discursive forms*, including narrative and thick description.

It makes formal sense, then, that Desmond turns to the instabilities of plotted narrative to convey precarity. When Arleen falls behind on rent, we wait in suspense as Sherrena prepares to evict her. But then chance intervenes. Sherrena shows the apartment to a young woman named Crystal, who says she will take it but agrees to allow Arleen to stay there with her. And so begins the complicated story of Arleen and Crystal, which ends in physical violence and another eviction. Along the way, Arleen loses everything she has ever owned because she cannot afford to store her things between evictions, and one of her rental apartments is robbed. Rents rise; her children move in with relatives, and she borrows money to bring them back to her.

In the final pages of the narrative, as the family settles into a new apartment without a stove or refrigerator, Arleen's son fantasizes about becoming a carpenter so that he can build her a home, and Arleen herself closes the chapter this way:

> I wish that when I be an old lady, I can sit back and look at my kids. And they be grown. And they, you know, become something. Something more than me. And we'll all be together, and be laughing. We be remembering stuff like this and laughing at it. (292)

Desmond here gives us the shape of the happy ending without its actual fulfillment. That is, Arleen imagines what it might be like to conclude her own story happily—laughing together at former troubles in a house built by her sons—while in fact she ends almost exactly where she began, in uncertain shelter with inadequate food. Desmond uses insufficiency and instability to structure the story around the *desire* for security, but as Arleen's endlessly precarious story makes clear, that desire cannot be properly satisfied. An ironic shadow of a happy ending, a fantasy, is all we will get for Arleen.

And yet, this is not quite the end of the story. Desmond's epilogue offers a second ending, which pulls together all of what we have learned about the consequences of the social forms we have encountered and proposes a single new social form, a well-designed universal housing voucher program, to change the shape of all of the lives we have followed here. The narrative arcs of the book, with their multiple quests for stable shelter, therefore set us up for a structural solution. Or to put this another way, Desmond borrows narratable insufficiency and desire from plotted narrative, and then gives us two versions of the ending: in the first, he shows that the conventional novelistic ending cannot be more than a fantasy under current conditions—the family at home, rewarded for the mother's sincere hard work and love, is well deserved, but tragically, cannot be realized; in the second ending, Desmond shows how the happy ending could in fact be fulfilled through large-scale social reform.

The plotted forms of popular fiction do not merely make *Evicted* entertaining for a broad audience. Desmond structures the propulsive movement of his text around precarious protagonists on a desperate quest to find a stable home. And in order to convince us that home should be a universal condition—a human right—Desmond teases us with the desire for a conventional family ending only to switch it for a large-scale political goal: stable shelter for all. Brilliantly, he has it both ways: he trains us to desire the security of regular food and protective shelter by showing us how much insecurity hurts without encouraging us to double down on the separation of some lives at the expense of others. He proposes housing security as a collective happy ending.

Modeling Systems

In this chapter so far, I have argued that certain aesthetic forms could help us to recognize and value infrastructure for collective continuance. Works of art can remind us of existing infrastructures that are essential to sustainable communities—such as routines of reliable work and food, smooth pathways, and stable shelter—and can show how these are too readily overlooked or unjustly distributed.

As we have seen throughout this book, this kind of reliability is not the usual focus of the aesthetic humanities, and the classroom is one institutional site that actively cultivates aesthetic values. In courses on art and literature, humanists often train students to pay their most alert attention to exciting and exceptional experiences: the introduction of a new technique, the sudden swerve away from an established pattern, or the subversion of generic expectations.[94] Standard survey courses are typically structured as stories of breaks and innovations. Students of American poetry, for example, are more likely to encounter Emily Dickinson and Walt Whitman on a syllabus than William Cullen Bryant and Henry Wadsworth Longfellow because their work is more innovative, less conventional. Most teachers would say simply: they are better poets. But my point here is that the valuing of rupture over stability is built into the selection of art objects usually understood to be worthy of study. This has had troubling consequences for artists from marginalized groups that do not fit the dominant story of progress. For example, when Simon J. Ortiz developed new courses on Native American literature in the 1970s, he wanted to combat two widespread assumptions: first, that Indigenous oral expression was "belated," belonging to a distant time before writing; and second, that contemporary Indigenous writing was "inauthentic," incorporating too much from the cultures of the colonizer. Being out of sync with the temporal patterns of the dominant national literature entailed invisibility. Ortiz opted to put continuity and rupture together in an unfamiliar way in his own survey course, presenting "an Indigenous oral literature as a form of cultural continuance, an incremental and still ongoing tradition that connected very different cultures and times," while also showcasing the "creative development" of Native writers, who have taken aspects of colonizing cultures and made these "meaningful in their own terms."[95]

Ortiz does not dispense with continuities or breaks; he rearranges them into an unfamiliar narrative arc. And it may be that both are necessary. After all, a focus on surprises can only emerge against its repetitive patterns. We must identify conventions—whether those are metrical regularity, generic expectations, or race and gender norms—in order to recognize exciting breaks from them, which means that the aesthetic humanities have always been covertly dependent on the conventions we condemn. We learn to read for routine in order to admire the rupture of routine. So: to turn our attention to the repetitive patterns that organize literary texts does not entail a huge break in method. But it could generate a very different set of values. If repetition became the interesting, meaningful foreground rather than the wearisome, constraining backdrop, would the aesthetic humanities value different works, different moments in those works, and different histories of aesthetic unfolding? I believe the answer is yes.

But revaluing continuity is only one contribution the arts can make. Aesthetic objects can also sketch out portable models to redesign social worlds—what Kenneth Burke called "equipment for living."[96] Julia Reinhard Lupton has made the argument that Shakespeare's dwellings—including material spaces, practices, and objects—are "designs for the theater of life."[97] For Mike Goode, similarly, Austen's households are "design experiments" that allow us to think about how specific organizations of land and property enable a range of actions and characters.[98] Digital games can model ecological worlds that require active participation and a recognition of the effects of our actions on others.[99] Virginia Woolf proposes a clear redesign of the social world in *A Room of One's Own*, where she argues that women have not been able to participate in the exciting work of making art because they have been financially dependent on men and subject to constant interruptions by others. Woolf recommends two specific forms: an enclosed space (a room of one's own) and a reliable routine of resources (£500 a year). One form affords solitude and shelter, the other autonomy and freedom from other work. And put together, these forms afford the entrance of women into the work of creativity.

I have argued elsewhere that most politically minded criticism implicitly relies on formal models like these.[100] Critics spin out generalizable conditions from specific textual instances. *Oliver Twist*, for example, ends with a moralizing individualism rather than a structural transformation, and so we call it conservative. From this perspective, blueprints for social life are everywhere: in the middle of a Rossetti poem, on the wall of the post office, in Austen fanfiction.

But as I argued in *Forms*, artworks do not only represent the social world; they also interact and intersect with all kinds of other forms, sometimes sustaining and sometimes rerouting social forms. This chapter ends, then, with two specific examples where aesthetic forms work together with infrastructural forms to produce sustainable models of collective life.

Plotted Transportation

In the 1970s and 1980s, short installments of Armistead Maupin's *Tales of the City* appeared five days a week in the *San Francisco Chronicle*. Featuring for the first time a range of gay and straight characters going about their daily lives, the series made a range of sexualities feel familiar and intimate. Maupin was one of the first writers to introduce a trans character into mainstream fiction and one of the first to represent the AIDS epidemic. The open-ended form of the serial narrative allowed Maupin to unfold unconventional household arrangements rather than driving toward traditional marriage like much domestic fiction.[101] Many of the columns ended with suspenseful cliffhangers that kept readers eager for the next installment. The daily rhythm of publication also meant that San Franciscans always had new material to discuss over the water cooler and at dinner parties. "Everybody who lived in San Francisco and its environs seemed to follow it avidly and talked as if its characters were their intimate friends," writes Laura Miller.[102] And then, Maupin's loving attention to the pathways and sites of San Francisco life—its streets, buses, supermarkets, neighborhoods, social circles, and queer and straight gathering places—brought a shared sense of the city to audiences who might otherwise have been unaware of the ways that their lives crisscrossed common spaces.

Perhaps most importantly, episodes of eight hundred words appeared each weekday in what for many readers became a "morning ritual." And this ritual, for lots of San Franciscans, took shape on their morning commute. Newspaper publication had long depended on multiple communication and transportation infrastructures, including telegraphs and railways. But the routine of daily news also fed into the experience of public transportation infrastructure, with commuters reading the paper on buses and trains to and from work.[103]

The introduction of the daily commute is usually told as a story of alienation, as industrial capitalism atomizes workers, standardizes time, and fosters suburban sprawl, which in turn reinforces patterns of social isolation, private property, and a diminished attention to public spaces and common goods.[104]

The classic commuter is the man in the gray flannel suit of the 1950s, living in the suburbs, alienated from his meaningless job, carrying his briefcase and waiting on the platform for the train to arrive. But *Tales of the City* suggests a more appealing set of affordances: the daily newspaper, the serialized novel, and the morning commute came together to shape and sustain San Francisco's identity as a queer public space. Thus the many readers who devoured installments in the *San Francisco Chronicle* on the bus in the morning joined routines and transportation and communications infrastructures in ways that reinforced an inclusive vision of collective life.

This model seems worth exploring at a moment when public transportation infrastructure is looking more and more essential to the stabilizing of our planetary temperatures. If commuters traveled to work by train instead of private car, they could cut a city's carbon emissions from transportation by more than half.[105] Since transportation accounts for a quarter of global carbon emissions, an embrace of public transportation infrastructure could clearly play a major role in reducing fossil fuel emissions worldwide. Nowadays, print newspapers have largely given way to electronic forms on mobile phones, and commuters are likely to be browsing social media, listening to podcasts and audiobooks, and playing video games. But could serialized narrative still play a role in sustaining public transportation routines?

In the 1990s, Japanese commuter trains successfully featured daily installments of illustrated stories hung on posters from the ceilings.[106] One might imagine that public transportation could gather new energy if new episodes of popular television serials—like *Game of Thrones*—were released first on subway cars, or suspenseful installments of mystery and adventure fictions appeared serially on bus routes. Plotted narrative has the potential to link shared daily pleasures to the patterns of sustainable public transportation.

Social Sculpture

My second example models an even more complex system of interacting social and aesthetic forms. In the early 1990s, a high school student from the historically Black Third Ward of Houston, Texas, asked visual artist Rick Lowe why he was making pictures of the neighborhood's problems instead of designing solutions. Lowe decided to change course.[107] He and six other African American artists raised money to buy a row of twenty-two shotgun houses in the Third Ward. These small narrow houses have often been slated for demolition, but the artists—inspired in part by the painter John Biggers, whose major

FIGURE 7. John Thomas Biggers, *Shotguns* (1983–1986). Photograph © 2023 Museum of Fine Arts, Boston.

works included images of shotgun houses in the Third Ward—saw them as worthy of preservation on both architectural and historical grounds.

They imagined them, too, as places to exhibit contemporary art and draw people to the neighborhood. Lowe says that he had worried about brain drain from Black communities: young people would leave, and they would not come back. He had done so himself.[108] But arts hubs in economically depressed neighborhoods can also end up hurting long-term residents. Prompting economic revitalization, a hip arts scene can spark racist processes of gentrification, forcing up property values and rents and so driving existing tenants away. Some commentators call this "artwashing."

Project Row Houses has set itself the project of revitalization without displacement.[109] They have focused on building, preserving, and sustaining affordable housing for people living in the Third Ward while also using row houses as exhibition spaces. They have raised money to buy properties around the original row—they now own over forty buildings—to prevent big developers from swooping in. And they have formed partnerships with existing institutions, including churches, museums, federal funding sources, and universities, to help them realize their vision. In one case, teams from Rice University's architecture school designed and built small, safe, attractive units using the existing row house structures, including a solar-powered home for visiting artists that has become a model for eco-friendly affordable housing elsewhere.[110] In 1996, Deborah Grotfeldt and Nelda Lewis started the Young Mothers Residential program, which provides housing to single women with children who are enrolled in education. It offers routines of regular childcare, counseling, tutoring, workshops on parenting, and employment training.

The artists-in-residence whose work is exhibited in Project Row Houses have developed creative ways to bring attention to the social and material infrastructure of the place and the people who have lived there for generations. Installation artist Autumn Knight, for example, responded to an article in the *Huffington Post* that called a street corner in the Third Ward "one of the worst in America" by hosting a Sunday social there, drawing on "rural/Southern/African American traditional picnics, socials, and jubilees that include dancing, live music, food, and socializing."[111] This work revalues the street corner as a pathway form that affords long-standing practices of creative interchange and social gathering.

At the same time, Project Row Houses does not limit its idea of art to the professional artists who visit and display their work. Rick Lowe embraces an expansive definition of art, one that builds on Joseph Beuys's notion of "social sculpture," which understands everyone as an artist and "the social organism as a work of art."[112] From this perspective, all residents of the Third Ward can shape and reshape the environment and the practices of collective life. Everyday activity, including cooking and caretaking, can count as art. A laundromat, Cookie Love's Wash N Fold, shares a building with artists' studios, and the Third Ward Bike Shop not only fixes old bicycles but teaches you how to repair your bike yourself. Even organizations like the Emancipation Economic Development Council, which joins together churches, local business owners, artists, nonprofit groups, and Third Ward residents to fight the gentrification of the community, can be considered an art group, committed to organizing, building, and preserving just and vibrant forms to keep this historic neighborhood going.

Dissolving the usual dividing lines between aesthetics and activism, Project Row Houses redefines collective life as a material and participatory art project that needs to be carefully designed, reshaped in response to changing needs and conditions, and, most importantly of all, sustained over time, with ongoing imagination, love, and labor.

5

Political Forms That Work

GOAL, TURNING POINT, HINGE

SCHOLARS ACROSS THE AESTHETIC HUMANITIES have often focused attention on exploitation and violence. This has been immensely important work. It is right to recognize, expose, and rage against injustice. It is right to refuse complacent stories of progress told by those who have profited off the suffering of others. It is right to resist the ongoing consequences of slavery, settler colonialism, and heteropatriarchy. It is right to refuse to turn away. Over the past decades, our fields have become highly skilled at exposing regimes of domination, revealing their impacts everywhere, including their disturbing effects within movements for social justice.

But understanding history as one long record of ruin presents its own kind of blockage. After all, if the forces of injustice always prevail, and if all wins are immediately co-opted, then why bother with political action at all? Bruce Robbins points out that Walter Benjamin's angel of history has appeared in criticism increasingly often since 1980, entrenching an understanding of the past as "unmitigated catastrophe."[1] And if we insist on a Benjaminian story "so grotesquely awful that we can only be redeemed from it by the coming of a messiah," the result, Robbins argues, "is not merely the dismissal of progress as a self-satisfied triumphalist meta-narrative, but hostility or indifference toward any putative achievement, however minor, that someone has had the temerity to claim as a step forward."[2] If there can be no successes, no victories, then political struggle is always and only howling into the wind.

A number of scholars in the aesthetic humanities have in fact explicitly warned us away from hopeful stories. Optimistic narratives can engender their own versions of distress, as Lauren Berlant makes clear.[3] For Roderick Ferguson, small institutional victories bewitch us with false solace, lulling us into passivity in the face of ongoing injustice and hidden violence.[4] And Lee Edelman contends, famously, that criticism should not rest on "the hope of forging a more perfect social order—such a hope, after all, would only reproduce the constraining mandate of futurism." The imperative, instead, is to "refuse the insistence of hope itself as affirmation."[5]

But what if the historical record is not all bleakness? What if there are victories to celebrate, at least here and there? Would those point us to an exciting, energizing relation to political struggle? And would it then make sense to figure out what has worked, and how—to take lessons from these examples to help us try to reduce the overwhelming suffering that has come and is still to come from climate change?

Those questions have guided this book. So far, I have been drawing attention to a range of examples where collectives have successfully built forms for sustainable justice. They prove that even in terrifying times, and even under regimes that are exploitative and cruel, history does not only offer up catastrophe. But now it is time to focus on what allowed those examples to be built in the first place. What values, what participants, what targets, what actions went into these struggles? What political methods have worked in the past, and why?

This chapter will argue for the value of formalist analysis in answering this question. Political movements rely on many different forms of organization—elections, committees, unions, marches, boycotts, occupations, petitions, speeches, debates, blockades, mutual aid infrastructure, alliances, coalitions, hierarchies, compromise, consensus, civil disobedience, armed struggle, media campaigns, and social networks, among others. For Roger Hallam, it is urgent to engage in mass, nonviolent civil disobedience, while for Andreas Malm, our only effective option is to start blowing up pipelines.[6] This chapter will argue that no single form will work for all political projects, but because each form has a limited range of affordances, some forms will be more effective than others in addressing the specific global challenges of climate justice.

Most importantly, current conditions point to the problem of political action at the largest scales. A campaign to address a shortage of sustainable shelter in one city could provide a model for other cities, for example, but it would not automatically spark systemic change. So: what forms afford large-scale social transformation? It is my argument here that we not only need to design and demand organizing forms that will sustain collective life; we also need to be smart about organizing *ourselves* on global scales for the sake of achieving meaningful global political change. This chapter will make a case for a particular constellation of organizing forms for mass collective action, including the shared goal, the turning point, and the hinge between networks. It will end with a look at a popular narrative form, which I call "the narrative of the struggling team," that showcases the forms necessary to successful political organizing and suggests that these are already appealing to publics on a vast scale.

The Myth of Spontaneity and the Form of the Goal

Haunted by the traumas of over-centralized and totalitarian models of left politics in the twentieth century, theorists and activists in our own time have moved to the opposite extreme: a celebration of spontaneity, leaderlessness, and the refusal of all hierarchy and teleology. Influential thinkers in the aesthetic humanities warn us of the dangers of organization and administration—what Jacques Rancière calls "the police" and Alain Badiou "the state." From this perspective, the only proper political strategy is a deliberate horizontalism, the spontaneous development of "small, multiple, and diffuse" local movements.[7]

I will turn to political theorist Rodrigo Nunes in this chapter to make the case that the anti-teleological impulse has in fact been an obstacle to success in political struggle. In the years after the financial crisis of 2008, a wave of deliberately horizontal political movements—Tahrir Square, the 15-M movement in Spain, Occupy Wall Street, Syriza in Greece, UK Uncut, student protests in Chile—promised an exciting new energy on the left. But as they unfolded, they also suffered from "fitfulness" and "an incapacity to sustain themselves over time," an "inability to scale up in a viable way, and a tendency to fall apart when they tried to do so," and a "propensity to demand large investments of time and energy from participants in return for little by way of clear strategy and decision-making."[8] Jodi Dean, like Nunes, argues for the importance of moving from "crowds"—"temporary collective beings" with affective intensities that transcend any individual feeling or experience—to more lasting and effective organizational forms. Her preferred form is the party, which "fits issues into a platform such that they are not so many contradictory and individual preferences but instead a broader vision for which it will fight."[9] The party is precisely not a spontaneous coming together but an institution that provides knowledge apart from what any single person can know and provides a lasting infrastructure for action. "Crowds amass," Dean argues, "but they do not endure."[10]

Spontaneity is itself illusion, according to Nunes: "However improvised and spur-of-the-moment a demonstration or a riot is, it never truly corresponds to the myth of a multitude of unconnected individuals joining together all at once, like a crowd in a musical magically breaking into song."[11] There is always some coordination of collective energies, a call to action, a time and space for gathering, a message passed through formal and informal networks. As with a musical performance, then, effective political change depends on development of skills through practice and coordination behind the scenes.[12]

I will build on Nunes's analogy between protests and musicals to make the case that we aesthetic formalists have the tools to read political forms in some of the same ways we analyze a work of art. For example, the primary form Occupy Wall Street took—the occupation of a bounded public space—was spatial. There was no organizing temporal shape, no narrative arc or rhythm. Enough people must simply continue to occupy the space indefinitely, withstanding forces of deterioration—including activist exhaustion, a lack of sympathy from a broad public, dwindling media interest—with no opportunity to declare or negotiate a victory. The movement could not change location or adopt a different major tactic without losing its identity, becoming something other than Occupy Wall Street.[13] For many, this freedom from linear temporality was the movement's special strength. But its commitment to the proliferation of many equally valid goals meant that there was no shared purpose to keep the movement going.[14] The fact that it did not have "a natural end point" meant that it had little option but to fizzle out without realizing any specific demands.[15]

As we have seen in this book, the aesthetic humanities—and activists and intellectuals of many stripes—have been, like the Occupy protestors, firmly resistant to teleological thinking. Working toward an end seems highly restrictive and normalizing, imposing too coherent an order on the contradictory stuff of reality. On these grounds we have fought for interruption, flux, and open-endedness. And yet, that means we have often missed the promising affordances of the form of the goal for leftist politics. After all, goals are forms that afford endurance, and the sheer length of a protest can contribute to its success.

Short demonstrations rarely work, as climate activist Daniel Hunter explains:

> Imagine you're a politician, and you're the target of a campaign. People are outside your office urging you to do something. You had to sneak in the back door so you wouldn't have to face them. You are feeling the pressure. But will they be around the next day? Will they keep the pressure on? If you can wait until the pressure is over, then you are unlikely to make the change. Government officials (and most targets) regularly just wait until people do their big action. If the activists are lucky, the official gets some bad press for

a few days. But the pressure does not stay. They wait until the heat blows over. Then they keep doing the bad thing.[16]

Historical examples bear out this hypothesis. Take the famous example of the Montgomery Bus Boycott, a thirteen-month-long nonviolent protest that ended in the desegregation of public buses. The boycott needed to draw large-scale participation and support, but it also needed to last long enough to shift sympathies and wear down the opposition. How best to keep this large group going through a lengthy campaign? "People must have something to look forward to," explained civil rights lawyer Fred D. Gray.[17] The form of the shared goal gave collective meaning and purpose to the arduous daily work of boycotting, inspiring people to persevere whenever they might be tempted to capitulate to the relative convenience of taking the bus. Winning the battle to desegregate the buses was far from a recipe for complacency, either: it helped to energize and empower other protests, marking the beginning of a series of crucial victories against Jim Crow laws across the South.

Another, more recent example comes from the small coastal community of Lamu, Kenya, where residents waged a long campaign of resistance against the building of a $2 billion coal-fired power plant.[18] Coordinating protests in Lamu and Nairobi, letter-writing campaigns, a poetry competition, a lawsuit, and frequent invitations to the media over a span of three years, local groups worked together with national and global environmental and human rights organizations, all in the interests of the same shared goal: to prevent the building of the plant.[19] In June 2019, they won: Kenya's National Environment Tribunal revoked the power company's license to build.[20] In these and many other cases, "sustained disruptions" are more powerful than brief outbursts.[21]

The Montgomery Bus Boycott and the Lamu coal plant protest both seemed hopeless when they began—battles against huge powers by relatively powerless people—and yet, they managed to pull off significant and enduring victories. As the Lamu organizers put it, they "stopped a giant in its tracks."[22] These successes make it clear, then, that goals do not only reinforce the status quo; they afford the realization of aspirations of all kinds.

And yet, one might still object that too much insistence on shared goals will afford rigidity and homogenization and the consolidation of power in the hands of leaders at the expense of the diverse voices and desires of the mass of participants. These are real dangers. But the answer is not less form but more. Nunes maintains that leftist movements have suffered specifically from an absence of *reciprocity* between leaders and participants—as when a powerful few organizers refuse to listen to constituent groups.[23] He argues that leaders are more likely to remain accountable to their base if there are constraints on the exercise of power: "fixed mandates, rotation of functions, permanent recallability, a limit to the amount of times an official might serve."[24] These are the kinds of routines of rotating and sharing decision making that, as we saw in an earlier chapter, have been central to Zapatista governance.

The Lamu coal plant movement developed its own routines to maintain reciprocity between global NGOs and local participants. In a concerted effort to keep the voices of Lamu residents front and center, local leaders held regular public meetings where they shared information and plans, and residents offered what they knew about the ongoing construction and contributed ideas for political tactics. The movement relied on regular routines of feedback.[25]

Many of us might still be drawn to the prospect of more sweeping and comprehensive transformations than a law here or a power plant there—fundamental shifts in living, feeling, and acting—but there is no magic, as far as I can tell, that gets us from here to there. It is a matter of doing the hard work of organizing ourselves for change. For Nunes, magical thinking has too often been a feature of the revolutionary left, the dim faith that at some hazy future moment when conditions are somehow and suddenly right, the people will rise up and change everything.[26] What this means, he argues, is that spontaneity is really just another version of teleology, but one that works mysteriously—by "some magic happening indifferently to our will."[27] This implicit teleology allows us to comfort ourselves with the illusion of a complete break to come, "the faint messianic hope of an event that could one day inaugurate an order that will not be an order, an actuality that will exclude no potential."[28] It also means that we can abdicate any responsibility to try to realize our collective potential now. This covert teleology can be highly seductive: it feels radical and virtuous, while it frees us from the messy practical work of addressing conflicting interests and delivers us from the responsibility to take action in the present.

Expanding Collective Power: Turning Points and Network Hinges

So far I have pointed to a few different temporal forms that have been useful tools for political movements: the first and most important is the clarity and purposiveness of a shared goal, which affords coordinated action over long stretches of time—long enough to put meaningful pressure on powerful groups and institutions. I have also mentioned the rotation of leadership to prevent the consolidation of decision-making power, and the feedback routine, where information and plans are shared between leaders and stakeholders. But none of these help us with the challenge of scaling a movement to sizes large enough to make a global difference.

Numbers do matter to the success of social movements. Size is not the only ingredient for success, to be sure: small groups of armed rebels managed to overthrow Cuban president Fulgencio Batista in 1958, and conversely, millions of Chinese people resisted the Japanese occupation in the 1930s and 1940s to no avail.[29] Still, large movements have structural advantages over small ones. As Erica Chenoweth and Maria J. Stephan argue, the larger and more diverse the campaign in terms of gender, age, religion, class, and ethnicity, the harder it is to isolate and discredit protestors, and the more likely participants are to bring a range of effective strategies and skills to the work.[30] As the crowd of protestors grows, the chance of retribution against them declines and momentum intensifies. When police and security forces are connected to protesters through kinship or social networks, they are less likely to commit violence against them for the sake of the regime. And the more widespread the sympathy and support for the campaign, the more likely those in power are to make concessions or to become divided.[31]

The occupation of a square is a form well suited to exhibiting and expressing mass resistance. It affords a spectacle that can draw media attention and widespread sympathy. Aerial photographs of Tahrir Square, for example, made front-page news around the world, revealing the tens of thousands of nonviolent protestors coming together, willing to risk their lives to rally against an authoritarian regime. This, in turn, brought widespread international interest and support. What square occupations cannot do easily, however, is to scale up even farther, to expand beyond the limits of the occupation itself.

In recent years, online platforms like Twitter and Weibo have allowed movements to reach large numbers of people quickly in ways that older forms could not. They are good at building mass support, sending messages of encouragement to those on the ground and amplifying their voices to the broader world. They have also been useful to offline actions, informing people about the logistics of protests, including meeting times and warnings about the presence of the police. But social media have troubling affordances, too: they can be readily monitored by state powers, who can use the information posted to send armed forces to subdue protestors, to plant provocateurs, and to identify and arrest participants.[32] Anyone may post, too, which means that social media presents low barriers to harassment and misinformation. The

FIGURE 8. Tahrir Square on November 27, 2012 (morning): https://commons.wikimedia.org/wiki/File:Tahrir_Square_on_November_27_2012_(Morning).jpg. Photo by Lilian Wagdy.

tweet as a form is also constrained by its brevity and cannot itself make lengthy, well-researched, and substantive arguments, although it can link to these.

The most troubling affordance of social media forms, perhaps, is what Malcolm Gladwell famously calls "slacktivism"—that is, supporters who make little effort or investment in a movement beyond retweeting or liking others' posts. Gladwell argues that this kind of engagement affords weaker and more fragile ties than offline movements, which build thick and sustainable bonds through shared skill-building, decision making, and routine, even tedious, work.[33] It is not clear that Gladwell is right; social media platforms have successfully boosted offline actions, and few movements operate today without a dedicated social media presence.[34] But what we do know is that quick and easy social media actions like online petitions and retweets do not *necessarily* invite long-term or energetic commitment. Even as they are able to reach large groups, they afford short bursts and easy fizzling.[35]

Since political movements benefit from the sustained commitment of many participants, it makes sense to ask what other forms afford the formation of a large, energetic, and dedicated base. For a long time, scholars assumed that people join social movements because they are motivated by deep values and beliefs, and especially outrage at injustice.[36] But it turns out that anger is not in itself a prompt to action. Nor is being informed. Many people who know a lot about the threat of fossil fuels, for example, are not engaged in environmental activism.[37]

To address the challenge of recruiting and sustaining large numbers of people in the struggle for collective continuance, I will focus on a form that crosses domains of technology, social relations, and the arts. Different fields give different names to it, but here I will refer to it as the *hinge*. Bruno Latour points out that ordinary household hinges solve a very basic problem: "The cleverness of the invention hinges upon the hingepin: instead of driving a hole through walls with a sledgehammer or a pick, you simply gently push the door. . . . furthermore—and here is the real trick—once you have passed through the door, you do not have to find trowel and cement to rebuild the wall you have just destroyed: you simply push the door gently back."[38] The hinge is a double connector: it is the piece that joins the wall to the door, which itself joins inside to outside.

There are many different ways to use this word metaphorically: a text can act as a hinge between periods of literary history; a nation can work as a hinge between geographical regions; and an argument can hinge on a concept. Rather than understanding these usages only as tropes, I want to suggest that these are all ways of referring to a particular form that organizes materials across different disciplines and domains. A hinge is a site that links two distinct things or spaces, each with its own identity.

I draw attention to the hinge here because I want to suggest that it is a crucial form for scaling up political actions to sizes large enough and durations long enough to change dominant structures and systems. When it comes to climate change, for example, no single activist group is likely to make revolutionary change on its own, and even a vast aggregation of specific actions will probably fail to add up to systemic transformation. For many of those watching the climate crisis, this is cause for despair. But separate campaigns and actions can have major structural impacts if they can be linked and coordinated, amplifying and extending each other to shared ends. This work of coordination does not have to be totally streamlined or even fully intentional. As Gilles Deleuze and Felix Guattari argue, the French Revolution was on the one hand the eruption of lots of "molecular" events, small peasant groups resisting in particular places, but on the other hand these would have been frustrated and powerless without an increasingly collective use of "molar" organizations to inscribe these molecular events into new legal and political forms. It is always the combination of "aggregate and collective action" that makes a revolution.[39]

What does this mean in practice? It means neither valorizing the small, local action over the massive revolutionary subject, or vice versa, but rather paying attention to the linkages between groups. It means focusing on the form of the hinge. Political theorists have long argued that social movements are most successful at recruiting new members when they tap into existing networks: families, workplaces, friendships, neighborhoods, unions, churches, schools, and colleges. A person might bring her new neighbor to a meeting, for example, and that neighbor will tell her cousin about it, who in turn gets so excited about the experience that she invites her whole youth group. As the social movement grows, its events and organizations create a vibrant new network of their own, which carries a sense of purpose and belonging that can make it attractive to new members.

The neighbor who invites the newcomer along acts as a hinge that links two small networks—the neighborhood and the activist organization. And that invitation, social scientists have argued, is much more important to political expansion than we might realize. Ziad Munson learned from interviews with pro-life activists in the United States that participants often joined the movement *before* they had developed strong views on abortion.[40] Many had vague or abstract opinions to start with; and some had even been pro-choice. The vast majority of activists who spoke to Munson said they had first attended meetings for social reasons. People then typically stuck with the type of activism they had first encountered and continued to justify it for years afterward. If they had begun by engaging in protests outside of abortion clinics, for example, they explained that these were the most effective tactics, and when they got tired of these, they quit the movement altogether rather than trying a different approach.[41] Meanwhile, those who worked for legislative change explained that screaming at abortion providers would undermine public support and argued that showing up in front of a clinic might save a few lives while leaving the system untouched. Again, they were more likely to leave the movement altogether than to switch tactics.[42] For most of these activists, the first encounter with the movement was more or less haphazard and arbitrary, but a whole belief system followed from it. The initial structure—whether it was taking to the street or registering voters—shaped the impassioned values to come. In this sense, form came first, with ideology, strangely, the afterthought.

Participants in the pro-life movement are of course a historically and culturally specific group, and it would be dangerous to generalize from a single case. But there is some evidence that their forms of expansion work elsewhere too.[43] And the goal of the analysis is not to determine, once and for all, what will work in all instances but to understand how organizing forms operate from past examples and to experiment with their affordances for our own ends.

According to Munson's account, two specific kinds of hinges afford the recruitment of new activists and expand the pool of dedicated activists, and both are useful for the work of social justice. The first hinge is a temporal form. Munson calls it the "turning point." The vast majority of activists who spoke to Munson said they had joined the movement when there was a gap or opening in the ordinary business of life—like going away to college, moving to a new town, or retiring from a job—and so were open to new activities suggested by acquaintances, church groups, roommates, or colleagues. It makes sense that people are most likely to be able to throw time and energy into political action when they are not already enmeshed in ongoing social worlds and work obligations. From this perspective, it is worth focusing recruitment efforts on newcomers to a community. And as people are looking around for new friends and activities, it is smart, too, to keep barriers to entry low. The pro-life movement has been especially good at welcoming everyone, regardless of their beliefs, and this hospitable, inclusive gesture itself has been a powerful engine of expansion. Movements that demand major sacrifices, risks, or litmus tests, by contrast, tend to stay too small to have the powerful effects afforded by widespread participation.[44]

This form, the turning point, has shaped the work of a team of faculty, staff, and students at Cornell who have introduced a course about climate change that is required of all incoming students before they arrive, called "Mission Sustainability."[45] We decided to direct the course at the college population that is moving here for the first time, eager to build new social contacts and not yet overwhelmed with obligations. The course invites these newcomers to browse through the wide range of courses that address sustainability and climate change, encouraging them to see how they can weave climate justice into any major. It also makes a case for the importance of collective action and asks students to look at a list of clubs and societies and to write about one way they might get involved in climate action. It is too soon to know whether this course has increased climate change activism at Cornell, but in 2022, nearly four thousand students took the course, and numerous respondents expressed enthusiasm for joining groups like Climate Justice Cornell, a student-led organization that was crucial to campus divestment, and Agua Clara, an engineering project focusing on sustainable water technologies.

The second kind of hinge is the link between existing networks. A network is a group of interconnected elements, a set of links between separable nodes. The nodes themselves might be anything, from neurons to social organizations.[46] In social networks, ties can be communicative, organizational, affective, or spatial; they can link people who know of each other or report to each other or live next door to each other.[47] A network needs a minimum of two nodes, but after that, at least in principle, it can expand indefinitely. It is possible to add new stops to a subway line, for example, or new members to a social club without disrupting the identity of the network. What network forms afford, that is, is expansion. Hinges between networks then allow these groups to join forces in potentially massive coalitions.

The divestment movement is an example of a strategic use of the hinge between networks. In July 2012, Bill McKibben, founder of the organization 350.org, published an article in *Rolling Stone* magazine called "Global Warming's Terrifying New Math," which explained the grave dangers of a global temperature rise above 2 degrees Celsius and warned that the amount of coal, oil, and gas already held in reserve by fossil fuel companies was five times higher than we could afford to burn to stay within that target.[48] McKibben then went on a lecture tour around the United States, appearing in city convention centers and on college campuses with other speakers, including Naomi Klein, Winona LaDuke, and Archbishop Desmond Tutu, and coordinating with local and national organizations to plan each event.[49] The following year, 350.org convened a weeklong gathering of young climate activists from around the world in Istanbul, offering trainings, support, and opportunities to connect. This event drew from a wide range of existing organizations, from Bolivia's Reacción Climatica to Itü, Turkey's technical university, which provided the infrastructure to connect global participants to each other.

The resulting campaign has not been a single, tightly structured operation, but nor has it been an agglomeration of entirely separate actions. Rather, 350.org acts as a hinge, encouraging, training, and linking local divestment groups as they build their own campaigns and then sharing accumulated lessons and contacts with all new groups that emerge. At the time of this writing, over a thousand institutions—churches, colleges, governments, and pension funds—have pledged to divest nearly $45 trillion from fossil fuels.[50] The movement not only makes an economic impact but sends a clear moral and public message about the companies most responsible for climate destruction, which shapes their social license to operate, and brings other institutions along. The sheer size of the movement is part of what makes both its financial and symbolic impacts significant.

To expand the movement for climate justice by understanding it as a network of networks has two beneficial effects. First, it allows each group its own structure, tactics, and identity, which means that participants may join organizations that are rooted in their own social networks and address local struggles or specific values. One person might join a group that allows them to make new friends at college; another might volunteer for a climate organization that deliberately centers gender justice. If networks like these are loosely coordinated toward shared ends, and at the same time each is able to draw new members by reaching into multiple *other* networks, the movement can be both effective and expansive. Second, in place of a single party or platform so centralized and large that it becomes disconnected from the base, this form encourages multiple centers of energy and leadership, which can shape the movement as a whole for the better—as when feminist and Indigenous groups argue against scientific assumptions about the autonomous human subject, and when public health experts circulate data about the health impacts of climate change.

Successful political struggles of many kinds in the past have depended on networks of networks. The Polish "Solidarity" movement brought together labor unions and the Catholic Church, which did not otherwise share the same ends and values. The union side reluctantly agreed to the Church's desire for a ban on Sunday shopping in return for financial and other support. Sociologist Christian Smith calls preexisting organizations that hinge to new groups *movement midwives*, "in recognition of their deliberate efforts to help in the 'birthing' of movements while retaining identities distinct from those of the resultant organizations."[51]

For a very different example, the movement for "natural childbirth" joined together a motley assortment of constituencies, each with its own organizations and different—even conflicting—values. The Catholic group La Leche League wanted to promote an ideal model of Marian motherhood.[52] Another enthusiastic constituency was made up of hippies, eager to embrace the body in its uncorrupted state. Ina May Gaskin was a leader in this stream, an influential popularizer of home births and midwifery who cofounded a counterculturalist commune in Tennessee.[53] A third network of activists, feminists, criticized the breakup of communities of women by masculinist models of science. In 1969, a feminist collective put together *Our Bodies, Ourselves,* soon to be a bestseller, which provided women-centered accounts and information about childbirth. Developing out of these different organizations were new institutions, including midwifery training, prenatal labor classes, and hospital birthing centers. It would not be long before these forms became mainstream.[54] While there is still a long way to go to ensure that this kind of care is widely affordable and available in the United States, there has been a substantial shift to woman-centered maternity care in many parts of the world.[55]

What these cases make clear is that hinged organizations can succeed, even if they are ideologically composite or even incoherent, because of their massive size. There is no need for purity or consistency. In fact, precisely the reverse may be true: movements grow large and powerful in part by linking groups with views that do not necessarily align perfectly. This conclusion may come as an unwelcome claim to activists on the left, many of whom have warned that we must radically remake our relations to ourselves and the world before we can have any meaningful effect. But how are we to get from here to there? We can start by focusing on forms that can join us together in powerful and meaningful numbers.

Working at large scales is a particular challenge for the aesthetic humanities, as I have suggested, in part because both our objects and our methods have so long valorized the distinctive moment, the exception, the minor gesture. But the hinge might be especially useful to us in this context, since it is a form whereby the small and the singular open into the collective or the general. The aesthetic humanities have in fact already theorized this form at work. It is one of the core assumptions of humanistic pedagogy that reading a passage or an image in the classroom acts as a hinge to an informed and responsible citizenry—that it can spark a set of recognitions about dominant values, collective life, and the operations of power that students will carry with them into lives beyond the literature class. And some aesthetic forms themselves do the work of hinging. Narrative, as Roman Jakobson argued long ago, is particularly well suited to "association by contiguity," the work of linking separate moments, agents, and ideas.[56] Emily Dickinson's dashes have been read as hinges too, alongside her repeated and explicit invocation of the word "hinge" ("Noon—is the Hinge of Day—").[57] For Nathaniel Mackey, the breaks, stutters, and limits in poetic language are hinges to possibility of change outside of language. "Doors are for going through," he writes at the end of his introduction, inviting us into the rest of the volume.[58]

Each aesthetic reading feels small-scale and specific, confined to expert readers and classroom discussions, and for this reason it is tempting to retreat to modesty as the proper scope of our disciplines, but a formalist training in reading works of art can also equip us to understand the importance of connecting forms, hinges between agents and sites that can gather our power on large scales rather than insisting on our continuing isolation and separation. This is a different kind of hinge to citizenship from the one we most often invoke. It is not a spark to consciousness but an invitation to address the practical challenge of organizing ourselves for collective action.

Goal, Hinge, Routine, Infrastructure

This chapter ends with two examples, one historical and the other aesthetic, which weave forms together to offer some working models for social movements. These are not imperatives or directives. They show how forms can intertwine to affirmative effect and so provide some know-how, some templates, some ideas for planning and use that can be revised and transformed.

Let's return, first, to the Montgomery Bus Boycott, which was organized not only around a clear goal, as we saw earlier, but also around a series of hinged pathways, institutions, and routines. Rosa Parks's refusal to give up her seat on the bus in December 1955 was not a spontaneous action. Parks was an experienced activist and a long-time NAACP member who had just attended a workshop on political organizing at the Highlander School in Tennessee, which she found inspiring and transformative. As the workshop ended, the organizers asked her what action she was prepared to take in Montgomery.[59]

The larger movement triggered by Parks's arrest was not spontaneous either. The Southern Christian Leadership Conference, so crucial to the U.S. civil rights movement, was really an organization of organizations, and they had been preparing for citywide action for some time. They had passed up the opportunity to mobilize around Claudette Colvin, a teenager who had been arrested for refusing to give up her seat on the bus back in March, because they worried about the fact that she was unmarried and pregnant, which was likely to draw disparaging attention that would undermine the cause. They were waiting for a better figurehead. Parks seemed like the ideal public face for a major political movement. The image of respectability, she was a regular churchgoer with no history of trouble with the law: quiet, married, and employed. The NAACP and the local Women's Political Council saw the occasion of Parks's arrest as a perfect opportunity to rally Montgomery's African American community.

A communications network got the boycott started. The night of Parks's arrest, the Women's Political Council (WPC) printed thirty-five thousand fliers announcing a citywide bus boycott. They had already mapped the city to find the best places to distribute the fliers. Jo Ann Robinson, leader of the WPC, who taught English at Alabama State College, got access to the college copy room through a business professor friend and with two students mimeographed thousands of pages through the night. In the early morning hours Robinson and the students moved through Montgomery, dropping off stacks of leaflets at beauty parlors, barber shops, bars, stores, and factories, and sending them home with children from schools.[60] One of the activists passed a flier to a white journalist, who ran a story in the daily *Montgomery Advertiser*, which helped to spread the news to the whole city.[61] The last line on the flier was an invitation to meet after the one-day boycott at Holt Baptist Church. That night, so many people tried to cram into the church that crowds spilled out into the streets, where they listened to the meeting through loudspeakers and shouted their enthusiasm for continuing the boycott. Activists formed the Montgomery Improvement Association and elected a young Martin Luther King Jr. its leader.

The text on the leaflets was neither original nor subtle. Brief and informative, offering clear instructions about what to do and when to gather, the message moved through the city's network of streets, pausing at major hubs of African American social life, only then to be dispersed back through those streets into homes around the city. Its reiteration and dissemination to thousands of people afforded the coordination of a massive crowd.

Another crucial form the movement needed was a robust alternative to riding the bus—a transportation infrastructure for the large numbers of people participating in the boycott. One of the greatest threats to mass participation was job insecurity; it was crucial to get workers to their jobs on time every day. Car owners organized carpools that picked up passengers along existing bus routes, coordinating schedules so that together they could transport workers during peak travel times.[62] This alternative pathway infrastructure was therefore built along the tracks of the old—it followed established bus routes and shaped itself to working routines. It was not a radically new organization in this respect. But in building on established routes and timetables, it was brilliantly effective in sustaining opposition to the status quo.

Several other routines kept the boycott going. At weekly mass meetings, King taught principles and practices of nonviolent resistance, including drill sessions where participants practiced techniques for surviving arrest. Protesters were trained to go limp and recite specific Bible verses if they were assaulted by the police. They repeated "dress rehearsals" for attacks often so that

This is for Monday, December 5, 1955

Another Negro woman has been arrested and thrown into jail because she refused to get up out of her seat on the bus for a white person to sit down.

It is the second time since the Claudette Colbert case that a Negro woman has been arrested for the same thing This has to be stopped.

Negroes have rights, too, for if Negroes did not ride the buses, they could not operate. Three-fourths of the riders are Negroes, yet we are arrested, or have to stand over empty seats. If we do not do something to stop these arrests, they will continue. The next time it may be you, or your daughter, or mother.

This woman's case will come up on Monday. We are, therefore, asking every Negro to stay off the buses Monday in protest of the arrest and trial. Don't ride the buses to work, to town, to school, or anywhere on Monday.

You can afford to stay out of school for one day if you have no other way to go except by bus.
You can also afford to stay out of town for one day. If you work, take a cab, or walk. But please, children and grown-ups, don't ride the bus at all on Monday. Please stay off of all buses [illegible]

FIGURE 9. Montgomery Bus Boycott leaflet. Civil Rights Movement Archive (www.crmvet.org/).

nonviolence, rather than anger, would become the instinctive first response.[63] The groups also sang songs to open every meeting, including "Onward Christian Soldiers" at the first meeting at Holt Baptist Church.[64] "We Shall Overcome" and "Lift Every Voice and Sing" encouraged boycotters to continue the protest.[65] Later civil rights activist Bruce Hartford explained: "The songs elevated our courage, The songs bonded us together, The songs forged our discipline, The songs shielded us from hate, The songs protected us from danger, And the songs kept us sane."[66]

Meanwhile, at the new local Montgomery NBC television affiliate, a young news director named Frank McGee decided that the boycott would make a dramatic ongoing story.[67] This was an unusual instance where a local station had its own film processing equipment, and McGee sent weekly newsreels to the national networks.[68] Routine coverage on daily local and national news sustained the boycott in two ways. It prompted a flow of donations that supported the transportation infrastructure, allowing the boycott organizers not only to pay for gas but also to pay drivers and buy new cars to transport people.[69] It also brought activists the strength to keep going, knowing that news of their struggle was reaching a sympathetic public.[70]

The boycott lasted 381 days, finally coming to a successful end when the Supreme Court ruled bus segregation unconstitutional and forced Montgomery to adopt a new ordinance. This success spurred King and the Southern Christian Leadership Conference to expand the emerging movement to new sites and new struggles. Though the backlash was quick and violent in Montgomery—and a lot of desegregating work still remains to be done today—the end of the boycott marked a victory in overturning the legal power of Jim Crow.

Unlike the Montgomery Bus Boycott, most consumer boycotts fail. They depend on multiple, separable acts of individual choice: "even consumers who are ideologically supportive of a boycott don't tend to follow through and support the boycott either because they don't want to change their behavior. It's just hard to actually stop buying a product that you're used to buying. Or because they never bought the product in the first place."[71] There is too little synchronization across bodies, too little of the practiced, planned, and disciplined coordination of actions. There is not enough form. The Montgomery Bus Boycott, by contrast, coordinated activist efforts around a shared goal. They worked through shared pathways of transportation and communication, repeated messages and Bible verses and sang songs over and over, practiced routines for nonviolence, and marshalled large networks of supporters through existing organizations. And they expanded by connecting existing networks, including local and national political associations, media outlets, the state college, elementary schools, city streets, and of course Black churches, which then built a foundation for other protests across the South. Though there is no question that civil rights needed brave and brilliant leaders, its power was also built through hinges that linked existing pathways and institutions.

The Narrative of the Struggling Team

While the most respected works of art rarely invite our attention to the nuts and bolts of creating institutions or planning action campaigns, there is a popular narrative that celebrates the forms we have seen organizing successful political movements. My example here is not a single text but a popular plot that crops up across media and national borders. I call it "the narrative of the struggling team." This is a plot that often revolves around sports, but it can focus on music, dance, or academic teams: Anglophone examples range from *Fame* (1980), *Stand and Deliver* (1988), and *The Sandlot* (1993) to *The Great Debaters* (2007), *Friday Night Lights* (2006–11), *The Get Down* (2016), *Overcomer* (2019), and *Pose* (2018–21). While I myself know English-language examples best, this story also gives shape to *Princess Iron Fan* (1941), the first full-length animated film in China, and the Hong Kong sports comedy *Shaolin Soccer* (2001).[72] There are Indian examples (*Iqbal*, 2005; *Say Salaam India*,

2007; *Victory*, 2013), the Argentinian-Spanish comedy *En fuero de juego* (2012), and more than one Japanese manga and anime series (*Akakichi No Eleven*, 1970–71; *Eyeshield 21*, 2002–9).

You know the drill. The story starts off with a motley assemblage of underdogs, seemingly unable to meet the challenges of the sports season or the performance competition. The group then encounters a series of obstacles, from an undisciplined member of the team to trouble at home. But the team submits to rigorous training and careful practice, thanks, often, to a charismatic coach. They pull together. And what is most important for my purposes here is that these popular stories foreground the very same organizing forms that we saw in the Montgomery Bus Boycott: goals, routines, and the building of new collectives by way of existing infrastructures.

The shape these narratives take is almost always the teleological arc. And since happy endings often restore dominant norms, teleological narrative, as we have seen, has often been critiqued as an engine of ideological conformity. Throughout this book, I have been working to revalue teleology, and here I will make the case that even popular and formulaic Hollywood endings have affirmative affordances for political action.

We saw in an earlier chapter how endings to novels like *Esther Waters* (1894) offer the promise of stable shelter and security to people whose lives have always been radically disrupted by economic precarity and violence. These endings value stability without being politically conservative. We have seen, too, how teleology can work in the service of radical social movements. For the Lamu and Montgomery protestors, the goal gave temporal shape to their arduous work so that it was not just an indefinite and hopeless slog. Having an end—in the sense of both an aim and an ending—helped to make it possible to sustain mass collective action for long stretches of time. To assume that all end-oriented narrative reinforces capitalism or sexism is to miss the fact that it can give shape to any aspiration or ambition, including work for justice. Teleology is not good for undecidability and open-endedness, but it does afford *all* ends. And that means that end-oriented narrative might sometimes be exactly right, and generative, for the project of realizing more just social forms than those we have now.

The end of *Fame* offers an affirmative example. The plot concludes with a final showcase performance of all of the students. This is a collective work of art, where the orchestra, solo singers, a chorus, and ballet and modern dancers come together to perform a piece that moves across styles, including classical, rock, jazz, and a capella, called "I Sing the Body Electric." This line from Walt

Whitman, self-styled poet of democracy, brings disparate characters and art forms together not into a sorting of winners and losers but into a coordinated act of beauty. If critics of teleological narrative have assumed that goals necessarily reinforce the status quo, what the ending of *Fame* suggests is that ends might afford the realization of aspirations of all kinds—like democracy, for example, or art itself.

Of course, the narrative of the struggling team is often organized around competition, and it would be easy to read a naturalizing of competitiveness as the ideological upshot of these plots. And yet, it is interesting that the protagonists do not always win, as in *Cool Runnings* (1993) and *Coach Carter* (2005). In *Ocean's Eleven* (2001) the crooks get away with their heist. And so formally speaking, the goal gives shape and purpose to the narrative, but it does not always offer up conventional versions of success. And in the long middle, these stories remain focused on the hard work of coming together.

What gets the team working well, usually, is a set of routines. There is a classic montage sequence that shows the repetitive drills involved in synchronizing bodies and actions behind-the-scenes: untold hours of free throw practice, pushup sequences, or dance rehearsals. One of many examples is a two-minute sequence in *Remember the Titans* (2000), which tells the story of a real Black coach, Herman Boone, who struggled to integrate a high school football team in Virginia in 1971. In the practice montage, we see teammates learning to move in perfectly coordinated formations. The soundtrack synchronizes musical rhythms with the bodily movements of the athletes as they train to hit, jump, do sit-ups, and roll together. Boone drags one laggard off the field. Becoming a unified team takes rigorous discipline and the deliberate channeling of anger and aggression, the coach explains, into "perfect" coordination.[73] In *Coach Carter*, an exhausted player cannot finish his pushups, so others volunteer to do them for him, abiding by the Coach's rule: "You will live, eat, breathe, and sleep as a team. The word I is no longer in your vocabulary do you understand?"[74]

In a neoliberal cultural context whose preferred pleasures are individual choice and consumption, the collective montage sequence is surprising: it reveals the arduous repetitiveness and sacrifice involved in drawing together as a collective. It shows that success is not the result of raw talent but of long stretches of practice, the monotonous work of trying again and again to bring separate bodies into shared actions. And perhaps most importantly, this celebration of disciplined collective action toward a common end sparks pleasures that do not have to wait for a revolution in consciousness: these are already revealed and expressed in popular culture.

The narrative of the struggling team not only valorizes routine; it is itself repetitive in its plotlines. Since Adorno and Horkheimer condemned the culture industry, literary and cultural studies have often imagined the repetitiveness of mass culture as anaesthetizing.[75] But I have suggested in this book that routines are also crucial to the projects of both social welfare—the ongoing, reliable provision of food, water, health care, and shelter—and environmental sustainability, the project of keeping the planet livable. There is nothing intrinsically unjust about repetition. And the narrative of the struggling team shows how the pleasures of repetition could become a model for political action—a blueprint for organizing ourselves into resilient and successful political collectives.

The narrative of the struggling team often shows us, too, that realizing goals brings exquisitely shared, *collective* pleasures—joining not only team members but also joyful audiences who leap from their seats to cheer the rousing performances that bring each story to a familiar end. The final action is often gloriously aesthetic—the ball caught elegantly in the end zone, or the song performed in breathtaking harmony, with gestures and voices perfectly coordinated across bodies.

If this popular plot is typically organized around goals and routines, it also foregrounds networks and institutional infrastructures: the sports league, the debating association, the performance circuit, the glee club, the public school. The struggle sometimes turns on inequities in material infrastructure: the sympathetic underdogs are poor and cannot find suitable equipment, practice spaces, uniforms, or time away from work and family responsibilities. Often, the rich group overflowing with resources appears as a foil for our protagonists. In *Stand and Deliver* (1988), for example, which is based on a true story, high school math teacher Jaime Escalante teaches at a majority Latinx school in East Los Angeles where students struggle with both racism and poverty.[76] He aims to teach Advanced Placement calculus to students whom other teachers do not believe are capable of understanding it. One of the key formal ingredients for success is repetition. The students take daily quizzes, practice with old tests, and come early to school every day for regular tutoring sessions. Another form at work is the goal: Escalante keeps everyone's focus tightly on the AP Exam. All of the students pass; they are accused of cheating; they retake the test, and finally, they succeed.

Like most other examples in this genre, *Stand and Deliver* does not give us an account of structural inequality—how segregation and economic dispossession emerged in the first place—but it does repeatedly mark the injustice of insufficient and decaying infrastructure and contrasts this to the comforts of wealthy white neighborhoods. And we do see Escalante rearranging institutional forms for his own ends. His students start out behind, and so he petitions the school to allow him to use existing classrooms during the summer. He requires the students to sign contracts agreeing to work on math on Saturday mornings. He negotiates with parents over their children's work schedules and with administrators over the use of the school's resources.

There are many reasons to be critical of *Stand and Deliver* and other narratives like it. Taking the standardized exam as the single sign of success, for example, Escalante does not change the whole system, and he certainly does not resolve vast disparities in wealth or racial injustice. The film can be used to convey the message that Latinx children need to be "saved" by heroic teachers.[77] All of this is persuasive and important. But *Stand and Deliver* is also one of many popular plots that reject myths of spontaneity and individual choice and consumption in favor of mutually sustaining collectives and celebrate the very forms that organized the Montgomery Bus Boycott: a clear goal to sustain people even through substantial sacrifices; disciplined, repetitive training to coordinate actions across bodies; building with existing institutional forms; and the pleasures of collective action, including the stunning achievements of underdogs who beat the odds. Interestingly, the bus boycott itself is not usually told as a story of the struggling team. It would be better if it were. The dominant narrative has it that one day, a tired Rosa Parks refused to give up her seat and so inspired a nation.[78] Spontaneity, individual heroism, and sudden inspiration thus displace discipline, routine, and teamwork.

The narrative of the struggling team already appeals to audiences on a massive scale—a source of pleasure for quite literally millions of people. Since Adorno, most scholarly readers have preferred to valorize discomfort, the unsettling of dominant regimes that comes from encounters with alterity and difficulty. But discomfort is not the only politically productive affect. Munson shows us how important hospitable openness can be to real social movements, since the moment of welcome can be so powerful that it holds more power than prior beliefs and ideologies. And this is also where popular culture offers a surprisingly promising field of models. It yokes the arduous work of collective coordination to social and aesthetic pleasures.

What if we grasped the work of coming together into coordinated groups not only as a sacrifice, demanding the subordination of impulses to a larger end, but also as a satisfying, exciting, and nourishing plot? What if progressive and radical movements emphasized the joy that comes with small victories, as well as large ones? This is not an argument for covering over the horrors of exploitation and violence, but a hypothesis and a gambit—that activism has some heady and exciting pleasures to offer and that a successful movement for change might work best from the joined promise of disciplined sacrifice and collective joy.

6

Three Weeks to Political Action

A WORKBOOK

Surprisingly small numbers of people are needed to make change. The few hundred people who regularly attended ACT UP meetings in the 1980s and 1990s succeeded in implementing vast and far-reaching changes, from ending insurance exclusions for people with AIDS to shifting the focus of infection research and fast-tracking experimental drugs.[1] Nonviolent revolutions over the past few decades have succeeded with the support of just 3.5 percent of the population.[2] These low thresholds suggest that sweeping social changes are within reach. But climate change has prompted a troublingly pervasive disengagement. One of the mysteries psychologists and communications scholars have tried to unravel is why more people who are fully convinced of the dangers of global warming do not translate those convictions into action.[3] Awareness does not in itself activate the work of change.

My own hypothesis is that when faced with climate injustice on the global scale, many of us—including me, for many years—don't know where to start. What actions could possibly have a sufficient impact? What are the dangers lying in seemingly persuasive proposals for change? A lot of us would like to be part of major structural transformations, but we worry that our efforts will amount to nothing or, worse, that we will do unintended harm. For this reason, many environmentalists turn to the small scale, reducing own individual carbon footprints, eating plant-based diets, cutting down on waste, and cycling to work, hoping that there are enough others like us to make a difference. Even when we feel passionately, almost all of us also feel too overworked, hopeless, cynical, harried, ineffective, or just shy to get involved on a larger scale. And so, the vast majority of those who are concerned or even alarmed about climate change remain bystanders, torn between wishing we could do more and not knowing where to begin.

This chapter is an experiment aimed at those readers. What follows here is a workbook, a deliberately plain, prosaic form borrowed from pedagogical practices going back at least as far as the eighteenth century.[4] Workbooks supplement lectures and other explanations, guiding you through a series of questions and exercises designed to help you deepen your understanding and practice your skills. This particular workbook builds on the theories and examples articulated in this book to help you get involved in political action and sustain this involvement over time. For a very long time, most academics have seen it as our job to step back from the world and to think and know, rather than to act. But like a lot of binaries that help sustain the status quo, the opposition between theory and practice is one of many forms that is now getting in the way of the struggle for climate justice.

This workbook will focus on forms that organize your experience, and it is organized as a set of forms (that is, the kind you fill out). It does not prescribe a particular set of actions or solutions: it is intended to be used for the values and purposes that mean the most to you. In this sense, it is open-ended. But the work outlined here is also end-oriented. In place of the "endless deferral" that so often shapes the question of political action across aesthetic humanities, I invite you here to choose some specific ends, and to make the transition from critique to action.[5] And that means that unlike most academic monographs, this book asks you to be the one who completes it.

Three Weeks to Political Action

Each week is broken into five days of workbook activity. Since most of us are very busy, and can't take on too much all at once, each day asks you to do some short and focused thinking and writing.

WEEK 1. *You've talked about politics on social media, you've had discussions of political issues in your classroom, and you've voted, but so far you haven't been involved in other kinds of political action. The first week is devoted to thinking about what experiences, skills, and strengths you can bring to this work.*

DAY 1:

1. What experiences have you had participating in groups in the past? Please check all that apply:

    ◦ sports
    ◦ musical groups
    ◦ work teams

- classes
- camping trips
- planning events
- other examples from your own experience (please describe)

---

2. Choose one of these that seemed especially effective.
   - What strategies most successfully motivated you and coordinated people in the group?
   - What different forms—spaces, schedules, goals, routines, connections, itineraries, hierarchies—organized this collective?

---

3. Choose one group that felt especially frustrating, unable to achieve its goals or to cohere as a collective.
   - What is your sense of what went wrong?
   - Do any particular forms or their absence—including schedules, goals, routines, connections, itineraries, hierarchies—strike you as particular problems for this group?

DAY 2:

1. Reflecting on your past experience of groups and collectives, what would you say are your strengths in working with other members of a team? Maybe you are patient with people struggling with new tasks, or tenacious, or good at connecting people. . . . It could be lots of things.

---

2. What do you see as your weaknesses when working with others?

---

3. What skills do you already have that might be useful to a political organization or movement? Please check all that apply.
   - writing
   - teaching
   - presenting
   - convening discussions
   - organizing events

- analyzing data
- making images
- doing research
- asking questions
- understanding institutions
- creating relationships
- listening
- other (please describe)

DAY 3:

1. What is your image of an activist? What skills and personality traits do you think they have or should have?

---

2. Do you see feel unsuited to political action? Do any of these descriptions capture why? (Check all that apply.)
    - You don't have the skills or personality that's right for this work.
    - You are overwhelmed with other obligations.
    - You find it draining to work with other people.
    - You just prefer academic or aesthetic activity.
    - You feel guilt around your own complicity and don't want to be hypocritical.
    - You think the title of "activist" belongs to people who are not like you.
    - Other (please describe).

---

3. What aspects of your personality seem to you to get in the way of political action? Examples might include:
    - You get easily stressed and overwhelmed.
    - You don't follow through on tasks.
    - You're disorganized.
    - You're introverted and prefer solitude.
    - You don't have enough energy to add more tasks to your list.
    - Anything else?

---

4. What if these are just neutral facts? Genuine and unalterable constraints? In this respect, they are helpful guides to finding the kinds of action that suit you best. They might also sometimes be strengths. Try redescribing these in a neutral way. For example:
   - I have enough time and energy to commit one hour per week.
   - I happily work for long periods alone.
   - External deadlines are essential to me when I have a task to complete.

DAY 4:

1. What do you *like* doing that might be relevant to political action? (Speaking for myself, I love writing all kinds of things, including reports and op-eds, and I like giving oral presentations. I like learning new things about people and institutions.)

---

2. What do you *hate* doing? (I absolutely dread making phone calls and going door-to-door. I get frustrated with slow processes. I hate taking minutes.)

DAY 5:

Take a few minutes to look back over your answers, and then draft an email introducing yourself to an imaginary group or organization. "Hi, I'm . . . I have experience in . . . I am good at . . . I willingly do . . . I would rather not . . ."

WEEK 2. *This week we will be focusing on keeping your involvement going over time. It is really hard, emotionally as well as practically, not to feel drained in the face of vast political challenges. The first hurdle is to build political action into the routines of ordinary life. The second is to sustain energy for this work over time.*

DAY 1:

To make political action sustainable, it will be important to build time for it into your **routines**.

1. If you map out an ordinary week and month, what obligations are immovable, like work and travel schedules? What times can you

reserve for activity that is important to your well-being (like exercise, time with friends, downtime)? Are there stretches of the month or year you know will be especially busy?

---

2. Write down an amount of time you can realistically commit to political work. It's good to start small.

---

3. Put political work into your calendar as a recurring obligation. If you know you can devote more time during some periods than others, put that in your calendar in advance.

All routines get interrupted sometimes by unanticipated events (illness, a plumbing disaster, an urgent work deadline). If this happens every so often, there is no need to change your schedule, but if these interruptions happen so often that they regularly derail your political action, then scale back your commitments to make sure they are realistic.

DAY 2:

One of the biggest surprises for me, since I started doing political work a few years ago, was how often friends, colleagues, and many other well-meaning people would actively *discourage* activist efforts. They would say that there is no point because this or that institution will never change; they would explain why a particular tactic would not work; they would argue that a different goal was more important or meaningful; they would dwell on the losses and failures of past movements. I cannot count the number of people who told me—with that breezy sense of assurance that always sways me—that it was hopeless to try to persuade the Cornell trustees to divest from fossil fuels. I managed to persevere only because another member of the team who knew a lot more than I did kept explaining how and why we had a good chance. Just a few months later, we won this battle. If you're anything like me, gloomy messages undermine whatever shaky confidence I have that the political work I am doing is worth the time and effort I am giving to it. So, maybe you, like me, would benefit from some strategies for responding to disheartening messages.

1. What thoughts about the world discourage you from taking political action? (You may check as many as you like.)

- ◦ You believe that activism doesn't work.
- ◦ You feel overwhelmed by the sheer scale of the wrongs of the world.
- ◦ You see dominant systems as inert and overpowering.
- ◦ You believe that politicians, CEOs, and other powerful people are unaccountable, and they have no reason to change.
- ◦ You think that only really radical change matters, and you don't know how to accomplish that.
- ◦ People are horrible: blinkered, bigoted, greedy, narcissistic.
- ◦ You don't know how to figure out which movements or organizations are making a real difference.
- ◦ You can only imagine change happening if huge numbers of people participate.
- ◦ Other (please describe).

---

2. Reflecting on the answers you checked, which of these are demonstrably true (and you would argue strenuously for them, using evidence), and which come out of fear or hopelessness or habit or temperament?

DAY 3:

What arguments might you use *against* the thoughts that most discourage you? (I am of course hoping that some of the other chapters in this book might prove useful here.)

DAY 4:

To quiet the voices of the naysayers in our heads, activists need to develop habits that sustain our work through challenges and obstacles. That is, we need to cultivate *routines of encouragement*. For me, what works best is being reminded of past victories, and especially those where small groups changed large structures. But what keeps me going might not work as well for you. So please brainstorm answers to these three final questions:

1. What routines could you practice to keep up your energy when things look bleak?

- ◦ repeating a slogan or mantra
- ◦ reminding yourself of past successes
- ◦ checking in with a supportive friend or ally
- ◦ imagining the joy of victory
- ◦ focusing on what you learn in every struggle
- ◦ making time for rest
- ◦ listening to words or songs that energize you
- ◦ other (please describe)

____

2. How will you build these into your schedule?

____

3. What will you say to the pessimists and wet blankets who try to dissuade you from your political goals?

____

DAY 5:

Friends and allies are crucial to most of us when it comes to sustaining energy, enthusiasm, and commitment over the long term. Reach out to one or two people who can be teammates, cheerleaders, or accountability partners—people who help you to follow through on your time commitments. Maybe they will join you in the work, or just check to see that you are doing what you've decided to do.

WEEK 3. *You have laid the groundwork for action. Now it's time to get started.*

DAY 1:

Let's focus on figuring out which particular issue you're going to address.

1. If you had lots of power, what political problems would you solve? Feel free to be as ambitious as you like here, but strive for some specificity. In other words, your first response might be "solve climate change," but then you might add, "especially environmental racism and the rate of fossil fuel emissions." This can be as long or short as you like.

____

2. Choose one of these problems. It should be one that you can imagine sustaining your interest and energy over time.

____

DAY 2:

Having chosen your field of action, write down a specific goal that seems to you ambitious but achievable. What does victory look like?

____

DAY 3:

You've made plans for incorporating political activity into the forms of your ordinary life, and you've articulated a goal. You could start your own movement, of course, but that is a heavy lift, and this book has argued for the importance of building with existing institutions, networks, and infrastructures. And so, at least for now, it probably makes sense to take one of two major routes:

A. Browse online and talk to friends and acquaintances about organizations that address the problem you chose. What goals do they articulate? Which organizations are striving for far-reaching structural impacts? Which are working at a scale larger than the individual consumer?

OR

B. Decide to work within an institution like a university or a town council to move it toward your goal. Are any of these already addressing the problem? (Maybe your college has a sustainability office, for example.)

DAY 4:

If you opted for A above, choose an existing organization that is already working toward the goal you have chosen. Before you commit to the organization, make sure it feels like a good match: the work should seem meaningful and exciting enough to keep your enthusiasm going.

If you chose B, write down any contacts you have or offices that are working on this. Do you know who has power to shape the institution—officers, trustees, bosses, leadership groups, committees, departments, watchdogs, advisory boards, democratic bodies, informal networks? How do the different bodies interrelate? Are there strict hierarchies, clear decision makers, a transparent flow of power? Or are there crisscrossing lines of authority, multiple networks, and different sites of decision making? Do you know of weak links, conflicting forms, surprising lines of influence, and decision makers who are not at the top of the hierarchy? How can you find out more?

DAY 5:

If you chose A, now it's time to introduce yourself to the organization, using your draft email from the first week. Get in touch by phone or email, outlining your specific skills, aptitudes, preferences, and time constraints.

If you chose B, reach out to three contacts and request a half-hour meeting. Prepare for the meeting with specific questions: How do certain policies work? What people or bodies have decision-making power? How have changes been made in the past? What are the most significant obstacles and opportunities to achieving your goal? Be sure to ask for names of other people who might be able to help you: is anyone currently working on this issue? As you listen, keep your analytical ear out for the interactions of multiple shapes and arrangements. Most people on the ground will give you a partial picture based on their own position, experience, and theories of change. You will need to piece together a bigger sense of how institutional change happens—and could happen—by paying attention to the ways that different departments, rules, and routines interact.

You're launched! Solidarity!

ACKNOWLEDGMENTS

You can't write a book about collective life and infrastructure without recognizing how very small you are. A vast number of people I have never met have made this thinking and writing possible, from the many public school teachers, counselors, and janitorial staff who have been taking care of my children to the sanitation workers who collect my household's trash every week. I wish, in the spirit of Mierle Laderman Ukeles, that I could shake all of these by the hand and express my gratitude directly—or at least thank them by name in these pages. But so much of the labor that goes into sustaining ordinary life remains invisible and anonymous, which means that the best I can do here is to acknowledge its enormity and its significance.

This book benefited from many responses to this work as it unfolded, and I thank colleagues at Oxford, Edinburgh, Bonn, Dundee, Leipzig, Gour Banga, Southern Denmark, Heidelberg, Chicago, Ulster, Penn State, Yale, the Cornell School of Criticism and Theory, UC-Santa Barbara, the Australasian Victorian Studies Association, Caen, University of East Anglia, the Freie Universität Berlin, Stanford-Duke Phil+Lit, the Research Center for Democratic Cultures and Politics at Groningen, the Netherlands Institute for Advanced Study in the Humanities and Social Sciences, Open University, Washington University in St. Louis, UC-Berkeley, McGill, Columbia, Goethe University, Muhlenberg College, University of Illinois-Chicago, the Knowlton School of Architecture, University of Colorado-Boulder, Skidmore College, University of Illinois at Urbana-Champaign, University of Connecticut, Loyola-Chicago, CUNY Graduate Center, University of Buffalo, Rutgers, New School for Social Research, Temple, Clemson, University of Toronto, the Berlin Center for Literary and Cultural Research, the North American Victorian Studies Association, and the University of Wyoming.

Pieces of the argument have appeared as "The Long Lure of Anti-Instrumentality: Politics, Aesthetics, and Climate Change," *Modern Fiction Studies* 67:2 (June 2021); "Model Thinking: Generalization, Political Form, and the Common Good," *New Literary History* 48:4 (autumn 2017): 633–53;

"The Enormity Effect: Realist Fiction, Literary Studies, and the Refusal to Count," *Genre* 50:1 (March 2017): 59–76; "'The Strange Familiar': Structure, Infrastructure, and Adichie's *Americanah*," *Modern Fiction Studies* 61:4 (winter 2015): 712–30; "Realism for Sustainability," in *Realism: Aesthetics, Experiments, Politics*, edited by Jens Elze (Bloomsbury, 2022); and "Endings and Sustainability," in *Beyond Narrative* (Transcript, 2022). Special thanks to Peter Kalliney and Michael Rubenstein for editorial comments that really sharpened my arguments.

Whole classes full of smart and curious students nourished and challenged the ideas I have developed in this book. I am especially grateful to the undergraduates who have taken "Communicating Climate Change" in its various iterations, my graduate seminar "Sustainable Forms," and the extraordinarily fun, collegial, and stimulating seminar I had the good fortune to teach at the Cornell School of Criticism and Theory in 2021. Matt Kilbane, while still a PhD student at Cornell, offered invaluable feedback on the manuscript.

The writing of this book coincided for me with chairing two academic departments, and I would not have been able to manage, much less write, without two extraordinary department managers who not only gave me the gift of their friendship but also reshaped my thinking about institutional fairness and care. I owe a deep debt to Spring Sherrod and Paula Epps-Cepero.

It has been an immense pleasure to learn from others in the fight for climate justice. Special thanks to Bob Howarth and Climate Justice Cornell for their work on divesting Cornell's endowment, Miranda Phillips and Nancy Jacobson for running the local chapter of Citizens Climate Lobby, and the TIAA-Divest! crew—especially Iris Marie Bloom, Bill Kish, Molly Ornati, Sheldon Pollock, and Dan Segal. Thanks also to Sarah Brylinsky, Kim Anderson, and Marianne Krasny, who have done incredible work on the ground at Cornell.

Anne Savarese has been an exceptional editor. She prompted me to rethink and rewrite this book from start to finish, and it's much the better for it. She also solicited two excellent readers' reports, one of which connected me to the wonderful Barbara Leckie.

It's not possible to express enough gratitude for the people close to me who have helped sustain me over the past few difficult years. Jessie Reeder and Devin Garofalo, beloved former students who make me so intensely proud, have been astute and generous readers. Liz Anker gave multiple rounds of perceptive feedback on drafts. I have been unimaginably lucky in having a long list of endlessly warm, supportive, and luminously intelligent friends, including Rachel Ablow, Rachel Adams, Tanya Agathocleous, Ayelet Ben-Yishai,

Susan Bernstein, Jan Caldwell, Ramzi Fawaz, Jane Gallop, Durba Ghosh, Rachel Harmon, Amy M. King, Anna Kornbluh, Venkat Mani, Masha Raskolnikov, and Lisa Sternlieb. Mary Pat Brady and Kate McCullough sustained me with glorious food as well as sympathy through some of the hardest times. Susan Stanford Friedman, generous friend and mentor, died as I was copy-editing this book. It was a question she asked that first prompted me to reconsider the value of stability. She will be deeply missed. Susan Wiser is a gifted therapist who has done more good for me than I could have ever imagined. My brother Peter got me thinking about politics in the first place, and he continues to provide insight and inspiration. My mother, Deedee Levine, has provided bountiful support. To beloved Moroccan friends, who made my sabbatical magical, Aziza Boulmessi and Abdelghani Tinzit: شكرًا

Amanda Claybaugh continues to be my best possible reader. Amanda, along with Rebecca Walkowitz and Martin Puchner, are the most incredible posse, always somehow joining intellectual brilliance with love, compassion, and insight. They have sustained me in more ways than I can count.

I was once asked why I didn't introduce my children as my greatest accomplishment. I just can't see myself taking credit for Eli McKenzie or Joe Levine. They always seem to be accomplishing themselves, becoming the most astonishing and impressive people—kind, interesting, smart, funny, thoughtful. There are no words for how much I love them.

I have saved two friends for the end. They have transformed my understanding of friendship over the past four years, providing the chosen family I have always longed for. Supporting, listening, venting, theorizing, cheerleading, emoting, joking, confessing, eating, walking, reading, commenting, and texting many times a day, they have been there for all of it. Tyler Bradway and Jen Spitzer, I dedicate this book to you.

NOTES

Preface

1. Donna J. Haraway, *Staying with the Trouble: Making Kin in the Chthulucene* (Durham: Duke University Press, 2016), 1.

2. Jeffrey Insko, "On Dismantling: A Report from Michigan," *Resilience* 8:1 (winter 2020): 149; Erin Manning, *The Minor Gesture* (Durham: Duke University Press, 2016); Anne-Lise François, "'Shadow Boxing': Empty Blows, Practice Steps, and Nature's Hold," *Qui Parle* 25:1 (fall/winter 2016): 164.

3. Owain Jones, Kate Rigby, and Linda Williams, "Everyday Ecocide, Toxic Dwelling, and the Inability to Mourn," *Environmental Humanities* 12:1 (2020): 388–405.

4. Stacy Alaimo, *Exposed: Environmental Politics and Pleasures in Posthuman Times* (Minneapolis: University of Minnesota Press, 2016), 3.

5. See, for example, Sarah Kanouse, "Staying with the Troubling, Performing in the Impasse," in *The Routledge Companion to Contemporary Art, Visual Culture, and Climate Change*, ed. T. J. Demos, Emily Eliza Scott, and Subhankar Banerjee (New York: Routledge, 2021), 153–63; and Thom van Dooren, *The Wake of Crows: Living and Dying in Shared Worlds* (New York: Columbia University Press, 2019).

6. Sarah M. Pike, "Mourning Nature: The Work of Grief in Radical Environmentalism," *Journal for the Study of Religion, Nature and Culture* 10:4 (2017): 419–41.

7. Anahid Nersessian, "Romantic Ecocriticism Lately," *Literature Compass* (January 2018): 2.

8. Caroline Levine, *Forms: Whole, Rhythm, Hierarchy, Network* (Princeton: Princeton University Press, 2015).

9. Anna Kornbluh, *The Order of Forms: Realism, Formalism, and Social Space* (Chicago: University of Chicago Press, 2019).

10. While feminist, Black studies, and queer activist-scholars have long struggled to make a case for activist work in the academy, an array of other humanities scholars recently have also been working against this foundational binary. See Elizabeth Ammons, *Brave New Words: How Literature Will Save the Planet* (Iowa City: University of Iowa Press, 2010); Shannon Jackson, *Social Works: Performing Art, Supporting Publics* (New York: Routledge, 2011); Doris Sommer, *The Work of Art in the World: Civic Agency and Public Humanities* (Durham: Duke University Press, 2014); Talia Schaffer, *Communities of Care: The Social Ethics of Victorian Fiction* (Princeton: Princeton University Press, 2021); and Barbara Leckie, *Climate Change, Interrupted* (Stanford: Stanford University Press, 2022).

Chapter 1

1. Lionel Trilling (1950), *The Liberal Imagination* (New York: New York Review of Books, 2008), 11–13; Fred Moten, *The Universal Machine* (Durham: Duke University Press, 2018), passim; Theodor Adorno, *Essays on Music*, trans. Susan H. Gillespie (Berkeley: University of California Press, 2002), passim; Gloria Anzaldúa, *Borderlands/La Frontera: The New Mestiza* (San Francisco: Aunt Lute, 1987), 68–69; Stephen Greenblatt, *Shakespearean Negotiations: The Circulation of Social Energy in Renaissance England* (Berkeley: University of California Press, 1988), 7; Bill Brown, "Thing Theory," *Critical Inquiry* 28:1 (autumn 2001): 1–22; Rosi Braidotti, *Transpositions: On Nomadic Ethics* (Malden, MA: Polity, 2006), especially 75–82; Kandice Chuh, *The Difference Aesthetics Makes: On the Humanities "After Man"* (Durham: Duke University Press, 2019), 1–25.

2. Max Weber, *Economy and Society*, vol. 1, ed. Guenther Roth and Claus Wittich (Berkeley: University of California Press, 1978), 24, 26, 63; György Lukács brings Weber's notion of instrumental rationality together with alienated labor in *History and Class Consciousness*, trans. Rodney Livingstone (Cambridge, MA: MIT Press, 1971), 88. Max Horkheimer, *Critique of Instrumental Reason*, trans. Matthew O'Connell (London: Verso, 2012); Herbert Marcuse, *Negations*, trans. Jeffrey J. Shapiro (Boston: Beacon, 1968); Max Horkheimer and Theodor W. Adorno, *Dialectic of Enlightenment*, trans. Edmund Jephcott (Stanford: Stanford University Press, 2002).

3. Mick Smith, *An Ethics of Place: Radical Ecology, Postmodernity, and Social Theory* (Albany: SUNY Press, 2001), 49.

4. Santiago Castro-Gómez, "The Missing Chapter of Empire," in *Globalization and the Decolonial Option*, ed. Walter D. Mignolo and Arturo Escobar (London: Routledge, 2010), 282–84.

5. Soren Hvalkof, "Progress of the Victims: Political Ecology in the Peruvian Amazon," in *Reimagining Political Ecology*, ed. Aletta Biersack and James B. Greenberg (Durham: Duke University Press, 2006), 195–232.

6. Michel Foucault, *Language, Counter-Memory, Practice*, trans. Donald F. Bouchard and Sherry Simon (Ithaca: Cornell University Press, 1977), 230.

7. "Something's Missing: A Discussion between Ernst Bloch and Theodor W. Adorno on the Contradictions of Utopian Longing," in Ernst Bloch, *The Utopian Function of Art and Literature*, trans. Jack Zipes and Frank Mecklenburg (Cambridge MA: MIT Press, 1988), 10, 12.

8. Fredric Jameson, *Archeologies of the Future* (New York: Verso, 2005), 289.

9. Jared Sexton, "Affirmation in the Dark: Racial Slavery and Philosophical Pessimism," *The Comparatist* 43 (October 2019): 105, 106.

10. Jack Halberstam, "The Wild Beyond: With and for the Undercommons," in Stefano Harney and Fred Moten, *The Undercommons: Fugitive Planning and Black Study* (Brooklyn, NY: Minor Compositions, 2013), 5.

11. See, for example, Vivasan Soni, "Can Aesthetics Overcome Instrumental Reason?" in *Mind, Body, Motion, Matter*, ed. Helen Mary McMurran and Alison Conway (Toronto: University of Toronto Press, 2016), 255–56; and Derek Attridge, *The Work of Literature* (Oxford: Oxford University Press, 2015), 98.

12. Jonathan Kramnick, *Paper Minds: Literature and the Ecology of Consciousness* (Chicago: University of Chicago Press, 2018), 27. See also Sandra Macpherson, "The Political Fallacy," *PMLA* 132:5 (2017): 1214–19.

13. Catherine Gallagher and Stephen Greenblatt, *Practicing New Historicism* (Chicago: University of Chicago Press, 2001), 19; Sara Ahmed, *The Cultural Politics of Emotion* (New York: Routledge, 2004), 202; Derek Attridge, *The Singularity of Literature* (London: Routledge, 2004), 137; Robert McRuer, *Crip Theory* (New York: New York University Press, 2006), 2008; Timothy Morton, *Hyperobjects: Philosophy and Ecology after the End of the World* (Minneapolis: University of Minnesota Press, 2013), 201; Dora Zhang, *Strange Likeness: Description and the Modernist Novel* (Chicago: University of Chicago Press, 2020), 52; Peter Boxall, *The Prosthetic Imagination* (Cambridge: Cambridge University Press, 2020), 354; Kevin Quashie, *Black Aliveness, or A Poetics of Being* (Durham: Duke University Press, 2021), 143; Tim Bewes, *Free Indirect: The Novel in a Postfictional Age* (New York: Columbia University Press, 2022), 18.

14. Ramzi Fawaz, *The New Mutants: Superheroes and the Radical Imagination of American Comics* (New York: New York University Press, 2016).

15. Helen Vendler, *The Breaking of Style* (Cambridge, MA: Harvard University Press, 1995), 7, 95.

16. Susan Stewart, *The Poet's Freedom: A Notebook on Making* (Chicago: University of Chicago Press, 2011), 16.

17. Attridge, *The Work of Literature*, 143.

18. Nan Z. Da, *Intransitive Encounter: Sino-U.S. Literatures and the Limits of Exchange* (New York: Columbia University Press, 2018), 221.

19. Taylor Littleton and Maltby Sykes, *Advancing American Art* (Tuscaloosa: University of Alabama Press, 1989), 41.

20. Frances Stonor Saunders, *The Cultural Cold War: The CIA and the World of Arts and Letters* (New York: New Press, 1999), 214. I tell this story at greater length in *Provoking Democracy: Why We Need the Arts* (Oxford: Blackwell, 2007), 73–102.

21. Peter Benson, *Black Orpheus, Transition, and Modern Cultural Awakening in Africa* (Berkeley: University of California Press, 1986), 23, 31.

22. Deborah N. Cohn, *The Latin American Literary Boom and U.S. Nationalism during the Cold War* (Nashville: Vanderbilt University Press, 2012), 20.

23. Bruce Cumings, "Boundary Displacement: The State, the Foundations, and Area Studies during and after the Cold War," in *Learning Places: The Afterlives of Area Studies*, ed. Masao Miyoshi and Harry Harootunian (Durham: Duke University Press, 2002), 261–302.

24. Eric Bennett, *Workshops of Empire: Stegner, Engle, and American Creative Writing during the Cold War* (Iowa City: University of Iowa Press, 2015).

25. Donna M. Binkiewicz, *Federalizing the Muse: United States Arts Policy and the National Endowment for the Arts, 1965–1980* (Chapel Hill: University of North Carolina Press, 2004), 147–78.

26. Peter Kalliney, "Modernism, African Literature, and the Cold War," *Modern Language Quarterly* 76:3 (2015): 337.

27. Susan Stanford Friedman, *Planetary Modernisms: Provocations on Modernity across Time* (New York: Columbia University Press, 2015), 3.

28. Nadja Popovich, Livia Albeck-Ripka, and Kendra Pierre-Louis, "The Trump Administration Rolled Back More than 100 Environmental Rules," *New York Times*, January 20, 2021, https://www.nytimes.com/interactive/2020/climate/trump-environment-rollbacks-list.html; Sue Branford and Thais Borges, "Brazil Guts Agencies, 'Sabotaging Environmental Protection' in

Amazon," *Mongabay*, February 1, 2021, https://news.mongabay.com/2021/02/brazil-guts-agencies-sabotaging-environmental-protection-in-amazon-report/; PIB Delhi, "Cabinet Approves Deregulation," June 29, 2022, https://pib.gov.in/PressReleasePage.aspx?PRID=1837892.

29. Eric M. Conway and Naomi Oreskes, *Merchants of Doubt* (New York: Bloomsbury, 2010).

30. Juliet Schor, William Attwood-Charles, and Mehmet Cansoy, *After the Gig* (Berkeley: University of California Press, 2020).

31. Wendy Brown, *Edgework: Critical Essays on Knowledge and Politics* (Princeton: Princeton University Press, 2005), 44.

32. Jenny Odell, *How to Do Nothing* (Brooklyn: Melville House, 2019), 201.

33. My thanks to Ryan Carroll for the language of gesture here. As I finish writing this book, I notice that some new books in the aesthetic humanities are beginning to sketch out practical programs. Talia Schaffer's *Communities of Care: The Social Ethics of Victorian Fiction* lays out a guide to creating care communities within the university (Princeton: Princeton University Press, 2021), 189–217. And Min Hyoung Song's *Climate Lyricism* (Durham: Duke University Press, 2022) seeks to move away from an emphasis on powerlessness and the dangers of agency toward "engaging the struggle as a daily practice" (15).

34. Stephanie LeMenager, *Living Oil: Petroleum Culture in the American Century* (Oxford: Oxford University Press, 2014), 183.

35. LeMenager, *Living Oil*, 195.

36. Rob Nixon, *Slow Violence and the Environmentalism of the Poor* (Cambridge, MA: Harvard University Press, 2011), 279–80.

37. Amitav Ghosh, *The Great Derangement: Climate Change and the Unthinkable* (Chicago: University of Chicago Press, 2016), 161–62.

38. Donna J. Haraway, *Staying with the Trouble: Making Kin in the Chthulucene* (Durham: Duke University Press, 2016), 5.

39. Haraway, *Staying with the Trouble*, 23–24.

40. Kathryn Yusoff, *A Billion Black Anthropocenes or None* (Minneapolis: University of Minnesota Press, 2018), 111.

41. Stacy Alaimo, *Exposed: Environmental Politics and Pleasures in Posthuman Times* (Minneapolis: University of Minnesota Press, 2016); Chelsea M. Frazier, "Troubling Ecology: Wangechi Mutu, Octavia Butler, and Black Feminist Interventions in Environmentalism," *Critical Ethnic Studies* 2:1 (spring 2016): 40; Kyle Devine, *Decomposed: The Political Ecology of Music* (Cambridge, MA: MIT Press, 2019), 189.

42. Barbara Leckie, *Climate Change, Interrupted* (Stanford: Stanford University Press, 2022), 131.

43. For a working definition of *res publica*, see Bonnie Honig, *Public Things* (New York: Fordham University Press, 2016), 3–5.

44. Ursula K. Heise, "Slow-Forward to the Future," in *Postmodern/Postwar and After*, ed. Jason Gladstone, Andrew Hoberek, and Daniel Worden (Iowa City: University of Iowa Press, 2016), 251–59.

45. Anna Lowenhaupt Tsing, *The Mushroom at the End of the World: On the Possibility of Life in Capitalist Ruins* (Princeton: Princeton University Press, 2015), vii–viii, 5. Donna J. Haraway, similarly, argues that species use each other all the time for survival, which means that "instrumental intra-action" is "intrinsic to bodily webbed mortal earthly being and becoming." *When Species Meet* (Minneapolis: University of Minnesota Press, 2008), 71.

46. Elizabeth Woody, "People of the River—People of the Salmon *Wana Thlama-Nusuxmí Tanánma*," in *Water and People: Challenges at the Interface of Symbolic and Utilitarian Values*, ed. Stephen McCool et al. (Portland, OR: U.S. Department of Agriculture, Forest Service, Pacific Northwest Research Station, 2008), 182. See also Nicholas James Reo and Kyle Powys Whyte, "Hunting and Morality as Elements of Traditional Ecological Knowledge," *Human Ecology* 40:1 (2012): 15–27.

47. Haraway, *When Species Meet*, 71. Barbara Johnson also reclaims use for ethics in her "Using People: Kant with Winnicott," in *The Turn to Ethics*, ed. Marjorie Garber, Beatrice Hannsen, and Rebecca L. Walkowitz (New York: Routledge, 2000), 262–74.

48. Kyle Powys Whyte, "Food Sovereignty, Justice, and Indigenous Peoples: An Essay on Settler Colonialism and Collective Continuance," in *The Oxford Handbook of Food Ethics*, ed. Anne Barnhill, Mark Budolfson, and Tyler Doggett (Oxford: Oxford University Press, 2018), 353.

49. See Elizabeth Hoover, "'Our Own Foods as a Healing': The Role of Health in the Native American Food Sovereignty Movement," *Journal for the Anthropology of North America* 24:2 (fall 2021): 89–97.

50. For recent responses by Native chefs and gardeners, see Hoover, "'Our Own Foods as Healing.'"

51. Whyte, "Food Sovereignty," 348–49.

52. Other philosophical traditions argue for the indissolubility of means and ends. Gandhi, for example, draws on the Hindu tradition of *Purusartha* to claim that since we can never know how things will turn out, the justice of the means is the only way to ensure justice at every moment. Mohandas Gandhi, *All Men Are Brothers* (Paris: UNESCO, 1958), 81–84. John Dewey writes: "The 'end' is merely a series of acts viewed at a remote stage; and a means is merely the series viewed at an earlier one. . . . The 'end' is the last act thought of; the means are the acts to be performed prior to it in time." *Human Nature and Conduct: An Introduction to Social Psychology* (New York: Modern Library, 1922), 34. If I hang a Black Lives Matter poster on my front door, I can say that I have accomplished an end, but if my larger end is racial justice, this act will look like only the smallest of steps in the right direction. Weber himself distinguished "instrumental rationality" from "value rationality," where the ends are moral, rather than based on the technical and efficient exploitation of resources for profit. *Economy and Society*, 25.

53. See, for example, Michelle C. Neely, *Against Sustainability* (New York: Fordham University Press, 2020).

54. Adrian Parr, *Hijacking Sustainability* (Cambridge, MA: MIT Press, 2009); Leerom Medovoi, "A Contribution to the Critique of Political Ecology: Sustainability as Disavowal," *New Formations* 69:10 (summer 2010): 129–43.

55. Amartya Sen, *The Idea of Justice* (Cambridge, MA: Harvard University Press, 2009), 288.

56. It seems worth noting that instrumental rationality itself often obscures the relation of means to ends. When states and corporations posit "efficiency" and "modernization" as ends, they conceal that these are in fact a means to another, deliberately obfuscated, end—profit-making for a small number of people. It is my argument here that if we can loosen the hold of an anti-instrumental purity, we can undertake the more challenging analytical work of differentiating ends that are more unjust and oppressive from those that are more just and capacitating.

57. See, for example, Lawrence Mead, *Beyond Entitlement* (New York: Simon and Schuster, 1986), 30–45; and Corey Robin on Friedrich Hayek in "Economics in the Materiality of Moral Choice," in *Economics after Neoliberalism*, ed. Joshua Cohen (Cambridge, MA: MIT Press, 2019), 30–35.

58. Kwame Anthony Appiah suggests that the real target should not be universals but the posturings of false universalisms. *In My Father's House: Africa in the Philosophy of Culture* (Oxford: Oxford University Press, 1992), 58.

59. Enzo Rossi and Olúfẹ́mi O. Táíwò, "What's New about Woke Racial Capitalism (and What Isn't)," *Spectre*, December 18, 2020, https://spectrejournal.com/whats-new-about-woke-racial-capitalism-and-what-isnt/.

60. José Esteban Muñoz, *Cruising Utopia* (New York: New York University Press, 2009), 20; Karen Pinkus, *Fuel: A Speculative Dictionary* (Minneapolis: University of Minnesota Press, 2016), 4.

61. Frank Wilderson III, for example, says that he is "only writing to the kind of black consciousness that is ready to burn it all down." Ena Grozdanic, "On Afropessimism," *The Monthly*, October 2, 2020.

62. For a history and counter to this argument, see Lisi Schoenbach, *Pragmatic Modernism* (Oxford: Oxford University Press, 2012), 8–9.

63. Karl Marx and Friedrich Engels, "Address of the Central Committee to the Communist League" (1850), in *The Marx-Engels Reader*, ed. Robert C. Tucker (New York: Norton, 1978), 501–11.

64. See *#accelerate#: The Accelerationist Reader* (Falmouth: Urbanomic, 2014).

65. *The Rosa Luxemburg Reader*, ed. Kevin B. Anderson and Peter Hudis (New York: Monthly Review Press, 2004), 129, 237–41.

66. Raymond Williams, *Politics and Letters*, ed. Geoff Dyer (London: Verso, 2015), 410–11.

67. Chantal Mouffe, *For a Left Populism* (London: Verso, 2018), 46.

68. Stuart Jeffries, "Interview: Angela Davis," *The Guardian*, December 14, 2014, https://www.theguardian.com/global/2014/dec/14/angela-davis-there-is-an-unbroken-line-of-police-violence-in-the-us-that-takes-us-all-the-way-back-to-the-days-of-slavery.

69. Sherry Wolf, "Why Gay Marriage Is a Civil Rights Issue," *Socialist Worker*, April 23, 2004, http://socialistworker.org/2004-1/496/496_07_GayMarriage.php.

70. Slavoj Žižek, *The Day after the Revolution: V. I. Lenin* (London: Verso, 2018), lxxvii.

71. Bruce Robbins, "Balibarism!" *n+1* (spring 2103), https://nplusonemag.com/issue-16/reviews/balibarism/.

72. Jordan Kinder, "The Coming Transition: Fossil Capital and Our Energy Future," *Socialism and Democracy* 30:2 (2016): 8–27.

73. Timothy Mitchell, *Carbon Democracy: Political Power in the Age of Oil* (London: Verso, 2013), 252.

74. David Bush, "The Socialist Case against the Carbon Tax," *Spring* (August 30, 2019): https://springmag.ca/the-socialist-case-against-the-carbon-tax.

75. Max Ajl, "Clean Tech versus a People's Green New Deal," *Earth Island Journal* (winter 2020), https://www.earthisland.org/journal/index.php/magazine/entry/clean-tech-versus-a-peoples-green-new-deal/; Vijay Kolinjivadi and Ashish Kothari, "No Harm Here Is Still Harm There: The Green New Deal and the Global South," *Jamhoor* 4 (May 20, 2020), https://www

.jamhoor.org/read/2020/5/20/no-harm-here-is-still-harm-there-looking-at-the-green-new-deal-from-the-global-south.

76. Kai Heron and Jodi Dean, "Revolution or Ruin," *e-flux* 110 (June 2020), https://www.e-flux.com/journal/110/335242/revolution-or-ruin/.

77. Jimmy Thomson, "Meet the Scientists Embracing Traditional Indigenous Knowledge," *The Narwhal*, June 20, 2019, https://thenarwhal.ca/meet-scientists-embracing-traditional-indigenous-knowledge/; Brandon Derman, "'Climate Change Is about Us': Fence-line Communities, the NAACP and the Grounding of Climate Justice," *Routledge Handbook of Climate Justice*, ed. Tahseen Jafry (London: Routledge, 2019), 407–19; Black Lives Matter, "Climate Justice Is Racial Justice," August 30, 2021, https://blacklivesmatter.com/climate-justice-is-racial-justice/.

78. Heron and Dean, "Revolution or Ruin." Ammons points out an uncanny similarity between the academic left and religious fundamentalism: "both preach that human agency is impotent, disaster is inevitable, and the future is out of our control." Elizabeth Ammons, *Brave New Words: How Literature Will Save the Planet* (Iowa City: University of Iowa Press, 2010), 10.

79. Marquis Bey, *Black Trans Feminism* (Durham: Duke University Press, 2022), 201.

80. See, for example, Sianne Ngai, *The Theory of the Gimmick: Aesthetic Judgment and Capitalist Form* (Cambridge, MA: Harvard University Press, 2020).

81. See, for example, Stuart Hall, "The Whites of Their Eyes: Racist Ideologies and the Media," in *Selected Writings on Race and Difference* (Durham: Duke University Press, 2021), 98.

82. The Birmingham tradition, like the Frankfurt School, remains robust in contemporary criticism. Queer theorist Ramzi Fawaz, for example, argues that in the 1960s and 1970s, the wonder and enchantment of comic books made a range of non-normative genders and sexualities seem desirable, and this not only widened the space for alternatives to normative models but actually encouraged participation in social activism. *The New Mutants*, 27–28.

83. Ghosh, *The Great Derangement*, 17–19.

84. Isiah Lavender (III) and Lisa Yaszek, *Literary Afrofuturism in the Twenty-first Century* (Columbus: Ohio State University Press, 2020).

85. Elizabeth Hope Chang, *Novel Cultivations: Plants in British Literature of the Global Nineteenth Century* (Charlottesville: University of Virginia Press, 2019), 1–2.

86. See the special issue on "climate realism" edited by Lynn Badia, Marija Cetinic, and Jeff Diamanti, *Resilience* 7:2–3 (spring–fall 2020): 1–199; and Sourit Battacharya, *Postcolonial Modernity and the Indian Novel: On Catastrophic Realism* (London: Palgrave Macmillan, 2020).

87. For example, Franco Moretti, *The Bourgeois: Between History and Literature* (London: Verso, 2013), 93.

Chapter 2

1. See Reuben Brower, "Reading in Slow Motion," *In Defense of Reading*, ed. Reuben Brower and Richard Poirier (New York: E. P. Dutton, 1962), 3–21; and Heather Love, "Close Reading and Thin Description." *Public Culture* 25:3 (2013): 401–34.

2. R. P. Blackmur, "A Critic's Job of Work" (1935), in *Language as Gesture* (London: George Allen and Unwin, 1954), 373; Gayatri Chakravorty Spivak, *Death of a Discipline* (New York: Columbia University Press, 2003), 20; Jane Gallop, "The Historicization of Literary Studies and

the Fate of Close Reading," *Profession* 6 (2007): 185; Nan Z. Da, "Disambiguation: A Tragedy," *nplusone* 38 (fall 2020).

3. Catherine Gallagher and Stephen Greenblatt, *Practicing New Historicism* (Chicago: University of Chicago Press, 2011), 6; Gilles Deleuze and Felix Guattari, *Anti-Oedipus: Capitalism and Schizophrenia*, trans. Robert Hurley, Mark Seem, and Helen R. Lane (Minneapolis: University of Minnesota Press, 1983), 315.

4. Janet Todd, *Feminist Literary History* (Cambridge: Polity Press, 1988), 98. See also Adela Pinch, "Recent Studies in the Nineteenth Century," *SEL: Studies in English Literature* 54:4 (autumn 2014): 944.

5. Caroline Levine, *Forms: Whole, Rhythm, Hierarchy, Network* (Princeton: Princeton University Press, 2015), 1–6.

6. Dipesh Chakrabarty, *Provincializing Europe* (Princeton: Princeton University Press, 2000), 8.

7. Jonathan Kramnick and Anahid Nersessian, "Form and Explanation," *Critical Inquiry* 43:3 (spring 2017): 650–69; Langdon Hammer, "Fantastic Forms," *PMLA* 132:5 (2017): 1200–1205; Sandra Macpherson, "The Political Fallacy," *PMLA* 132:5 (2017): 1214–19.

8. Barbara Fuchs, *Knowing Fictions: Picaresque Reading in the Early Modern Hispanic World* (Philadelphia: University of Pennsylvania Press, 2021); Juliana Hu Pegues, *Space Time Colonialism* (Chapel Hill: University of North Carolina Press, 2021), 121; Hongmei Sun, *Transforming Monkey: Adaptation and Representation of a Chinese Epic* (Seattle: University of Washington Press, 2018), 62; Anthony Reed, *Freedom Time: The Poetics and Politics of Black Experimental Writing* (Baltimore: Johns Hopkins University Press, 2014), 109.

9. We find the valuing of excess, flux, and ephemerality all over the aesthetic humanities, from Julia Kristeva's *Revolution in Poetic Language*, trans. Margaret Waller (New York: Columbia University Press, 1984), 79–80, to Rosi Braidotti's *Nomadic Subjects* (New York: Columbia University Press, 2011), 58; Andre Lepecki's *Singularities: Dance in the Age of Performance* (New York: Routledge, 2016), 3; Ramzi Fawaz's "fluxability," in *The New Mutants: Superheroes and the Radical Imagination of American Comics* (New York: New York University Press, 2016); and C. Namwali Serpell's "Weird Times," *PMLA* 132:5 (2017): 1238. Queer theorists have urged us to understand sexuality as "fluid, open ended, constructed" rather than as a set of fixed categories: Ian Barnard, *Queer Race* (New York: Peter Lang, 2008), 10; Gayatri Gopinath, *Unruly Visions: The Aesthetic Practices of Queer Diaspora* (Durham: Duke University Press, 2018). Much affect theory has also been focused on evanescence. See, for example, Gregory J. Seigworth and Melissa Gregg, "An Inventory of Shimmers," in *The Affect Theory Reader* (Durham: Duke University Press, 2010), 1–25. One fascinating exception is Jonathan Flatley's "How a Revolutionary Counter Mood Is Made," *New Literary History* 43:3 (2012): 503–25.

10. Ronjaunee Chatterjee, Alicia Mireles Christoff, and Amy R. Wong, "Undisciplining Victorian Studies," *Victorian Studies* 62:3 (2020): 378.

11. Anna Kornbluh, *The Order of Forms: Realism, Formalism, and Social Space* (Chicago: University of Chicago Press, 2019), 5.

12. Levine, *Forms*. My own definition deliberately departs from the original theorization, which is J. J. Gibson's. I put a much stronger emphasis on material constraint. Paul B. Armstrong is one of several critics who have taken issue with this redefinition. See his *Stories and the Brain: The Neuroscience of Narrative* (Baltimore: Johns Hopkins University Press, 2020), 217.

13. The push against formalism was particularly strong for counterculturalists, including Beat poet Michael McClure, who writes in "Flowers of Politics I": "OH BREAK UP THE FORMS AND FEEL NEW THINGS," in *The New American Poetry, 1945–1960*, ed. Donald Allen (Berkeley: University of California Press, 1960), 349.

14. See Kornbluh, *Order of Forms*, 3–4.

15. Lauren Berlant and Michael Warner, "Sex in Public," in Michael Warner, *Publics and Counterpublics* (New York: Zone Books, 2002), 194.

16. Catriona Mortimer-Sandlands and Bruce Erickson, "A Genealogy of Queer Ecologies," in *Queer Ecologies* (Bloomington: University of Indiana Press, 2010), 13–14.

17. Matthew Flisfeder, "Renewing Humanism against the Anthropocene: Towards a Theory of the Hysterical Sublime," *Postmodern Culture* 32:1 (September 2021), https://doi.org/10.1353/pmc.2021.0012.

18. Min Hyoung Song, *Climate Lyricism* (Durham: Duke University Press, 2022), 3.

19. Barbara Epstein, "The Rise, Decline, and Possible Revival of Socialist Humanism," in *For Humanism*, ed. David Alderson and Robert Spencer (London: Pluto, 2017), 18.

20. Amitav Ghosh, *The Great Derangement: Climate Change and the Unthinkable* (Chicago: University of Chicago Press, 2016), 127.

21. Alex Woloch, *The One v. The Many* (Princeton: Princeton University Press, 2003).

22. Katie Trumpener argues that the female *Bildungsroman* is more collective than the critical tradition has recognized, though the group remains modest in size—a "small sibling or friend group." "Actors, Puppets, *Girls*: Little Women and the Collective *Bildungsroman*," *Textual Practice* 34:12 (2020): 1911–31.

23. Karen A. Keely, "Marriage Plots and National Reunion: The Trope of Romantic Reconciliation in Postbellum Literature," *Mississippi Quarterly* 51:4 (fall 1998): 621–48.

24. Janice Ho, *Nation and Citizenship in the Twentieth-Century British Novel* (Cambridge: Cambridge University Press, 2015), 3.

25. See, for example, Janice Radway, *Reading the Romance* (Chapel Hill: University of North Carolina Press, 1984), 61.

26. See, for example, Elizabeth Maddock Dillon, *New World Drama: The Performative Commons in the Atlantic World, 1649–1849* (Durham: Duke University Press, 2014).

27. Federal Housing Administration, *Underwriting Manual* (Washington: GPO, 1938), part 2, section 9.

28. Anne Mellyn Cassebaum calls this "septic racism" in *Down Along the Haw: The History of a North Carolina River* (Jefferson, NC: McFarland, 2011), 86–87.

29. As Detroit NAACP director Heaster Wheeler explains: "One out of three Detroit households don't own cars and they rely very heavily on public transportation. Unfortunately, our current transportation system does not take you anywhere. You cannot get to the airport, you cannot get to the megamalls on the outskirts of the region." Quoted in Robert D. Bullard, *Growing Smarter: Achieving Livable Communities, Environmental Justice, and Regional Equity* (Cambridge, MA: MIT Press, 2007), 40.

30. Cecilia Rocha and Iara Lessa, "Urban Governance for Food Security: The Alternative Food System in Belo Horizonte, Brazil," *International Planning Studies* 14:4 (2009): 389–400.

31. M. Jahi Chappell, *Beginning to End Hunger: Food and the Environment in Belo Horizonte, Brazil, and Beyond* (Berkeley: University of California Press, 2018).

32. Cecilia Delgado, "Integrating Food Distribution and Food Accessibility into Municipal Planning," in *Integrating Food into Urban Planning*, ed. Yves Cabannes and Cecilia Marocchino (London: UCL Press, 2018), 209–28.

33. Chappell, *Beginning to End Hunger*, 66.

34. M. Jahi Chappell et al., "Participation in a City Food Security Program May Be Linked to Higher Alpha- and Beta-Diversity," *Agroecology and Sustainable Food Systems* 40:8 (2016): 804–29.

35. Cecilia Rocha, quoted in Anita Makri, "How Belo Horizonte's Bid to Tackle Hunger Inspired Other Cities," *Nature*, September 24, 2021, https://www.nature.com/articles/d41586-021-02412-x. One theory for the program's longevity is that it involves different municipal departments, the private sector, and members of key communities, including activists, educators, farmers, and professional organizations, and this broad range of groups has helped to build public trust. Corinna Hawkes and Jess Halliday, "What Makes Urban Food Policy Happen?" *iPES Food* (June 2017): 21–31. Another hypothesis is that the city shifted from providing the most minimal necessities—"poor food for poor people"—to "a consistent preoccupation with 'quality.'" Rocha and Lessa, "Urban Governance for Food Security," 398.

36. Chappell, *Beginning to End Hunger*, 88–89.

37. I am thinking here of Yopie Prins, "Robert Browning, Transported by Meter," in *The Traffic in Poems: Nineteenth-Century Poetry and Transatlantic Exchange*, ed. Meredith L. McGill (New Brunswick, NJ: Rutgers University Press, 2008), 205–30.

38. Danielle Venton, "Mother Nature as Engineer," *Wired*, August 16, 2011, https://www.wired.com/2011/08/biomimicry-gallery/. I make this argument at greater length in "Model Thinking: Generalization, Political Form, and the Common Good," *New Literary History* 48:4 (autumn 2017): 633–53.

39. Nancy Morris, "New Song in Chile," in *The Militant Song Movement in Latin America*, ed. Pablo Vila (Plymouth: Lexington, 2014), 42.

40. Makri, "How Belo Horizonte's Bid to Tackle Hunger Inspired Other Cities."

41. Guy Julier, *Economies of Design* (London: Sage, 2017); Arden Stern and Sami Siegelbaum, eds., "Design and Neoliberalism," a special issue of *Design and Culture* 11:3 (2019).

42. See, for example, Tony Bennett, *Pasts beyond Memory: Evolution, Museums, Colonisation* (London: Routledge, 2004); Steph Schem Rogerson, "I, Mabel Hampton: Political Power and the Archive," *Public* 29:57 (June 2018): 80–87; and Hannah Turner, *Cataloguing Culture: Legacies of Colonialism in Museum Documentation* (Vancouver: University of British Columbia Press, 2020).

43. Frank Wilderson III, *Afro-Pessimism* (New York: Liveright, 2020), 194.

44. Stefano Harney and Fred Moten, *The Undercommons: Fugitive Planning and Black Study* (Brooklyn, NY: Minor Compositions, 2013), 20.

45. Dylan Rodríguez, "Racial/Colonial Genocide and the 'Neoliberal Academy': In Excess of a Problematic," *American Quarterly* 64:4 (December 2012): 812.

46. Nikki Sullivan, *A Critical Introduction to Queer Theory* (New York: New York University Press, 2003), v.

47. Shannon Jackson, *Social Works: Performing Art, Supporting Publics* (New York: Routledge, 2011), 14.

48. Jodi Dean, *Crowds and Party* (London: Verso, 2016); Jackson, *Social Works*; Benjamin Kohlmann, *British Literature and the Life of Institutions: Speculative States* (Oxford: Oxford

University Press, 2021); Lisi Schoenbach, *Pragmatic Modernism* (Oxford: Oxford University Press, 2012); Robyn Wiegman, *Object Lessons* (Durham: Duke University Press, 2012).

49. James G. March and Johan P. Olsen, "Elaborating the 'New Institutionalism,'" in *The Oxford Handbook of Political Institutions*, ed. R.A.W. Rhodes et al. (Oxford: Oxford University Press, 2006), 3.

50. Elaine Gan and Anna Tsing, "How Things Hold: A Diagram of Coordination in a Satoyama Forest," *Social Analysis: The International Journal of Anthropology* 62:4 (December 2018): 103–45.

51. Julian Josephson, "The Promise of Cleaner Coal," *EPA Journal* 11:8 (October 1985), 7–9; Gene T. Harris and Edwin Harre, *World Fertilizer Situation and Outlook, 1978–1985* (March 1979), 38.

52. Rodríguez, "Racial/Colonial Genocide and the 'Neoliberal Academy,'" 811; see also Nathan Snaza and Julietta Singh, "Introduction: Dehumanist Education and the Colonial University," *Social Text* 39:1 (March 2021): 1–19.

53. See J. Jeffrey Williams, "The Need for Critical University Studies," in *A New Deal for the Humanities: Liberal Arts and the Future of Public Higher Education*, ed. Gordon Hutner and Feisal G. Mohamed (New Brunswick, NJ: Rutgers University Press, 2016), 145–57; and Christopher Newfield, *The Great Mistake: How We Wrecked Public Universities and How We Can Fix Them* (Baltimore: Johns Hopkins University Press, 2016).

54. Roderick Ferguson, *The Reorder of Things* (Minneapolis: University of Minnesota Press, 2012), 12.

55. Sociologist Marc Schneiberg theorizes "holdover" forms in "What's on the Path?" *Socio-Economic Review* 5:1 (March 2006): 47–80.

56. Raymond Williams, *Marxism and Literature* (Oxford: Oxford University Press, 1977), 122.

57. https://blacklivesmatter.com/about/what-we-believe/.

58. For a surprising range of thinkers even within the aesthetic humanities, the terms "form" and "structure" are interchangeable. Cleanth Brooks, the quintessential formalist in literary studies, actually uses the term "structure." *The Well-Wrought Urn: Studies in the Structure of Poetry* (New York: Harcourt, 1947).

59. James K. Boyce and Mark Paul, "Making Them Pay," *Jacobin*, December 5, 2016, https://www.jacobinmag.com/2016/12/carbon-pricing-fossil-fuel-climate-environment.

60. David Bush, "The Socialist Case against the Carbon Tax," *Spring*, August 30, 2019, https://springmag.ca/the-socialist-case-against-the-carbon-tax; Jessica F. Green, "It's Time to Abandon Carbon Pricing," *Jacobin*, September 24, 2019, https://jacobinmag.com/2019/09/carbon-pricing-green-new-deal-fossil-fuel-environment.

61. Daniel Vock, "Washington State Rejects What Would Have Been Nation's First Carbon Tax," *Governing*, November 9, 2016, https://www.governing.com/archive/gov-washington-carbon-tax-ballot-measure.html.

62. Jason Margolis, "Sweden's Capital Is on Its Way to Becoming Fossil Free by 2040," *The World*, February 18, 2016, https://www.pri.org/stories/2016-02-18/swedens-capital-its-way-becoming-fossil-fuel-free-2040.

63. Scott Nystrom and Patrick Luckow, "The Economic, Climate, Fiscal, Power, and Demographic Impact of a National Fee-and-Dividend Carbon Tax" (2014): 35, https://11bup83sxdss

1xze1i3lpol4-wpengine.netdna-ssl.com/wp-content/uploads/2018/05/The-Economic-Climate-Fiscal-Power-and-Demographic-Impact-of-a-National-Fee-and-Dividend-Carbon-Tax-5.25.18.pdf.

64. Ibid., 18–19.

65. Caroline Levine, "Building Bridges on Climate Change," *Ithaca Journal*, August 20, 2018, https://www.ithacajournal.com/story/opinion/2018/08/10/turn-building-bridges-climate-change/37096819/.

66. Yale Program on Climate Change Communication, "Americans Are Increasingly 'Alarmed' about Global Warming" (February 2019), https://climatecommunication.yale.edu/publications/americans-are-increasingly-alarmed-about-global-warming/.

67. "The Princeton Review Guide to Green Colleges," https://www.princetonreview.com/press/green-guide/press-release.

68. "Fossil Fuel Divestment: An FAQ for the Cornell Community," February 13, 2020, https://statements.cornell.edu/2020/20200213-fossil-fuel-divestment-faq.cfm.

69. Campus Infrastructure Committee, "White Paper on Divestment" (for resolution passed through university assemblies January–March 2020), https://assembly.cornell.edu/sites/default/files/cic_divestment_white_paper_0.pdf.

70. Tamara Kamis, "Climate Justice Cornell Blocks Statler Crosswalk in Demand for Divestment," *Cornell Daily Sun*, February 19, 2020, https://cornellsun.com/2020/02/19/climate-justice-cornell-blocks-statler-crosswalk-in-demand-for-divestment/; Tamara Kamis, "Climate Justice Cornell Protests Occupy North and South Campus Bridges, Disrupt Traffic," *Cornell Daily Sun*, March 10, 2020, https://cornellsun.com/2020/03/10/climate-justice-cornell-protests-occupy-north-and-south-campus-bridges-disrupt-traffic/.

71. Mihika Badjate, "Students Silently Protest in University Libraries, Demand Divestment from Fossil Fuels," *Cornell Daily Sun*, February 19, 2020, https://cornellsun.com/2020/02/19/students-silently-protest-in-university-libraries-demand-divestment-from-fossil-fuels/; "Fossil Fuel Divestment Day Brings Protestors into the Streets," February 20, 2020, https://cornellsun.com/2020/02/20/fossil-fuel-divestment-day-brings-protestors-into-the-streets/.

72. Emma Dietz, "Cornell University Leads Schools Nationwide in Push for Carbon Neutrality," EESI, March 6, 2017, https://www.eesi.org/articles/view/cornell-university-leads-schools-nationwide-in-push-for-carbon-neutrality.

73. https://sustainablecampus.cornell.edu/about/reports-awards-facts/stars.

74. Bill McKibben, "Money Is the Oxygen on Which the Fire of Global Warning Burns," *New Yorker*, September 17, 2019, https://www.newyorker.com/news/daily-comment/money-is-the-oxygen-on-which-the-fire-of-global-warming-burns.

Chapter 3

1. For example, Ai-Jen Poo, *The Age of Dignity* (New York: New Press, 2015); and U.S. Congress H.R. 1911, Child Care is Infrastructure Act, 117th Cong. (2021–22), https://www.congress.gov/bill/117th-congress/house-bill/1911.

2. AbdouMaliq Simone, "People as Infrastructure: Intersecting Fragments in Johannesburg," *Public Culture* 16:3 (2004): 407–29; David Alff, "Make Way for Infrastructure," *Critical Inquiry* 47 (summer 2021): 626.

3. Susan Leigh Star, "The Ethnography of Infrastructure," *American Behavioral Scientist* 43 (1999): 379.

4. Fonna Forman and Veerabhadran Ramanathan, "Unchecked Climate Change and Mass Migration," in *Humanitarianism and Mass Migration*, ed. Marcelo Suarez-Orozco (Berkeley: University of California Press, 2019), 46.

5. See Elleke Boehmer and Dominic Davies, eds., *Planned Violence Post/Colonial Urban Infrastructure, Literature and Culture* (Houndsmills: Palgrave, 2018); Michelle Kooy and Karen Bakker, "(Post)Colonial Pipes: Urban Water Supply in Colonial and Contemporary Jakarta," in *Cars, Conduits, and Kampongs: The Modernization of the Indonesian City, 1920–1960*, ed. Freek Colombijn and Joost Coté (Leiden: Brill, 2015), 72–75; and Jessica Hurley, *Infrastructures of Apocalypse: American Literature and the Nuclear Complex* (Minneapolis: University of Minnesota Press, 2020).

6. Daniel Nemser, *Infrastructures of Race: Concentration and Biopolitics in Colonial Mexico* (Austin: University of Texas Press, 2017), 20.

7. Rebecca Evans, "Geomemory and Genre Friction: Infrastructural Violence and Plantation Afterlives in Contemporary African American Novels," *American Literature* 93:3 (September 2021): 449.

8. Jessica Hurley and Jeffrey Insko, "Introduction: The Infrastructure of Emergency," *American Literature* 93:3 (2021): 351.

9. Winona LaDuke and Deborah Cowen, "Beyond Wiindigo Infrastructure," *South Atlantic Quarterly* 119:2 (April 2020): 245.

10. Hurley and Insko use this phrase to argue against it. "Introduction," 351.

11. Ricia Chansky, "Mi Maria," *Voices of Witness*, https://voiceofwitness.org/stories-puerto-rico/.

12. Sergio M. Marxuach, *The Threefold Challenge to the Puerto Rican Economy* (San Juan: Center for a New Economy, 2021).

13. Marie T. Mora et al., *Hurricane Maria in Puerto Rico: Disaster, Vulnerability, and Resiliency* (Lanham, MD: Lexington Books, 2021).

14. Antina von Schnitzler, "Infrastructure, Apartheid Technopolitics, and Temporalities of 'Transition,'" in *The Promise of Infrastructure*, ed. Nikhil Anand, Akhil Gupta, and Hannah Appel (Durham: Duke University Press, 2018), 139.

15. Antina von Schnitzler, "Citizenship Prepaid: Water, Calculability, and Techno-Politics in South Africa," *Journal of Southern African Studies* 34:4 (2008): 899–917.

16. Julia Hornberger, "Nocturnal Johannesburg," in *Johannesburg: The Elusive Metropolis*, ed. Sarah Nuttall and Achille Mbembe (Durham: Duke University Press, 2008), 288.

17. Jeremy Seekings, *UDF: History of United Democratic Front in South Africa, 1983–1991* (Athens: Ohio University Press, 2000); Glen Mills, "Space and Power in South Africa: The Township as a Mechanism of Control," *Ekistics* 56:334/335 (1989): 65–74. See also Sarah Gibson, "Railing against Apartheid," in *Mobilities, Literature, Culture*, ed. Marian Aguiar et al. (Cham: Springer, 2019), 35–64.

18. Dean Spade, "Solidarity Not Charity: Mutual Aid for Mobilization and Survival," *Social Text* 38:1 (March 2020): 135.

19. Lydia Sargent, "New Left Women and Men: The Honeymoon Is Over," in *Women and Revolution: A Discussion of the Unhappy Marriage of Marxism and Feminism* (Montreal: Black Rose Books, 1981), ix.

20. Spade, "Solidarity Not Charity."

21. Quoted in Spade, "Solidarity Not Charity," 136.

22. bell hooks, *Feminist Theory: From Margin to Center* (New York: Routledge, 2015), 133–34.

23. Ralph Waldo Emerson, "Circles" (1841), in *Essays and Lectures: Nature, Addresses and Lectures* (New York: Library of America, 1983), 413.

24. Alison Kafer, *Feminist, Queer, Crip* (Bloomington: Indiana University Press, 2013), 15.

25. Friedrich Engels, *The Condition of the Working-Class in England in 1844*, trans. Florence Kelley Wischnewetsky (London: Swan Sonnenschein, 1892), 119.

26. Studs Terkel, *Working* (New York: New Press, 1972), 160.

27. Chin-Ju Tsai, "Boredom at Work and Job Monotony: An Exploratory Case within the Catering Sector," *Human Resource Development Quarterly* 27:2 (summer 2016): 210.

28. Elaine Gan and Anna Tsing, "How Things Hold: A Diagram of Coordination in a Satoyama Forest," *Social Analysis: The International Journal of Anthropology* 62:4 (December 2018): 132.

29. The terms "routine" and "habit" have different genealogies and connotations, but both point us to repetitive actions that sustain everyday life over time. Neurologists and biologists study habit, considering it part of human embodiment—although they recognize that different habits will take shape for humans in different social contexts. Routines are more likely to be studied by sociologists, and associated with the troubling mechanization and standardization of social life in modernity. But it is not always easy to tell these apart. Is falling asleep at night a habit or a routine, or both? I opt for routine in this chapter to put an emphasis on the constructedness—the artifice—of these repetitions.

30. Philomena Essed, *Understanding Everyday Racism* (Newbury Park: Sage, 1991).

31. Lance D. Laird et al., "Looking Islam in the Teeth," *Medical Anthropology Quarterly* 29:3 (2015): 334–56.

32. *About Faces*, U.S. Public Health Service, 1941, https://www.youtube.com/watch?v=uN6V8JKiitQ.

33. Kerry Segrave, *America Brushes Up* (Jefferson, NC: McFarland, 2010), 15–16.

34. Prudence M. Rice, *Maya Calendar Origins: Monuments, Mythohistory, and the Materialization of Time* (Austin: University of Texas Press, 2007), 200, 202.

35. Amory Starr, María Elena Martínez-Torres, and Peter Rosset, "Participatory Democracy in Action: Practices of the Zapatistas and the Movimento Sem Terra," *Latin American Perspectives* 38:1 (January 2011): 105.

36. Richard Lee, "Politics, Sexual and Non-Sexual, in an Egalitarian Society," in *Politics and History in Band Societies* (Cambridge: Cambridge University Press, 1982), 53–54. This is now old work, but Lee's argument that egalitarianism takes regular effort is still garnering praise from anthropologists. Jacqueline Solway, *The Politics of Egalitarianism: Theory and Practice* (New York: Berghahn Books, 2006), 1.

37. William James, *Habit* (New York: Henry Holt, 1914), 51.

38. William James, *The Principles of Psychology*, vol. 1 (New York: Henry Holt, 1905), 122.

39. James, *Principles of Psychology*, 122.

40. See Reiner Stach, *Kafka: The Decisive Years* (Princeton: Princeton University Press, 2013), 116.

41. Toni Morrison, "The Art of Fiction No. 134," interviewed by Elissa Schappell, *The Paris Review* 128 (fall 1993).

42. Claudia Tate, "Conversations with Maya Angelou," interview conducted in 1983 and published in 1989: http://aas.princeton.edu/publication/conversations-with-maya-angelou/.

43. A. Joan Saab, *For the Millions: American Art and Culture between the Wars* (Philadelphia: University of Pennsylvania Press, 2004), 40–41.

44. Laura Hapke, *Labor's Canvas: American Working-Class History and the WPA Art of the 1930s* (Newcastle: Cambridge Scholars, 2008), 3.

45. Nicholas Xavier, "Interview with Jacob Lawrence, *Callaloo* 36:2 (spring 2013): 260–67, 507.

46. Thadious Davis, "Becoming: Richard Wright and the WPA," *The Black Scholar* 39 (summer 2009): 11–16.

47. Robert Nozick, *Anarchy, State and Utopia* (New York: Basic Books, 1974), 172.

48. Theodore Brainard Terry, *Our Farming* (Philadelphia: The Farmer Company, 1893), 335.

49. Adekami O. Suleiman et al., "Worker Perspectives on the Impact of Non-Standard Workdays on Worker and Family Well-Being," *BMC Public Health* 21:2230 (December 2021): 1.

50. Benjamin H. Snyder, *The Disrupted Workplace* (Oxford: Oxford University Press, 2016), 7.

51. Guy Standing, *The Precariat: The Dangerous New Class* (London: Bloomsbury, 2016), 141–47.

52. As one female corrections officer says: "You miss out on so much. . . . Your family events . . . holidays. . . . You feel like—you're a bad mom. You're a bad friend. You're a bad family member because you can't be there for a lot of people's things." See Suleiman et al., "Worker Perspectives," 5.

53. Jaeseung Kim et al., "Workplace Flexibility and Worker Well-Being by Gender," *Journal of Marriage and Family* 82 (June 2020): 892–910.

54. Susan J. Lambert, "When Flexibility Hurts," *New York Times*, September 19, 2012, https://www.nytimes.com/2012/09/20/opinion/low-paid-women-want-predictable-hours-and-steady-pay.html.

55. See Richard Sennett, *The Corrosion of Character: The Personal Consequences of Work in the New Capitalism* (New York: W. W. Norton, 1998), 23; and Snyder, *Disrupted Workplace.*

56. Tsai, "Boredom at Work and Job Monotony," 220–21.

57. Terkel, *Working*, 30.

58. William H. Form, "Auto Workers and Their Machines: A Study of Work, Factory, and Job Satisfaction in Four Countries," *Social Forces* 52:1 (September 1, 1973): 4, 12.

59. Jim Hale, "On Writing: When Typewriters Roamed the Earth," *Juneau Empire*, December 25, 2014.

60. Alix Kates Shulman, *Drinking the Rain: A Memoir* (New York: Farrar, Straus and Giroux, 1995), 183–84.

61. Mary Weismantel, foreword to *Kitchenspace: Women, Fiestas, and Everyday Life in Central Mexico*, by Maria Elisa Christie (Austin: University of Texas Press, 2009), xiv.

62. Barbara Garson, *All the Livelong Day: The Meaning and Demeaning of Routine Work* (New York: Doubleday, 1975), 27.

63. Stephanie Wakefield, "Infrastructures of Liberal Life: From Modernity and Progress to Resilience and Ruins," *Geography Compass* 12:7 (2018): 8; Paul N. Edwards, "Infrastructure and Modernity," in *Modernity and Technology*, ed. Thomas J. Misa, Philip Brey, and Andrew Feenberg (Cambridge, MA: MIT Press, 2003), 191. For architectural historian Swati Chattopadhyay (*Unlearning the City: Infrastructure in a New Optical Field* [Minneapolis: University of Minnesota Press, 2012]), "infrastructure is the central trope of modern urban thought" (x).

64. Yuri Gorokhovich, Larry Mays, and Lee Ullmann, "A Survey of Ancient Minoan Water Technologies," *Water Supply* 11:4 (2011): 388–99.

65. James A. O'Kon, "Computer Modeling of the Seventh Century Maya Suspension Bridge at Yaxchilan," *Proceedings of the 2005 ASCE International Conference on Computing in Civil Engineering*, 1307–20.

66. Tricia Toso, "'Keeping the Road Clear between Us': Indigenous Infrastructure and the Potential for Transformative Design," *Stream: Inspiring Critical Thought* 10:1 (2018): 14.

67. Sam Markwell, "The Colonial Hydropolitics of Infrastructure in the Middle Rio Grande Valley," *Wiley Interdisciplinary Reviews: Water* (March 2015): 426.

68. Markwell, "Colonial Hydropolitics," 427.

69. Markwell, "Colonial Hydropolitics," 427–28; for a similar story in Namibia, see Emmanuel Kreike, *Environmental Infrastructure in African History* (Cambridge: Cambridge University Press, 2013), 204.

70. Jules Law, *The Social Life of Fluids* (Ithaca: Cornell University Press, 2010), 49–52; Brian Larkin, *Signal and Noise: Media, Infrastructure, and Urban Culture in Nigeria* (Durham: Duke University Press, 2008), 17.

71. A few scholars have recently been drawing attention to the duration of infrastructures across long periods, including Maren Loveland, "The Aesthetics of Water Reclamation: Cinema and the Irrigated West," in *Resilience: A Journal of the Environmental Humanities* 8:3 (fall 2021): 40–70; and Evans, "Geomemory and Genre Friction."

72. Susan Leigh Star, "This Is Not a Boundary Object," *Science, Technology, and Human Values* 35:5 (2010): 611.

73. My thanks to Del Maticic for filling out my understanding of this inscription. See Edmund Thomas, *Monumentality in the Roman Empire: Architecture in the Antonine Age* (Oxford: Oxford University Press, 2007), 203.

74. Laine Kaplan-Levenson, "'The Monster': Claiborne Avenue before and after the Interstate," in *Tripod: New Orleans at 300*, May 5, 2016, podcast, https://www.wwno.org/podcast/tripod-new-orleans-at-300/2016-05-05/the-monster-claiborne-avenue-before-and-after-the-interstate.

75. See Robert Bullard et al., eds., *Highway Robbery: Transportation Racism and New Routes to Equity* (Cambridge, MA: South End Press, 2004), 4.

76. Regan F. Patterson and Robert A. Harley, "Effects of Freeway Rerouting and Boulevard Replacement on Air Pollution Exposure and Neighborhood Attributes," *International Journal of Environmental Research and Public Health* 21 (2019): 4072.

77. Quoted in Kate McAlpine, "Transportation Is a Form of Freedom," *University of Michigan News*, April 22, 2021, https://news.engin.umich.edu/2021/06/transportation-is-a-form-of-freedom-how-to-make-it-more-equitable/. The uneven distribution of pathways organizing many cities has given rise to movements for "transportation justice," which focus on the intertwining of environmental and social equity. See, for example, Kafui Ablode Attoh, *Rights in Transit: Public Transportation and the Right to the City in California's East Bay* (Athens: University of Georgia Press, 2019).

78. Julie Cidell, *An Introduction to Transportation Geography: Transport, Mobility, and Place* (Lanham, MD: Rowman and Littlefield, 2021), 165–66.

79. Myung-Rae Cho, "The Politics of Urban Nature Restoration," *International Development Planning Review* 32:2 (April 2010): 145–65; Jong Youl Lee and Chad David Anderson, "The Restored Cheonggyecheon and the Quality of Life in Seoul," *Journal of Urban Technology* 20:4 (2013): 3–22.

80. Judith Dellheim and Jason Prince, eds., *Free Public Transit: And Why We Don't Pay to Ride Elevators* (Montreal: Black Rose Books, 2018), 29–56.

81. John D. Nelson and Steve Wright, "Flexible Transport Services," in *The Routledge Handbook of Public Transport*, ed. Corinne Mulley, John D. Nelson, and Stephen Ison (New York: Routledge, 2021), 224–35.

82. Jarrett Walker, *Human Transit: How Clearer Thinking about Public Transit Can Enrich Our Communities and Our Lives* (Washington, DC: Island Press, 2012), 85.

83. https://www.cnu.org/publicsquare/2019/04/09/time-restore-grid.

84. Manfred Hafner and Simone Tagliapietra, eds., *The Geopolitics of the Global Energy Transition* (Cham: Springer Open, 2020).

85. Vijaya Ramachandran, "Blanket Bans on Fossil Fuels Will Entrench Poverty," *Nature* 592 (April 20, 2021).

86. Debajit Palit et al., "Energising Rural India Using Distributed Generation," *Green Energy and Technology* (May 2014): 1–12. See also Jonathan Cloke et al., "Imagining Renewable Energy," *Energy Research and Social Science* 31 (September 2017): 269.

87. See David McDermott Hughes, *Who Owns the Wind?* (London: Verso, 2021).

88. Catherine Hausman and Lucija Muelenbachs, "Price Regulation and Environmental Externalities: Evidence from Methane Leaks," *Journal of the Association of Environmental and Resource Economists* 6:1 (January 2019): 73–109.

89. Stefano Harney and Fred Moten, *The Undercommons: Fugitive Planning and Black Study* (Brooklyn, NY: Minor Compositions, 2013), 18.

90. Richard D. Kahlenberg, "How Minneapolis Ended Single-Family Zoning," *Century Foundation Report*, October 24, 2019, https://tcf.org/content/report/minneapolis-ended-single-family-zoning/?agreed=1.

91. Setha Low, *Behind the Gates: Life, Security, and the Pursuit of Happiness in Fortress America* (New York: Routledge, 2003).

92. Chaitawat Boonjubun, "Also the Urban Poor Live in Gated Communities: A Bangkok Case Study," *Social Sciences* 8:7 (July 2019): 219–35.

93. G. L. Ream and N. Forge, "Homeless Lesbian, Gay, Bisexual, and Transgender (LGBT) Youth in New York City: Insights from the Field," *Child Welfare* 93:2 (2014): 7–22; Deborah Coolhart and Maria T. Brown, "The Need for Safe Spaces: Exploring the Experiences of Homeless LGBTQ Youth in Shelters," *Children and Youth Services Review* 82 (November 2017): 230–38.

94. Scott Lucas, "A Green House Divided," *San Francisco Magazine*, April 17, 2018.

95. Estimates vary widely, but a 2021 report from the World Bank projects that over 143 million people just in sub-Saharan Africa, Latin America, and South Asia will be forced to migrate by 2050. Kanta Kumari Rigaud et al., *Operational Experiences and Lessons Learned at the Climate Migration Development* (Washington, DC: World Bank, 2021).

96. Abrahm Lustgarten, "The Great Climate Migration," *New York Times Magazine*, July 23, 2020, https://www.nytimes.com/interactive/2020/07/23/magazine/climate-migration.html.

97. Susan Fraiman, *Extreme Domesticity: A View from the Margins* (New York: Columbia University Press, 2017), 39.

98. Fraiman, *Extreme Domesticity*, 41.

99. Edward Goetz, *New Deal Ruins: Race, Economic Justice, and Public Housing Policy* (Ithaca: Cornell University Press, 2013); Nicholas Dagen Bloom, Fritz Umbach, and Lawrence J. Vale, eds., *Public Housing Myths: Perception, Reality, and Social Policy* (Ithaca: Cornell University Press, 2015).

100. Gautam Bhan, "Notes on a Southern Urban Practice," *Environment and Urbanization* 3:2 (2019): 639–54.

101. Precarious shelter, of course, is not exclusively a human problem. Vast numbers of species worldwide are now facing the disruption or total loss of their habitats.

102. Importantly, what threatens to shut down this program is not its price or its success rate but a relative lack of public support. Deborah Padgett, Benjamin F. Henwood, and Sam J. Tsemberis, *Housing First: Ending Homelessness, Transforming Systems, and Changing Lives* (Oxford: Oxford University Press, 2016), 58.

103. Lawrence J. Vale, *Reclaiming Public Housing* (Cambridge, MA: Harvard University Press, 2002), 279–361.

104. G. J. Coates, "The Sustainable Urban District of Vauban," *International Journal of Design and Nature and Ecodynamics* 8:4 (2013): 265–86.

105. Coates, "The Sustainable Urban District of Vauban," 278.

106. Coates, "The Sustainable Urban District of Vauban," 269.

107. Jonas Rabinovitch, "Curitiba: Toward Sustainable Urban Development," *Environment and Urbanization* 4:2 (October 1992): 62–73.

108. Nicole Mikesh, "Curitiba: People-Centric Planning on a Budget," *ICELI*, https://depts.washington.edu/open2100/Resources/1OpenSpaceSystems/OpenSpaceSystems/Curitiba%20Case%20Study.pdf.

109. Hiroaki Suzuki et al., *Eco2 Cities* (Washington, DC: World Bank, 2010), 173.

110. Peter Rosset et al., "The *Campesino*-to-*Campesino* Agroecology Movement of ANAP in Cuba," *Journal of Peasant Studies* 38:1 (January 2011): 161–91.

111. "After 3-Year Delay, Government Releases Farmer Suicide Data," *The Wire*, November 8, 2019, https://thewire.in/agriculture/farmer-suicides-data.

112. http://indianricecampaign.org/event/view/Nel-Thiruvizha-2019-53393685.

113. Ashlesha Khadse and Peter M. Rosset, "Zero Budget Natural Farming in India: From Inception to Institutionalization," *Agroecology and Sustainable Food Systems* 43:7–8 (April 2019): 848–71.

114. See Divya Veluguri et al., "Political Analysis of the Adoption of the Zero-Budget Natural Farming Program in Andhra Pradesh, India," *Agroecology and Sustainable Food Systems* 45:6 (2021): 907–30.

115. Norman Uphoff, "Systems Thinking on Intensification and Sustainability," *Current Opinion in Environmental Sustainability* 8 (October 2014): 89–100.

116. Paul Hawken, *Drawdown* (New York: Penguin, 2017), 49.

117. Judith A. Carney, *Black Rice: The African Origins of Rice Cultivation in the Americas* (Cambridge, MA: Harvard University Press, 2011).

118. Susie Protschky, "The Empire Illuminated," *Journal of Colonialism and Colonial History* 13:3 (2012).

119. Sandy Isenstadt, *Electric Light: An Architectural History* (Cambridge, MA: MIT Press, 2018), 15.

120. Antoine Halff et al., *Energy Poverty: Global Challenges and Local Solutions* (Oxford: Oxford University Press, 2014), 61, 64, 73, 284.

121. https://littlesun.org/stories/.

122. Jerry Farrell, "Promoting Literacy and Protection with Solar Lamps in Yemen," *Stability* 3:1 (2014): 1–7; Michelle Dynes et al., "Handheld Solar Light Use, Durability, and Retention among Women and Girls in Internally Displaced Persons Camps in Haiti, 2013–2014," *International Journal of Disaster Risk Reduction* 18 (September 2016): 162–70.

123. Lupin Rahman and Vijayendra Rao, "The Determinants of Gender Equity in India: Examining Dyson and Moore's Thesis with New Data," *Population and Development Review* 30:2 (June 2004): 254. The authors warn that the effects may be more correlation than cause.

124. Hawken, *Drawdown*, 80–82.

125. Jaime Lerner, "Cities, Agency and Change," *Perspecta* 45 (2012): 42–43.

126. Aleksandra Pluta, "Jaime Lerner," *Culture.PL* (June 2015), https://culture.pl/en/artist/jaime-lerner.

Chapter 4

1. Rob Nixon, *Slow Violence and the Environmentalism of the Poor* (Cambridge, MA: Harvard University Press, 2011), 2.

2. John Oliver, "Last Week Tonight," *HBO*, March 2, 2015.

3. Susan Leigh Star, "The Ethnography of Infrastructure," *American Behavioral Scientist* 43 (1999): 380.

4. Stephen Graham, Simon Marvin, *Splintering Urbanism: Networked Infrastructures, Technological Mobilities* (London: Routledge, 2001), 47.

5. David Sneath, "Reading the Signs by Lenin's Light: Development, Divination and Metonymic Fields in Mongolia," *Ethnos* 74:1 (2009): 72–90.

6. Nikhil Anand, Akhil Gupta, and Hannah Appel, eds., *The Promise of Infrastructure* (Durham: Duke University Press, 2018), 11. See also David Alff, "Make Way for Infrastructure," *Critical Inquiry* 47 (summer 2021): 625–43.

7. Lauren Berlant, "The Commons: Infrastructures for Troubling Times," *Society and Space* 34:3 (2016): 403.

8. AbdouMaliq Simone, "People as Infrastructure: Intersecting Fragments in Johannesburg," *Public Culture* 16:3 (2004): 407–29.

9. Casper Bruun Jensen, "Pipe Dreams: Sewage Infrastructure and Activity Trails in Phnom Penh," *Ethnos* 82:4 (2017): 629.

10. Anand, Gupta, and Appel, *Promise of Infrastructure*, 16–17.

11. Theo Reeves-Evison writes that it is the "disposition" of infrastructure to "downplay its powerful role in orchestrating activities that typically gain more attention than the infrastructure itself." "The Art of Disciplined Imagination: Prediction, Scenarios, and Other Speculative Infrastructures," *Critical Inquiry* 47 (summer 2021): 721.

12. Some examples include the collapse of highway bridges, like one over the Mississippi River in Minneapolis in 2007, and one in Genoa, Italy, in 2018; aging electrical grids across the

United States and Europe; and the struggles of the fifty-year-old Takasago Thermal Power Plant in Japan.

13. Nicole Starosielski, *The Undersea Network* (Durham: Duke University Press, 2015).

14. Brian Larkin, "The Politics and Poetics of Infrastructure," *Annual Review of Anthropology* 42 (2013): 329.

15. Percy Shelley, "A Defence of Poetry" (1821), in *The Prose Works*, vol. 3, ed. Harry Buxton Forman (London: Reeves and Turner, 1880), 139.

16. Viktor Shklovsky, "Art as Technique" (1917), in *Russian Formalist Criticism: Four Essays*, trans. Lee T. Lemon and Marion J. Reis (Lincoln: University of Nebraska Press, 1965), 3–24.

17. John Dewey, *Art as Experience* (New York: Perigree, 1980), 104.

18. Quoted in David Maclagan, *Outsider Art: From the Margins to the Marketplace* (London: Reaktion, 2009), 49.

19. Theodor Adorno and Max Horkheimer, "The Culture Industry: Enlightenment as Mass Deception" (1944), in *Dialectic of Enlightenment*, trans. Edmund Jephcott (Stanford: Stanford University Press, 2002), 94.

20. Elaine Auyong, *When Fiction Feels Real* (Oxford: Oxford University Press, 2018), 36. Liesl Olson makes a powerful case for the overlooked role of the ordinary in Modernism. *Modernism and the Ordinary* (Oxford: Oxford University Press, 2009), 6.

21. Derek Attridge, *The Singularity of Literature* (New York: Routledge, 2004), 2.

22. Quoted in Katie Hagan, "Art Needs to Disrupt People's Daily Routines," *Dance Art Journal*, August 7, 2019, https://danceartjournal.com/2019/08/07/art-needs-to-disrupt-peoples-daily-routines-an-interview-with-alka-nauman/.

23. Fred Moten, *Black and Blur* (Durham: Duke University Press, 2017), 3.

24. Carolyn Lesjak, *Working Fictions* (Durham: Duke University Press, 2006), 2.

25. Catherine Gallagher, *The Industrial Reformation of English Fiction* (Chicago: University of Chicago Press, 1988); Lesjak, *Working Fictions*.

26. Stewart O'Nan's 2008 novel, *Last Night at the Lobster* (New York: Penguin, 2007), opts for a similar strategy, though in a kind of neat chronological reversal of Zola. The novel tells the story of the last day at work for the manager of a Red Lobster chain restaurant. Even *Jeanne Diehlman* (dir. Chantal Ackerman, 1975), a film that lingers on the repetitive routines of housekeeping, shows us a single day, implying that many of the same actions recur every day for the protagonist.

27. Gerard Genette, *Narrative Discourse*, trans. Jane Lewin (Ithaca: Cornell University Press, 1980). 116.

28. Elaine Scarry, *Resisting Representation* (Oxford: Oxford University Press, 1994), 68.

29. Thomas Hood, "Song of the Shirt," *Punch* (London, December 1843).

30. Susan P. Casteras, "'Weary Stitches': Illustrations and Paintings for Thomas Hood's 'Song of the Shirt' and Other Poems," in *Famine and Fashion: Needlewomen in the Nineteenth Century*, ed. Beth Harris (Abingdon: Ashgate, 2005), 21.

31. Elizabeth Barrett Browning, "The Cry of the Children" (1844); Caroline Norton, "The Voice from the Factories" (1836); and William Morris, "The Voice of Toil" (1884).

32. Christina Rossetti, *Complete Poems*, ed. Betty S. Flowers (Harmondsworth: Penguin, 1990), 10.

33. Friedrich Engels argues that traditional farmworkers in England "were comfortable in their silent vegetation, and but for the industrial revolution they would never have emerged

from this existence, which, cosily romantic as it was, was nevertheless not worthy of human beings." *The Condition of the Working-Class in England in 1844*, trans. Florence Kelley Wischnewetzky (London: Swan Sonnenschein, 1892), 3.

34. Casteras, "'Weary Stitches,'" 21.

35. Keith Jones, "Music in Factories," *Social and Cultural Geography* 6:5 (2005): 723–44.

36. Joel Dinerstein, *Swinging the Machine: Modernity, Technology, and African American Culture between the Two World Wars* (Amherst: University of Massachusetts Press, 2003), 6.

37. Michael Pickering, Emma Robertson, and Mark Korczynski, "Rhythms of Labour: The British Work Song Revisited," *Folk Music Journal* 9:2 (2007): 231.

38. Marek Korczynski, *Songs of the Factory: Pop Music, Culture, and Resistance* (Ithaca: Cornell University Press, 2015), 64–65.

39. Sam Cooke, "Chain Gang" (RCA Studio, 1960).

40. Cooke's deictics, which refer to "this" sound and the need for now to work "right here," pointedly fuse or conflate the repetitive rhythms of music and dance with the routinized work rhythm the singer longs to leave, as if they were indistinguishable.

41. As Theodor Adorno famously does: "All 'light' and pleasant art has become illusory and mendacious." "The Fetish Character of Music and the Regression of Listening," in *The Essential Frankfurt School Reader*, ed. Andrew Arata and Eike Gebhardt (New York: Continuum, 1985), 274.

42. Thomas C. Jones and Robert Tombs, "The French Left in Exile," in *A History of the French in London*, ed. Debra Kelly and Martyn Cornick (London: Institute for Historical Research, 2013), 186.

43. Carolyn Christensen Nelson, ed., *Literature of the Women's Suffrage Campaign in England* (Plymouth: Broadview, 2004), 170–71.

44. Richard Taruskin, *Russian Music at Home and Abroad* (Oakland: University of California Press, 2016), 244–45; *Reds* (1981), dir. Warren Beatty; Tony Babino, closing credits of *Capitalism: A Love Story* (2009), dir. Michael Moore.

45. Peter Höyng, "'The Gospel of World Harmony'; or, Beethoven's Transformation of Schiller's 'An die Freude' into World Music Literature," *Modern Language Quarterly* 74:2 (2013): 261–76.

46. Quoted in Greg Mitchell, "Tiananmen Square Massacre: How Beethoven Rallied the Students," Billmoyers.com, November 14, 2013, http://billmoyers.com/content/tiananmen-square-massacre-how-beethoven-rallied-the-students/.

47. Aisha Francis, "Lift Every Voice and Sing," *Encyclopedia of Black Studies*, ed. Molefi Kete Asante and Ama Mazama (London: Sage, 2005), 309–12.

48. Francis, "Lift Every Voice," 311.

49. John Kennedy, "Kendrick Lamar's 'Alright' Should Be the New Black National Anthem," *BET*, March 31, 2015, https://www.bet.com/news/music/2015/03/30/kendrick-lamar-alright-new-black-national-anthem.html.

50. Jamilah King, "The Improbable Story of How Kendrick Lamar's 'Alright' Became a Protest Anthem," *MIC*, February 11, 2016, https://www.mic.com/articles/134764/the-improbable-story-of-how-kendrick-lamar-s-alright-became-a-protest-anthem.

51. Joe Coscarelli, "Kendrick Lamar on the Grammys," *New York Times*, December 29, 2015, https://www.nytimes.com/2016/01/03/arts/music/kendrick-lamar-on-a-year-of-knowing-what-matters.html?r=0.

52. Gotthold Ephraim Lessing, *Laokoon* (1767), trans. E. C. Beasley (London: George Bell, 1888), 111.

53. Norman Bryson, *Vision and Painting: The Logic of the Gaze* (New Haven: Yale University Press, 1983), 94. See also Susie Protschky, *Images of the Tropics: Environment and Visual Culture in Colonial Indonesia* (Leiden: Brill, 2011), 82.

54. Barbara Haskell, *Vida Americana: Mexican Muralists Remake American Art, 1925–1945* (New York: Whitney Museum, 2020), 20.

55. Bartholomew Ryan, "Manifesto for Maintenance: A Conversation with Mierle Laderman Ukeles," *Art in America*, March 18, 2009, https://www.artinamericamagazine.com/news-features/interviews/draft-mierle-interview/.

56. Mierle Laderman Ukeles, "Manifesto for Maintenance Art" (1969), *The Act* 2:1 (1990), 84–85; also available at the Queens Museum website: https://queensmuseum.org/wp-content/uploads/2016/04/Ukel:s-Manifesto-for-Maintenance-Art-1969.pdf.

57. Ukeles, "Manifesto."

58. Randy Kennedy, "An Artist Who Calls the Sanitation Department Home," *New York Times*, September 21, 2016, https://www.nytimes.com/2016/09/22/arts/design/mierle-laderman-ukeles-new-york-city-sanitation-department.html and https://www.brooklynmuseum.org/eascfa/feminist_art_base/mierle-laderman-ukeles; Patricia Phillips, Tom Finkelpearl, and Larissa Harris, *Mierle Laderman Ukeles: Maintenance Art* (London: Prestel, 2016).

59. Ukeles, "Manifesto."

60. Eugene Anderson, *Caring for Place: Ecology, Ideology, Emotion* (London: Routledge, 2014), 17.

61. These are the words of Karuk Ceremonial Leader and Director of the Department of Natural Resources Leaf Hillman, in Kari Marie Norgaard, "Karuk Traditional Ecological Knowledge and the Need for Knowledge Sovereignty" (Karuk Department of Natural Resources, 2014), 16, https://cpb-us-e1.wpmucdn.com/blogs.uoregon.edu/dist/c/389/files/2010/11/Final-pt-1-KARUK-TEK-AND-THE-NEED-FOR-KNOWLEDGE-SOVEREIGNTY-1phd94j.pdf.

62. Anne-Christine Hornborg, "Protecting Earth? Rappaport's Vision of Rituals as Environmental Practices," *Journal of Human Ecology* 23:4 (2008): 275–83.

63. YiShan Lea, "The Praxis of Cultural Sustainability: A Q'eqchi' Maya Case of Cultural Autonomy and Resistance against the Monsanto Law in Guatemala," *Theory in Action* 11:4 (October 2018): 44–73.

64. Leah Namugerwa, "School Strike for the Climate," June 6, 2019, https://www.earthday.org/2019/06/06/school-strike-for-climate-a-day-in-the-life-of-fridays-for-future-uganda-student-striker-leah-namugerwa/.

65. In 2014, Delaney Parish estimated that "77 percent of infrastructure workers are involved with operating infrastructure, compared to only 15 percent with construction." "14.2 Million Americans Work in Infrastructure. What Does That Mean?" *Brookings Now*, May 12, 2014, https://www.brookings.edu/blog/brookings-now/2014/05/12/14-2-million-americans-work-in-infrastructure-what-does-that-mean/.

66. Shklovksy, "Art as Technique," 12.

67. Rita Felski, "Introduction: Everyday Life," *New Literary History* 33:4 (2002): 608.

68. Franco Moretti, *The Bourgeois: Between History and Literature* (London: Verso, 2013), 93.

69. Min Hyoung Song makes a similar case for lyric, poems which "demand attunement to the everyday in original and often estranging ways." *Climate Lyricism* (Durham: Duke University Press, 2022), 5.

70. George Eliot, *Middlemarch* (1871–72) (Harmondsworth: Penguin, 1994), 194.

71. Charles Dickens, *Bleak House* (1853–54) (Oxford: World's Classics, 1996), 668.

72. Dickens, *Bleak House*, 572.

73. Chimimanda Ngozi Adichie, *Americanah* (New York: Anchor, 2014), 94. I will simply refer to page numbers from this edition for the rest of this section.

74. Kohlmann is paraphrasing Tony Judt here: *British Literature and the Life of Institutions: Speculative States* (Oxford: Oxford University Press, 2021), 5.

75. *Call the Midwife*, season 1, episode 1, dir. Philippa Lowthorpe (January 15, 2012).

76. Frank Prochaska, *Christianity and Social Service in Modern Britain: The Disinherited Spirit* (Oxford: Oxford University Press, 2006), 128, 139.

77. *Call the Midwife*, season 1, episode 5, dir. Jamie Payne (February 12, 2012).

78. *Call the Midwife*, season 1, episode 5.

79. For recent scholarship on the political affordances of serial forms, see Derrick R. Spires, "Sketching Black Citizenship on Installment after the Fifteenth Amendment," in *African-American Literature in Transition, 1865–1880*, ed. Eric Gardner (Cambridge: Cambridge University Press, 2021); and Clare Pettitt, *Serial Forms: The Unfinished Project of Modernity, 1815–1848* (Oxford: Oxford University Press, 2020).

80. Susan Fraiman, *Extreme Domesticity: A View from the Margins* (New York: Columbia University Press, 2017), 50.

81. Roland Barthes, *The Pleasure of the Text*, trans. Richard Miller (New York: Noonday, 1975); Terry Eagleton, *Myths of Power* (London: Macmillan, 1975); D. A. Miller, *The Novel and the Police* (Oakland: University of California Press, 1988); Ronald R. Thomas, *Detective Fiction and the Rise of Forensic Science* (Cambridge: Cambridge University Press, 1999); Jared Sexton, "The Social Life of Social Death: On Afro-Pessimism and Black Optimism," *Tensions Journal* 5 (2011): 31; Valerie Rohy, "Queer Narrative Theory," in *The Cambridge Companion to Narrative Theory*, ed. Matthew Garrett (Cambridge: Cambridge University Press, 2018), 169–82.

82. Hillary Chute, *Why Comics? From Underground to Everywhere* (New York: Harper Collins, 2017), 25.

83. Ramzi Fawaz, "A Queer Sequence: Comics as a Disruptive Medium," *PMLA* 143:3 (2019): 593.

84. Tyler Bradway, "Queer Narrative Theory and the Relationality of Form," *PMLA* 136:5 (October 2021): 711–27.

85. Pettitt, *Serial Forms*; Spires, "Sketching Black Citizenship on Installment after the Fifteenth Amendment," 36.

86. As James MacDowell argues, we have so readily assumed the intelligibility and predictability of happy endings that we have not spent enough time understanding their range and how they work. *Happy Endings in Hollywood Cinema* (Edinburgh: Edinburgh University Press, 2013).

87. D. A. Miller, *Narrative and Its Discontents* (Princeton: Princeton University Press, 1981), 265.

88. Michael Parrish Lee, *The Food Plot in the Nineteenth-Century British Novel* (London: Palgrave Macmillan, 2016).

89. Charles Dickens, *Oliver Twist* (1838) (Oxford: Oxford World's Classics, 1986), 14.

90. Dickens, *Oliver Twist*, 253.

91. George Moore, *Esther Waters* (1894) (Oxford: Oxford World's Classics, 2012), 322, 324.

92. Moore, *Esther Waters*, 325.

93. Matthew Desmond, *Evicted: Poverty and Profit in the American City* (New York: Crown, 2016), 267. Hereafter I will refer to page numbers from this edition.

94. Terry Eagleton, building on Yuri Lotman, brings together rhyme, rhythm, metaphor, and syntax as repetitive systems that create "a background against which their differences become all the more perceptible." *How to Read a Poem* (Malden, MA: Blackwell, 2007), 54. Brian Cheadle argues that "the critic's most important task" may be "to attend afresh to those 'pleasant surprises' which unendingly afford the pleasure Ashbery called happiness." "*Four Quartets*: Structure and Surprise," *Cambridge Quarterly* 44:3 (September 2015): 233–50.

95. Rachel Sagner Buurma and Laura Heffernan, *The Teaching Archive: A New History for Literary Study* (Chicago: University of Chicago Press, 2020), 183, 194; Simon J. Ortiz, "Towards a National Indian Literature: Cultural Authenticity in Nationalism," *MELUS* 8:2 (summer 1981): 8. For the difficulty of incorporating orature into conventional literary histories, see also my essay, "The Great Unwritten: World Literature and the Effacement of Orality," *MLQ* 74:2 (June 2013): 217–37.

96. Kenneth Burke, *The Philosophy of Literary Form* (Berkeley: University of California Press, 1973), 296.

97. Julia Reinhard Lupton, *Shakespeare Dwelling: Designs for the Theater of Life* (Chicago: University of Chicago Press, 2018).

98. Mike Goode, *Romantic Capabilities: Blake, Scott, Austen, and the New Messages of Old Media* (Oxford: Oxford University Press, 2020).

99. Alenda Y. Chang, *Playing Nature: Ecology in Video Games* (Minneapolis: University of Minnesota Press, 2019), 26.

100. Caroline Levine, *Forms: Whole, Rhythm, Hierarchy, Network* (Princeton: Princeton University Press, 2015), 110–11; Caroline Levine, "Model Thinking: Generalization, Political Form, and the Common Good," *New Literary History* 48:4 (autumn 2017): 633–53.

101. Robyn R. Warhol, "Making 'Gay' and 'Lesbian' into Household Words: How Serial Form Works in Armistead Maupin's 'Tales of the City,'" *Contemporary Literature* 40:3 (autumn 1999): 378–402.

102. Laura Miller, "My *Tales of the City*," *Slate*, June 13, 2019, https://slate.com/culture/2019/06/netflix-tales-city-maupin-review.html.

103. Daniel Allington et al., *The Book in Britain: A Historical Introduction* (Oxford: Wiley Blackwell, 2019), 306–7.

104. The classic source is Wolfgang Schivelbusch, *The Railway Journey* (Berkeley: University of California Press, 1977), 31, 67.

105. Meidad Kissinger and Ariel Reznik, "Detailed Urban Analysis of Commute-Related GHG Emissions to Guide Urban Mitigation Measures," *Environmental Impact Assessment Review* 76 (May 2019): 26–35.

106. Alisa Freedman, *Tokyo in Transit* (Stanford: Stanford University Press, 2011), 13–14.

107. Michael Kimmelman, "Home Is Where the Art Is," *New York Times*, December 17, 2006, https://www.nytimes.com/2006/12/17/arts/design/17kimm.html.

108. Tom Finkelpearl, *What We Made: Conversations on Art and Social Cooperation* (Durham: Duke University Press, 2015), 140.

109. "Community Development," *Project Row Houses*, https://projectrowhouses.org/our-work/neighborhood-development/community-development/.

110. Linda Day, "Revitalizing Lives: Architecture and the Third Ward," *Rice Magazine* 9 (2011): 26–29.

111. Carriemarie Schneider, "Emancipation Park, Emancipatory Art: Flipping the Gentrification Playbook," *Rice Design Alliance*, June 19, 2017, https://www.ricedesignalliance.org/emancipation-park-emancipatory-art-flipping-the-gentrification-playbook.

112. David Adams, "Joseph Beuys: Pioneer of a Radical Ecology," *Art Journal* 51:2 (1992): 26–34.

Chapter 5

1. Bruce Robbins, *Criticism and Politics: A Polemical Introduction* (Stanford: Stanford University Press, 2022), 155.

2. Robbins, *Criticism and Politics*, 154–55.

3. Lauren Berlant, *Cruel Optimism* (Durham: Duke University Press, 2011).

4. Roderick Ferguson, *The Reorder of Things* (Minneapolis: University of Minnesota Press, 2012), 224. For an account of this tradition in criticism, see Christopher Castiglia, *The Practices of Hope: Literary Criticism in Disenchanted Times* (New York: New York University Press, 2017).

5. Lee Edelman, *No Future: Queer Theory and the Death Drive* (Durham: Duke University Press, 2004), 4.

6. Andreas Malm, *How to Blow Up a Pipeline* (London: Verso, 2021); Roger Hallam, *Common Sense for the 21st Century* (New York: Chelsea Green, 2019).

7. Rodrigo Nunes, *Neither Vertical nor Horizontal: A Theory of Political Organization* (London: Verso, 2021), 29.

8. Nunes, *Neither Vertical nor Horizontal*, 1.

9. Jodi Dean, *Crowds and Party* (London: Verso, 2016), 25–26.

10. Dean, *Crowds and Party*, 26.

11. Nunes, *Neither Vertical nor Horizontal*, 122.

12. And it is impossible to draw a clear distinction between what is organically inside a group and what is impressed from outside. Nunes, *Neither Vertical nor Horizontal*, 128. See also Jo Freeman, "The Tyranny of Structurelessness," *Ms.* (July 1973): 76–78, 86–89.

13. Daniel Hunter, *Climate Resistance Handbook* (350.org, 2019), 47–48, https://trainings.350.org/wp-content/uploads/2019/05/Climate-Resistance-Handbook-PDF.pdf.

14. Craig Calhoun, "Occupy Wall Street in Perspective," *British Journal of Sociology* 64:1 (March 2013): 26–38.

15. Calhoun, "Occupy Wall Street in Perspective," 31.

16. Hunter, *Climate Resistance Handbook*, 23.

17. Fred D. Gray, *Bus Ride to Justice* (Montgomery: New South Books, 2013), 70.

18. UN Environment Programme, "Lamu Coal Plant Case Reveals Tips for Other Community-Led Campaigns," August 22, 2019, https://www.unenvironment.org/news-and-stories/story/lamu-coal-plant-case-reveals-tips-other-community-led-campaigns.

19. Organizations that worked with the Lamu group included the Decoalanize Campaign, the Katiba Institute, Heinrich-Böll-Stiftung, 350 Africa, the Centre for Human Rights and Civic Education, Sauti Ya Wanjiku, Muhuri-Muslims for Human Rights, Natural Resources Alliance

of Kenya, the American Jewish World Service, and the Center for Justice Governance and Environmental Action. Dana Ullman, "When Coal Comes to Paradise," *Foreign Policy*, June 19, 2019, https://foreignpolicy.com/2019/06/09/when-coal-came-to-paradise-china-coal-kenya-lamu-pollution-africa-chinese-industry-bri/.

20. Otsieno Namwaya, "Tribunal Stops Kenya's Coal Plant Plans," *Human Rights Watch*, July 1, 2019, https://www.hrw.org/news/2019/07/01/tribunal-stops-kenyas-coal-plant-plans.

21. Erica Chenoweth and Maria J. Stephan, *Why Civil Resistance Works* (New York: Columbia University Press, 2012), 41.

22. Justin Jacobs, "Corporations Aren't Demi-Gods," *American Jewish World Service*, https://ajws.org/blog/corporations-arent-demigods-the-kenyan-movement-to-stop-coal-wins-in-court/.

23. Nunes, *Neither Vertical nor Horizontal*, 128.

24. Nunes, *Neither Vertical nor Horizontal*, 197.

25. UN Environment Programme, "Lamu Coal Plant Case."

26. Nunes, *Neither Vertical nor Horizontal*, 151.

27. Nunes, *Neither Vertical nor Horizontal*, 227.

28. "A potential that remains indefinitely open will always be more radical than whatever actually exists; by not being invested in anything finite and limited, it excludes no possibilities and cannot be subject to perversion or decay. . . . To be radical is then not to transform positive reality, but to have no truck with it: to negate it so thoroughly, to exceed it so completely, that nothing could ever be done here and now that would ever be adequate" (Nunes, *Neither Vertical nor Horizontal*, 274; see also p. 275).

29. Chenoweth and Stephan, *Why Civil Resistance*, 39.

30. Chenoweth and Stephan, *Why Civil Resistance*, 40.

31. Chenoweth and Stephan, *Why Civil Resistance*, 46.

32. John T. Jost et al., "How Social Media Facilitates Political Protest," *Advances in Political Psychology* 39, supplement 1 (February 2018): 85–118.

33. Malcolm Gladwell, "Small Change: Why the Revolution Will Not Be Tweeted," *New Yorker*, October 4, 2010.

34. Jost, "How Social Media." See also Zeynep Tufekci, *Twitter and Tear Gas: The Power and Fragility of Networked Protest* (New Haven: Yale University Press, 2017); and Elizabeth Brunner, *Environmental Activism, Social Media, and Protest in China* (Lanham, MD: Lexington Books, 2019).

35. Sandra Gonzalez-Bailon, Javier Borge-Holthoefer, and Yamir Moreno argue that even online groups tend to centralize and organize around hierarchies increasingly over time: "Broadcasters and Hidden Influentials in Online Protest Diffusion," *American Behavioral Scientist* 57:7 (2013): 943–65.

36. Robert D. Benford and David A. Snow argue that there is little evidence for this assumption in "Framing Processes and Social Movements," *Annual Review of Sociology* 26 (2000): 615–16.

37. Anneleen Kenis and Erik Mathijs, "Beyond Individual Behaviour Change," *Environmental Education Research* 18:1 (2012): 45–65.

38. Bruno Latour, "Where Are the Missing Masses?" in *Shaping Technology/Building Society: Studies in Sociotechnical Change*, ed. W. E. Bijker and J. Law (Cambridge, MA: MIT Press, 1992), 227–28.

39. Nunes, *Neither Vertical nor Horizontal*, 24–25.

40. Ziad W. Munson, *The Making of Pro-life Activists* (Chicago: University of Chicago Press, 2009).

41. Munson, *Making*, 126.

42. Munson, *Making*, 127.

43. Andrew G. Walder has found similar structures at work in the Cultural Revolution in China. See *Agents of Disorder: Inside China's Cultural Revolution* (Cambridge, MA: Harvard University Press, 2019). Robert J. Norris's account of the U.S. "innocence movement" also shares similarities with the pro-life example. *Exonerated: A History of the Innocence Movement* (New York: New York University Press, 2017), 148–49.

44. Chenoweth and Stephan, *Why Civil Resistance*, 37–38.

45. Cornell Campus Sustainability Office, "Sustainability and Climate Literacy Module Added to First-Year Orientation," September 14, 2020, https://sustainablecampus.cornell.edu/news/sustainability-and-climate-literacy-module-added-first-year-orientation.

46. Mark Newman, Albert Lazlo Barabasi, and Duncan J. Watts, *The Structure and Dynamics of Networks* (Princeton: Princeton University Press, 2006), 2.

47. Nancy Katz et al., "Network Theory and Small Groups," *Small Group Research* 35:3 (June 2004): 308.

48. Bill McKibben, "Global Warming's Terrifying New Math," *Rolling Stone*, July 19, 2012, https://www.rollingstone.com/politics/politics-news/global-warmings-terrifying-new-math-188550/.

49. "Do the Math," 350.org, https://math.350.org/?ga=2.196779749.839743416.1631884554-1879378477.1626790689#tour-dates.

50. Stand Earth and 350.org, "The Database of Fossil Fuel Divestment Commitments Made by Institutions Worldwide," https://gofossilfree.org/divestment/commitments/.

51. Christian Smith, *Resisting Reagan: The U.S. Central America Peace Movement* (Chicago: University of Chicago Press, 2014), 109.

52. See Lauri Umansky, *Motherhood Reconceived: Feminism and the Legacies of the Sixties* (New York: New York University Press, 1996), 52–76; and Jule Dejager Ward, *La Leche League: At the Crossroads of Medicine, Feminism, and Religion* (Chapel Hill: University of North Carolina Press, 2000).

53. Ina May Gaskin, *Spiritual Midwifery* (Summertown, TN: Book Publishing, 1976).

54. In 2000, the American Public Health Association encouraged all health care systems and professional associations to recognize the value and training of midwives. "Position Paper 7924: Alternatives in Maternity Care," *APHA Public Policy Statements, 1948 to Present* (Washington, DC: APHA, n.d.).

55. L. Attanasio and K. B. Kozhimannil, "Relationship between Hospital-Level Percentage of Midwife-Attended Births and Obstetric Procedure Utilization," *Journal of Midwifery and Women's Health* 63:1 (January 2018): 14–22.

56. Roman Jakobson and Krystyna Pomorska, *Dialogues*, trans Christian Hubert (Cambridge, MA: MIT Press, 1983), 128.

57. See Eileen John, "Dickinson and Pivoting Thought," in *The Poetry of Emily Dickinson*, ed. Elisabeth Camp (Oxford: Oxford University Press, 2021), 182.

58. Nathaniel Mackey, *The Paracritical Hinge* (Iowa City: University of Iowa Press, 2018), 7, 18.

59. Kim Ruehl, *A Singing Army: Zilphia Horton and the Highlander Folk School* (Austin: University of Texas Press, 2021), 225–31.

60. Jo Ann Gibson Robinson, *The Montgomery Bus Boycott and the Women Who Started It* (Knoxville: University of Tennessee Press, 1987).

61. Donnie Williams and Wayne Greenhaw, *The Thunder of Angels: The Montgomery Bus Boycott and the People Who Broke the Back of Jim Crow* (Chicago: Lawrence Hill Books, 2006), 65.

62. Robinson, *The Montgomery Bus Boycott*.

63. Cheryl Fisher Phibbs, *The Montgomery Bus Boycott: A History and Reference Guide* (Santa Barbara: Greenwood, 2009), 64.

64. Robert Darden, *Nothing but Love in God's Water: Volume 1* (University Park: Penn State University Press, 2021), 119–36.

65. Robyn Bradley Litchfield, "Music and Fellowship Sustained Montgomery Bus Boycotters," *Montgomery Advertiser*, December 4, 2018, https://www.montgomeryadvertiser.com/story/news/2018/12/04/montgomery-bus-boycott-voices-ripley-street-baptist-churchs-dorothy-jones/2211818002/.

66. Bruce Hartford, "Nonviolent Training" (2004), https://www.crmvet.org/info/nv3.htm.

67. Sasha Torres, *Black, White, and in Color: Television and Black Civil Rights* (Princeton: Princeton University Press, 2018), 27.

68. Joseph Boyett, *Getting Things Done in Washington: Lessons for Progressives from Landmark Legislation* (Bloomington: ASJA Press, 2011), 295.

69. Robinson, *The Montgomery Bus Boycott*, 94.

70. Robinson, *The Montgomery Bus Boycott*, 100.

71. Stephen J. Dubner, "Do Boycotts Work?" *Freakanomics Radio*, episode 234, produced by Greg Rosalsky (January 21, 2016).

72. For more, see Hongmei Sun, *Transforming Monkey: Adaptation and Representation of a Chinese Epic* (Seattle: University of Washington Press, 2018), 60–90.

73. *Remember the Titans*, dir. Boaz Yakin (2000).

74. *Coach Carter*, dir. Thomas Carter (2005).

75. Max Horkheimer and Theodor W. Adorno, *Dialectic of Enlightenment*, trans. Edmund Jephcott (Stanford: Stanford University Press, 2002).

76. *Stand and Deliver*, dir. Ramón Menéndez (1988).

77. Adriana Heidiz, "Please Stop Talking about 'Stand and Deliver,'" *New America*, June 29, 2017, https://www.newamerica.org/weekly/please-stop-talking-about-stand-and-deliver/.

78. One example is Brad Meltzer's *I Am Rosa Parks*, a popular children's book (New York: Dial Books, 2014).

Chapter 6

1. Sarah Schulman, *Let the Record Show: A Political History of ACT UP New York, 1987–1993* (New York: Farrar, Straus and Giroux, 2021), 9.

2. Erica Chenoweth, *Civil Resistance: What Everyone Needs to Know* (Oxford: Oxford University Press, 2021), 114–19.

3. See, for example, Matthew J. Hornsey and Kelly S. Fielding, "Understanding (and Reducing) Inaction on Climate Change," *Social Issues and Policy Review* 14:1 (2020): 3–35.

4. Anglophone examples include Thomas Simpson's *Select Exercises for Young Proficients in the Mathematicks* (London: J. Nourse, 1752) and Lindley Murray's 1797 *English Exercises* (New York: Collins, 1819), which went through dozens of editions.

5. Barbara Leckie, *Climate Change, Interrupted* (Stanford: Stanford University Press, 2022), 137.

INDEX

Page numbers in *italics* refer to figures and tables

A NOTE ON THE TYPE

This book has been composed in Arno, an Old-style serif typeface in the classic Venetian tradition, designed by Robert Slimbach at Adobe.

Printed and bound by CPI Group (UK) Ltd, Croydon, CR0 4YY

21/10/2024

14577032-0002